WOMEN AND THE LABOUR MOVEMENT
IN SCOTLAND 1850–1914

Women and the Labour Movement in Scotland 1850–1914

ELEANOR GORDON

CLARENDON PRESS · OXFORD
1991

Oxford University Press, Walton Street, Oxford OX2 6DP
Oxford New York Toronto
Delhi Bombay Calcutta Madras Karachi
Petaling Jaya Singapore Hong Kong Tokyo
Nairobi Dar es Salaam Cape Town
Melbourne Auckland
and associated companies in
Berlin Ibadan

Oxford is a trade mark of Oxford University Press

Published in the United States
by Oxford University Press, New York

British Library Cataloguing in Publication Data
(data available)

Library of Congress Cataloging in Publication Data
Gordon, Eleanor.
Women and the labour movement in Scotland, 1850–1914/Eleanor
Gordon.
Includes bibliographical references and index.
1. Women—Employment—Scotland—History. 2. Women in trade
unions—Scotland—History. 3. Jute industry—Scotland—Dundee—
History. I. Title.
HD6137.G67   1991
331.4′7′09411—dc20   90-26540
ISBN 0-19-820143-5

Typeset by Dobbie Typesetting Limited, Tavistock, Devon
Printed and bound in Great Britain by
Bookcraft Ltd, Midsomer Norton, Bath

To the memory of my mother,
Jean Gordon

Acknowledgements

I SHOULD like to thank the ESRC, the Institute of Historical Research, and the Carnegie Trust for funding the various stages of this research. My two supervisors, Keith Burgess and Anne Crowther, offered guidance, support, and constructive criticism which went beyond the call of duty. I have also benefited from discussions with and comments from Arthur McIvor, Alan McKinlay, Sian Reynolds, Pat Thane, and Chris Wrigley. Alistair Reid and Paul Johnson also made helpful comments. I am particularly grateful to Barbara Littlewood, who has given generously of her time to make insightful and supportive comments. Thanks are also due to Linda Craig and Blythe O'Driscoll for typing the manuscript.

Many individuals have contributed in some way to the completion of this book, especially family and friends, who have encouraged and supported me throughout its duration. I gained practical support and encouragement from Callum Brown, Basilia Griffin, Peter Griffin, Jackie Gulstad, and Joan MacKenzie, whilst Ian Mitchell read the final draft with his customary perceptiveness and wit.

Special thanks are due to Jack Law for his support and forbearance. Above all I would like to acknowledge the debt I owe to my mother, Jean Gordon, whose open and inquiring mind set me a fine example.

Contents

List of Tables

Abbreviations and Conventions

ASE	Amalgamated Society of Engineers
DARC	Dundee Archives and Record Centre
DDUJFW	Dundee and District Union of Jute and Flax Workers
DMFOH	*Dundee Mill and Factory Operatives' Herald*
DMFOU	Dundee and District Mill and Factory Operatives' Union
DSU	Dundee Social Union
DUA	Dundee University Archives
GCWT	Glasgow Council for Women's Trades
GLHW	Glasgow Labour History Workshop
GTC	Glasgow Trades Council
GUWW	Glasgow Union of Women Workers
ILP	Independent Labour Party
IWGB	Industrial Workers of Great Britain
LC	Lamb Collection, National Library of Scotland
MLG	Mitchell Library, Glasgow
NFCWT	National Federal Council for Women's Trades
NFWW	National Federation of Women Workers
NLS	National Library of Scotland
SCWG	Scottish Co-operative Women's Guild
SCWT	Scottish Council for Women's Trades
SDF	Social Democratic Federation
SDP	Social Democratic Party
SLP	Socialist Labour Party
SNAOT	Scottish National Association of Operative Tailors
SRA	Strathclyde Regional Archives
STA	Scottish Typographical Association
STUC	Scottish Trades Union Congress
SUA	Strathclyde University Archives
SWPEC	Scottish Workers' Parliamentary Elections Committee
WCE	Webb Collection E, British Library of Political and Economic Science
WLL	Women's Labour League
WPPL	Women's Protection and Provident League
WSPU	Women's Social and Political Union
WTUL	Women's Trade Union League
WTUR	*Women's Trade Union Review*

Introduction

THIS book is about working women in Scotland in the period 1850–1914, and is concerned with the pattern of their employment, their involvement in and relationship to trade-unionism, and the forms of their workplace resistance and struggles. It is part of the wider project of redressing the balance of labour history, which for so long has omitted the history of working women. In recent years there has been a concerted effort by feminist historians to retrieve women from historical obscurity and reinsert them into the historical landscape. Early research concentrated on this task of reclamation and produced a number of monographs and studies of women's lives. However, the emphasis has shifted towards viewing the sexual division of labour as a central object of study and a tool of analysis, and evaluating its impact on the historical process. It is argued that in this way feminist history can transform our knowledge of the past and contribute to a greater understanding of the process of historical change. Therefore, whilst the study focuses on Scotland, the intention is to shed light on some of the key debates which have emerged in the historical and theoretical literature on women and work, as well as to contribute to the much neglected history of Scotland's women workers.

The third quarter of the nineteenth century has long been regarded as a watershed in Britain's economic, political, and social history. Politically it has been portrayed as the beginning of a period of relative quiescence and stability, particularly when contrasted with the social upheavals and class conflict of the Chartist era, and economically it is viewed as the period of consolidation of industrial capitalism, the mechanized factory system, and Britain's dominance of world trade and manufacture. The historiography of this period has tended to exaggerate the contrast between the Chartist and post-Chartist period, and underplay the continuities, particularly in its representation of radical political consciousness. In Scotland in the 1830s and 1840s, the challenge of the working class was to gain political representation to redress economic grievances, rather than to seize political power in order fundamentally to restructure existing economic relationships.[1] Similarly, the mid-Victorian labour movement was neither so quiescent nor so politically subordinate to liberalism as it has been portrayed.[2] It is therefore important to trace the continuities as well as the discontinuities in the historical process and to recognize the legacy of earlier traditions in order fully to comprehend the development of the labour movement.

Continuities and adaptations of existing ideologies and practices to the changing economic and social circumstances are also evident in attitudes to the role of women and sexual divisions. The Victorian formulation of the ideology of domesticity stressed the division of the world into a private and a public sphere, which corresponded to the division between home and work.[3] The Victorian domestic ideal regarded the family as a haven from the harsh and sinful public world and assigned to women the role of moral guardian who was to be the embodiment of Christian purity. Women, therefore, became associated with the 'private' realm of the household and the family, and men with the public world of work. Women's pivotal role in the household was not a new phenomenon, but the confinement of women to the exclusively private realm of the home, which was also physically separated from the workplace, and her exclusion from the commercial and industrial world was a new strand in the reconstruction of gender relations. The identification of women with the home and family and men with work was so powerful and pervasive that the social origins of the division became obscured so that it appeared as a natural phenomenon.

However, this domestic ideology was essentially a middle-class notion and, whilst the increasingly important economic

---

[1] T. Dickson and T. Clarke, 'Class and Class Consciousness in Early Industrial Capitalism', in T. Dickson (ed.), *Capital and Class in Scotland* (Edinburgh: John Donald, 1982).

[2] See Ch. 2 for a fuller discussion of this.

[3] C. Hall, 'The Butcher, the Baker, the Candlestickmaker: The Shop and the Family in the Industrial Revolution', in E. Whitelegg *et al.. The Changing Experience of Women* (Oxford: Martin Robertson, in association with the Open University, 1982); C. Hall, 'The Early Formation of Victorian Domestic Ideology', in S. Burman (ed.), *Fit Work for Women* (London: Croom Helm, 1979).

and social role of the middle classes ensured the hegemony of bourgeois ideas and ideologies in society, it is by no means clear that the ideology of domesticity in its middle-class form was unreservedly embraced by the working class. As Gray's study of Edinburgh's labour aristocracy demonstrated, the transmission of dominant ideologies is a complex process of accommodation and negotiation mediated by the material conditions of working-class life and work, which differed considerably from the middle-class experience.[4] Working-class accommodation or adaptation to the dominant domestic ideology is therefore a matter of empirical investigation and cannot be assumed from its primacy in the ideological armoury of the middle class, whose everyday experience legitimized and reinforced it. None the less, because the ideology of domesticity and separate sexual spheres was at its apogee in the Victorian era, historians have tended to assume the actuality of this ideology and incorporate it into their analysis. They have tended to view women through the filter of Victorian domestic ideology and have concluded that women were firmly located in the home, that they had withdrawn from the public sphere, and that any variation on this pattern was the exception which proved the rule. Thus one leading historian could unequivocally state: 'The fact of the withdrawal from public activity by the women of the working class is incontrovertible.'[5]

The force of this ideology of separate sexual spheres, coupled with the symbolic significance of the machine and hard physical labour, which is associated with the Industrial Revolution, has meant that work has generally been defined as something which men do, and indeed 'working class' has generally been defined as 'working men'.[6] Women's work, whether waged or in the home as unpaid domestic labour, has until recently been neglected as a serious area of study and relegated to a peripheral

[4] R. Q. Gray, *The Labour Aristocracy in Victorian Edinburgh* (Oxford: Clarendon Press, 1976).

[5] D. Thompson, 'Women and Nineteenth Century Radical Politics: A Lost Dimension', in J. Mitchell and A. Oakley (eds.), *The Rights and Wrongs of Women* (Harmondsworth: Penguin, 1976), 137.

[6] S. Alexander, 'Women's Work in Nineteenth Century London: A Study of the Years 1820–1850', in Mitchell and Oakley (eds.), *The Rights and Wrongs of Women*, 59.

role, while women have been written about primarily as the dependants of working men. Labour historicans have implicitly accepted the view of working-class woman that 'Once married, she belonged to the proletariat not as a worker, but as the wife, mother and housekeeper of workers.'[7]

Assertions by historians that women did not inhabit the world of work or were marginal to it in the Victorian era are usually based on the strength of assumptions rather than on systematic investigations of the historical reality. These assertions are not simply the product of slipshod scholarship, but reflect the pervasiveness and tenacity of the ideology of separate sexual spheres which imbues the sexual division of labour with the status of a 'natural' or biological fact. Consequently, sexual divisions have been taken for granted rather than viewed as social constructs which are legitimate objects of historical inquiry. Historians have been content to resort to bland and unsubstantiated assertions to describe them: 'Typically it was the male who had to leave the home every day to work for wages and the women who did not.'[8]

There have been, however, an increasing number of studies by feminist historians whose findings have questioned the validity of such sweeping generalizations of women's role by revealing that women's involvement in waged labour was more extensive than has previously been supposed, that usually their earnings were central to the family economy, and that frequently women were family bread-winners.[9]

Just as work has been defined according to a masculine conception, struggle has also been defined in a narrow, partial fashion. The pre-industrial struggles of the common people encompassed and reflected the heterogeneity of that category and consisted of direct action on the streets, and women's role

[7] E. J. Hobsbawm, 'Men and Women in Socialist Iconography', *History Workshop Journal*, 6 (Autumn 1978), 131. [8] Ibid. 130.

[9] Alexander, 'Women's Work in Nineteenth Century London'; J. Liddington and J. Norris, *One Hand Tied Behind Us* (London: Virago, 1978); A. V. John, *By the Sweat of their Brow: Women Workers at Victorian Coal Mines* (London: Croom Helm, 1980); S. Taylor, 'The Effects of Marriage on Job Possibilities for Women, and the Ideology of the Home, Nottingham 1890–1930', *Oral History*, 5(2) (Autumn 1977); J. Lown, 'Not so much a Factory, more a Form of Patriarchy: Gender Division and Domestic Ideology in a Nineteenth Century Essex Silk Mill', in E. Garmarknikow *et al.* (eds.), *Class, Gender and Work* (London: Heinemann, British Sociological Association, 1983).

in these struggles has been well documented.[10] However, with
the consolidation of industrial capitalism, the dominant form of
proletarian struggle and organization became trade-unionism,
which was based on occupational categories and was therefore
a more exclusive form of struggle than in the pre-industrial
era, when membership of the common people was the sole
criterion for involvement.

Although trade-unionism became the established form of
struggle, historians have tended to regard it as encompassing
all collectivist tendencies and women's low level of participation
in trade unions has been taken variously as evidence of their
apathy, passivity, and disunity, and of their disinclination for
collective action. Resistance and struggle which do not take male
forms have been ignored or seen as insignificant, irrelevant,
or anachronistic. Instances of such assumptions amongst
traditional labour historians are too numerous to document,
but evidence of the pervasiveness of the view is its presence
in the work of feminist historians who challenge other long-
standing assumptions about gender divisions. For example,
Barrett and MacIntosh in an article which seeks to debunk the
myth of the male bread-winner can still assert of working women
in the nineteenth century: 'Their voices were little heard in the
debates, for they were unorganised and unrepresented, it was
left to others to speak of their rights or of their sufferings—
even when it was recognised that their exploitation at work
was so great because they were unorganised and disunited.'[11]

An important aspect of the present study is an attempt
to challenge empirically such entrenched assumptions by
rediscovering women in the world of work and making visible
the forms of their workplace resistance. However, as feminist
historians have argued, feminist history is defined by its
approach rather than its subject matter and therefore means

[10] E. P. Thompson, *The Making of the English Working Class* (Harmondsworth:
Penguin, 1968); B. Taylor, 'The Early Socialists', in S. Lipshitz (ed.), *Tearing the
Veil* (Routledge & Kegan Paul, 1978); K. T. Logue, *Popular Disturbance in Scotland
1780–1815* (Edinburgh: John Donald, 1979); D. Thompson, 'Women and Nineteenth
Century Radical Politics' in J. Mitchell and A. Oakley (eds.), *The Rights and Wrongs
of Women* (London; Penguin, 1976).
[11] M. Barrett and M. MacIntosh, 'The Family Wage: Some Problems for Socialists
and Feminists', *Capital and Class*, 11 (Summer 1980), 56.

much more than researching a group or category which has previously been ignored and grafting on the acquired knowledge to an already constituted history.[12] Whilst there clearly has to be a concern with excavating women's history from the layers of neglect, bias, and preconceptions, this should involve theorizing about the implications for our understanding of the past. Assumptions about gender divisions have remained virtually untouched and unexplored by traditional historians, and feminist history, by placing them in the centre stage of historical investigation, should raise new questions and so transform our knowledge of the past and contribute to a greater understanding of the process of historical change. It is, therefore, intended in this book to move beyond reclaiming and salvaging working women's past to considering the impact of gender ideologies and family structures on women's experience of work and to questioning the adequacy of traditional forms of labour organization.

Recent feminist theorizing has taken issue with accounts which subsume women's experience under the category of class, arguing that it does not adequately explain the basis of women's subordination in society, the different forms which it has assumed, and the differential experience of men and women of both the working class and middle class. Much of this debate has been generated by critiques of *The Origin of the Family, Private Property and the State*, the seminal work by Engels which is seen to exemplify the approach which reduces gender to class.

Engels's central task was to offer a materialist explanation of women's subordination by relating it to certain developments in private property, the state, and the family. He argued that in pre-class societies there was a natural but complementary sexual division of labour with women responsible for food. This state was changed by the first major developments in the productive forces, namely, the domestication of animals, which enabled the creation of a surplus and eventually the development

---

[12] Alexander, 'Women's Work in Nineteenth Century London', 59; Editorial, *History Workshop Journal*, 19 (Spring 1985); A. Davin, 'Feminism and Labour History', in R. Samuel (ed.), *People's History and Socialist Theory* (London: Routledge & Kegan Paul, 1981).

of private property. Because it was men who hunted and procured the other necessities of life, the herd became the private property of men rather than women.

Therefore, with the domestication of animals and the expansion of trade, men became the sole owners of the strategic resources of society, and women became dependent individuals:

[The] division of labour [in the family] remained unchanged, and yet it now put the former domestic relationship topsy-turvy simply because the division of labour outside the family had changed. The very cause that had formerly made the woman supreme in the house, namely, her being confined to domestic work, now assured supremacy in the house for the man: the woman's housework lost its significance compared with the man's work in obtaining a livelihood; the latter was everything, the former an insignificant contribution.[13]

Engels also argued that the overthrow of mother right, the shift to a patrilineal clan system, and the development of the monogamous family had their origins in the development of private property. As the establishment of inheritance became crucial in order to safeguard property, monogamy, which applied only to women, evolved as the surest way of establishing paternity by enforcing their chastity. Engels's analysis of marriage in capitalist society concludes that it is only within the proletarian family, where there is no property to preserve, that there is no material basis for male supremacy and therefore the possibility of equality.[14] However, crucially, he argues that a further condition of women's emancipation, which is only possible for women of the working class, is their re-entry into social production in large numbers.

This necessarily schematic presentation of Engels's theory omits many aspects of his analysis which have been subjected to a sustained critique by a number of authors.[15] However, the central criticism of Engels's work is of his postulation of women's subordination as a side-effect of economic class

[13] Engels, *The Origin of the Family, Private Property and the State* (New York: Pathfinder Press, 1972), 152.   [14] Ibid. 132.
[15] R. Delmar, 'Looking Again at Engels's *Origin of the Family, Private Property and the State*, in Mitchell and Oakley (eds.), *The Rights and Wrongs of Women*; L. Vogel, *Marxism and the Oppression of Women: Towards a Unitary Theory* (London: Pluto, 1983), ch. 6; P. Aaby, 'Engels and Women', *Critique of Anthropology*, 9–10 (1979).

relations and the uncritical insertion of this analysis into subsequent Marxist theorizing. Feminists have argued that this analysis fails to account for a number of factors, including the trans-historical and cross-cultural character of women's oppression, and the historical and cultural character of women's subordination in the modern capitalist working-class family when according to the theory there is no longer any material basis for it.

Feminist attempts to offer an alternative interpretation of the specific nature of women's oppression fall into two broad categories. The first approach stresses the persistence of male domination throughout history and its autonomous nature, that is, its separateness from other forms of oppression and exploitation in society.[16] The second or Marxist feminist approach attempts to analyse the relationship between male domination and female subordination and different modes of production or different forms of class society.[17] Within both approaches there are a variety of ways of conceptualizing both the power relationship between men and women and modes of production.[18]

The position taken in this study is that inequalities of gender and capitalist socialist social relations are not two separate systems whether interlocking or mutually accommodating,[19] but that they are integrated into one single process, so that it is possible to speak of patriarchal capitalist social relationships. By this it is meant that capitalism has developed on the basis of pre-existing sexual divisions, which are in turn adapted and transformed in the process of struggles between both capital and labour and struggles within the working class and become

[16] Perhaps the principal exponent of this approach is K. Millett, *Sexual Politics* (New York: Doubleday, 1969).

[17] There are myriad contributions which take this broad approach. Both Z. R. Eisenstein (ed.), *Capitalist Patriarchy and the Case for Socialist Feminism* (New York: Monthly Review Press, 1979) and A. Khun and Ann Marie Wolpe (eds.), *Feminism and Materialism* (London: Routledge & Kegan Paul, 1978) contain a number of articles which attempt to relate patriarchy and different modes of production.

[18] V. Beechey, 'On Patriarchy', *Feminist Review*, 3 (1979) provides a useful analysis of the different ways in which patriarchy and modes of production have been conceptualized.

[19] H. Hartman, 'Capitalism, Patriarchy and Job Segregation by Sex', in Eisenstein (ed.), *Capitalist Patriarchy and the Case for Socialist Feminism*.

deeply imbricated into the fabric of the social relations of capitalism.[20]

This approach has important implications for an analysis of women's paid labour in capitalism as it rejects the orthodox Marxist definition of class, which is narrowly conceived in terms of the production process or the relations of exploitation within the workplace. A central assumption of the orthodox Marxist argument is that in an industrially based capitalist society waged labour is a gender-free and age-free category and the social relations of the workplace are governed by the impersonal criteria of the cash nexus and the market. Indeed this is the basis of the primacy which Engels placed on the potentially liberating force of women's involvement in social production, as it involved the replacement of woman's domination by her husband with the depersonalized power of capitalist over workers. According to the traditional Marxist analysis class experience is determined by one's position in the relations of production as waged labour. However, feminists have pointed up the inadequacy of this analysis for an understanding of the specificity of women's employment and its salient characteristics, for example: the existence of a horizontal division of labour which concentrates women in certain well-defined sectors of the economy; the existence of a vertical division of labour which largely confines women to unskilled jobs and a subordinate position in the hierarchical structures of the workplace; and women's low pay in relation to the male workforce. It has been argued that the divergent experience of female waged labour, and indeed different categories of waged labour, cannot be understood by reference to the realm of production only, but require to be analysed in terms of the wider social relations of production which include the family and the relations between men and women.[21]

---

[20] Alexander, 'Women's Work in Nineteenth Century London', Beechey, 'On Patriarchy', and M. Barrett, *Women's Oppression Today* (London: Verso and New Left Books, 1980) all adopt this perspective.

[21] This argument relates to wider debates within Marxism concerning definitions of key Marxist concepts such as 'class', 'class consciousness', 'modes of production', and 'relations of production'. For a full discussion of this debate see R. Johnston, 'Thompson, Genovese, and Socialist Humanist History', *History Workshop Journal*, 6 (Autumn 1978) and the responses from K. McLelland, G. Williams, and T. Putnan in *History Workshop Journal*, 7 (Spring 1979).

Consequently, it is posited that women's entry into the labour market and their status as waged labour is patterned by and mediated by their subordination as a gender.

It is important to stress that the significance attached to gender ideologies in explaining the concentration and segregation of women's work into low-status, low-skilled, and low-paid occupations and sectors does not imply a correspondence between domestic labour and the types of waged labour performed by women; nor is it intended to supplant all other explanations of occupational segregation with one based on domestic ideology. The redrawing of the boundaries of women's work over time is an important feature of the process of occupational segregation, as are the regional variations in women's work, and clearly the pervasiveness of domestic ideology cannot account for this. However, the contention is that any satisfactory understanding of the gendered segmentation of the labour market must take account of and integrate gender ideologies into the explanation.

Whilst it is accepted that prevailing notions of women's appropriate cultural role were critical in shaping their subordinate labour market position, this study takes issue with accounts which assume that their labour market position explains the pattern of women's workplace behaviour and which conflate a subordinate labour market position with subordination and submission in the workplace. Clearly it is important to recognize the impact of social processes outside the workplace on orientations to work and experience of work. However, in terms of women workers, the interconnections of work and home have usually been discussed in the context of providing explanations for women's 'lesser trade union organization', simply because it has been assumed that in the workplace women have been unorganized, passive, and submissive. It is not in dispute that to be concentrated in sectors which are classed as unskilled and are low-paid places constraints on successful combination, but the assumption of the docility of women workers is not based on historical investigation of the specific context of women's employment, but on a general theory of gender which associates women with the domestic realm, equates domesticity with passivity and submission, and assumes that women's primary commitment is to the family and that they therefore lack the motivation to combine in order to improve their lot at the point of production.

As ideologies of gender and the form of the sexual division of labour vary historically, their precise impact on women's experience of work is a matter for historical investigation. It is therefore the purpose of this study specifically to examine the connections between gender ideologies, the family, and production in the period 1850–1914 in Scotland, and how this affected women's experience of work, their consciousness, and the forms of their workplace resistance.

Chapter 1 charts the pattern of women's employment in Scotland between 1850 and 1914, both regionally and nationally, and examines the various factors which shaped this pattern. It focuses on the specific characteristics of women's employment and argues that these cannot be understood solely by reference to changes in the economy and the sectoral distribution of employment but requires consideration of ideological factors. It considers the extent to which dominant gender ideologies play a role in determining women's changing participation rates in the labour force and the lower wages of women workers and in constituting certain kinds of work as 'women's work'.

Chapter 2 looks at the development and form of Scottish trade-unionism and discusses the extent to which trade union ideology and practices were influenced by ideologies of gender. It is argued that, by incorporating these ideologies into their practices, trade unions played a significant role in maintaining and reinforcing the sexual division of labour in work and women's status as cheap labour. Women's involvement in trade unions is outlined in Chapter 3 and traditional explanations which have been offered to explain their lack of involvement are critically discussed. It is suggested that one explanation which is overlooked lies in the structure and practice of trade unions themselves, which usually developed in response to the needs and interests of skilled male workers. This chapter examines the relevance of traditional forms of trade-unionism to women workers and presents evidence to illustrate that, far from being apathetic and docile, women workers often took collective action to resolve their grievances. However, as these forms of resistance did not conform to accepted male models of organization and took place outside them, they were usually discounted.

Having discussed these arguments in a general fashion, the next two chapters focus on women workers in one particular industry in one town, namely, the jute workers of Dundee. These chapters reconstruct the detail of working women's lives including the labour process in the jute industry, the division of labour, the culture of the mill and factory, household structures, marriage patterns, and recreational life. The particular ways in which women's subordination as a gender were reflected in the workplace is highlighted, as are the strategies adopted in the workplace and the community to ensure that women's role as workers did not subvert Victorian domestic ideology and the conception of women as the embodiment of the virtues of modesty and chastity. Whilst the pervasive influence of patriarchal control is stressed, attention is also drawn to the ways in which women resisted this control. Women's disputes in the jute industry are examined to illustrate how the sexual division of labour created the basis for conflict between male and female workers and contributed to the fragmentation of the working class. It is also argued that women's experience of waged labour as a gender, as well as as workers, generated particular forms of struggle.

Chapter 6 discusses the trade union organizations which were created specifically for women and observes that, although they recognized the need to relate directly to women, the structure and ideology of these organizations replicated those of male unions in that they regarded women's presence in the labour market as a problem and an anomaly. Although women continued to take collective action and made a significant contribution to the upsurge in industrial militancy in the years before the First World War, the dominant view continued to be that women could not be organized in trade unions because of their weakness and apathy. However, it is argued that the failure of trade unions to organize around women's problems and issues explains the difficulties in sustaining organization amongst them.

Chapter 7 examines how an ideology of gender divisions was reproduced in working-class politics and socialist organizations in the early twentieth century. It is demonstrated that, whilst this ideology operated to generate struggles amongst working-class women and drew them into political activity, working women were in practice excluded from working-class politics as women were only related to in their capacity as wives and mothers. It is suggested that this inhibited the potential of the early socialist movement to transcend significant divisions within the working class.

In one sense there are no purely technical problems of data collection in writing feminist history, as it is primarily concerned with peeling off the layers which distort so much of the evidence concerning women. There are, however, a number of practical problems involved in such research, the most immediate being that of invisibility. Usually women's past goes unrecorded by both others and themselves, admittedly a common problem with the powerless. There is no cache of records which can be unearthed and simply consulted and the information is usually scattered and the nature of research piecemeal and fragmentary. The problem of invisibility, however, is compounded by the problem of bias. Labour and social historians have long confronted the bias of class, which imbues so many of the sources of information on the working class and the poor. However, the study of women is often distorted by the filters of both class and gender, which often has the consequence of reinforcing women's invisibility.

Although the census has been used as the major source of statistical information on women's employment, census statistics are produced and constructed according to male definitions of work, that is full time, permanent, and outside the home. As much of women's work was temporary, seasonal, casual, part time, or performed in the home, women are seriously under-represented as their work did not conform to the male defined norm. An additional problem is that the classification of women's work is vague and imprecise in comparison with men's work, which is usually subdivided into a number of categories. Consequently, one often has to approach the research from an oblique angle and supplement this information with data gleaned from sources which were designed for other purposes. As regards women's employment, I have relied on parliamentary reports, census schedules, and the surveys of official bodies and philanthropic organizations to flesh out the skeletal outline provided by the census. Oral sources and the records of philanthropic organizations have been used for details of working women's daily life in the workplace and the community.

Trade union records reveal very little about the nature of working women's collective resistance; however, if one places assumptions about gender and sexual divisions to the fore of investigations, these records provide illuminating examples of the ways in which issues, policies, and problems were defined according to the interests and points of view of men. In this way we can begin to question the relevance and adequacy of official trade union organization to women; this in turn leads to the reformulation of standard definitions and conceptions of work and struggle and points to alternative ways of interpreting the evidence. Thus trade union reports of strikes or disputes by women can be re-evaluated and these, coupled with newspaper accounts of women's strikes, can provide a wealth of material on the particular forms of women's resistance and organization.

The task of rediscovering women in the world of work is not a sterile one, for the evidence does exist. However, it is to a great extent an exercise which involves asking different questions of the evidence in order to explore deep-rooted assumptions about gender divisions.

1.   Women's Employment in Scotland, 1850–1914

ALTHOUGH industrialization had a major impact on economic and social organization, it has commonly been argued that the process was altogether more gradual than implied by the term 'Industrial Revolution'. Moreover, recent research on the process of industrial change in England has stressed that its impact was uneven and incomplete, and that the expansion of traditional processes and skills was an integral part of industrialization and that technical change was confined to certain industries.[1] This revised picture has particular relevance for Scotland. Although industrialization began later, and was a more dramatic and telescoped process than south of the border, consequently it was more uneven in its impact.

By 1850 the twin processes of industrialization and urbanization had advanced to the stage that Scotland had been transformed from a predominantly agrarian society to a robust industrial economy within the space of half a century. None the less the industrial structure continued to be dominated by small-scale employers, and workshops rather than factories predominated. Less than 3 per cent of employers engaged more than 100 workers[2] and even in cotton textiles, the archetypal factory industry, just over one-third of those involved in cotton manufacture were employed in mills and factories, illustrating the importance of the home and the small workshop in production.[3]

The coexistence of a variety of forms of work organization and loci of industrial production had important implications

---

[1] Raphael Samuel, 'The Workshop of the World: Steam Power and Hand Technology', *History Workshop Journal*, 3 (Spring 1977); N. F. R. Crafts, *British Economic Growth during the Industrial Revolution* (Oxford University Press, 1985).

[2] Richard Rodgers, 'Mid Victorian Employers' Attitudes', *Social History*, 2 (1986), 78.

[3] J. Butt, 'Industrial Relations in the Cotton Industry', in J. Butt and K. Ponting (eds.), *Scottish Textile History* (Aberdeen University Press, 1987), 140.

for the pattern of women's employment and suggest a more complex reality than that which has dominated both historical accounts and popular consciousness.

The conventional wisdom that industrialization brought about the complete separation of home and work and the retreat of women from the public sphere generally and the world of work in particular has been challenged by the evidence of a number of recent English-based studies which have revealed that women's involvement in waged and unwaged production was more extensive than has previously been supposed.[4] The evidence for Scotland is more sparse and therefore the best single source available for analysing changing occupational patterns and work participation rates of Scottish women remains the census. There are, however, a number of problems associated with the use of the census which make it a particularly inadequate tool for uncovering the pattern of women's employment.

The difficulties and pitfalls one encounters when dealing with census data have been well documented,[5] the problems ranging from straightforward methodological ones to those of theory. This latter approach has been taken up by some sociologists of the ethnomethodological school, notably Cicourel, who argues that official statistics tell one more about the statistics-producing agencies and their values and assumptions than they do about the subject of the statistics.[6] Cicourel's position leads him to dismiss the validity of official statistics as reflections of the real world and to shift his focus of study to the construction process of statistics in order to ascertain what this reveals about those producing the statistics. Whilst we need not adopt the relativism of this approach, it does alert us to

[4] S. Alexander, 'Women's Work in Nineteenth Century London: A Study of the Years 1820–1850', in J. Mitchell and A. Oakley (eds.), *The Rights and Wrongs of Women* (Harmondsworth: Penguin, 1976); E. Hoestettler, 'Gourley Steel and the Sexual Division of Labour', *History Workshop Journal*, 4 (Autumn 1977); A. V. John, *By the Sweat of their Brow: Women Workers at Victorian Coal Mines* (London: Croom Helm, 1980); J. Lown, 'Not so much a Factory, more a Form of Patriarchy', in E. Garmarknikow *et al.* (eds.), *Gender, Class and Work* (London: Heinemann, British Sociological Association, 1983).

[5] E. A. Wrigley (ed.), *Nineteenth Century Society: Essays in the Use of Quantitative Methods for the Study of Social Data* (Cambridge University Press, 1972).

[6] J. Kituse and A. Cicourel, 'A Note on the Use of Official Statistics', *Social Problems*, 2 (1963).

the fact that census statistics are socially constructed, that is, they embody assumptions about the nature of work and reflect prevailing ideologies, particularly with regard to attitudes to women and their role in society.

By the middle of the nineteenth century the ideology of domesticity and separate sexual spheres was firmly entrenched and this was reflected in the construction of census statistics. The census report of 1861 stated that 'As the home duties of the wife are by far the most important to the community in which a wife is engaged, every wife ought to have been tabulated under that head no matter what trade or occupation she might occasionally follow.'[7] Although this was not a fiat issued to enumerators and householders, it seems fair to conclude that it expressed a shared perception that a woman's household work was her 'true' occupation and presumably this influenced enumerators and householders when completing the census schedules.

The definition of women as dependants of a male bread-winner was made explicit in the 1871 Scottish census, which attempted to experiment with a new method of classification by abstracting 'wives, children and scholars', and assigning them to the various orders and suborders as 'dependants on those who were the actual bread-winners'.[8] Although this was partly to enable the enumerators to establish differential mortality rates in the different classes and occupations, it also reflected the belief that women should be defined primarily in relation to a male head of household.

The prevalence of the assumption that women did not work is evident in the 1871 census, which instructed enumerators to note the number of men and boys on Scottish farms, no mention being made of women and girls. The census report noted that almost half of the farmers did in fact supply the number of adult female labourers; however, no returns were obtained regarding the numbers of girls employed.[9]

Changing definitions of work were also reflected in the census and contributed to the marginalization of women's work in the official snapshot of employment patterns. By 1881

---

[7] Census of Scotland, 1861, Enumerator's Report, p. xlvi.
[8] Census of Scotland, 1871, p. xxxvii.   [9] Ibid., p. xlvii.

unwaged work in the household, whether for family consumption or for the market economy, no longer constituted 'work'
for the purposes of the census. In the 1871 census and in
all subsequent censuses, the working population did not
include shopkeepers' wives, farmers' wives, innkeepers' wives,
shoemakers' wives, butchers' wives, etc., although they had
previously been included. This meant that many women who
assisted in family businesses and who did not receive any
formal payment were classified as 'dependants' in 1871, and
'unoccupied' thereafter.[10] In the 1881 census women engaged
in domestic duties in the home were assigned to a residual
category termed the 'non-productive and unoccupied' class, and
included with 'persons of property and rank'. In previous
censuses they had been placed in the 'domestic' class and
included in the main body of the Tables of Occupations.[11]
These changing census classifications no doubt reflected the
pervasiveness of market forces during the second half of the
nineteenth century and the fact that work was increasingly
defined as an activity which was carried out for a wage
outside the home and which was governed by market
relations.

Work also tended to be defined as a 'regular' activity,
implying continuity if not permanency. For example, the census
report of 1881 explained that wives, daughters, and other
dependants 'without any *special* occupation' (my italics) should
be assigned to the 'unoccupied and non-productive class'.[12] As
many women were engaged in casual and seasonal work or
might only work when their husbands were unemployed or
underemployed, it is likely that their work was omitted from
census figures which related to one day in the year and which
were based on a conception of employment defined by a male
norm of stable, full-time work outside the home.

Therefore, in addition to the usual problems associated with
the census stemming from the various modifications to the
classification system, there are a number of problems relating
to women, the overall effect of which is to underestimate the
extent of their involvement in occupations other than domestic

---

[10] Census of Scotland, 1871, p. xlvii.
[11] Census of Scotland, 1881, p. xxv.   [12] Ibid.

TABLE 1.1. *Women as a percentage of the total labour force,*
1851–1911

1851	1861	1871	1881	1891	1901	1911
36.29	36.81	31.73	31.31	31.30	29.8	28.7

Source: Census of Great Britain and Scotland, 1851–1911.

service.[13] This problem of under-representation is particularly acute for married women, whose employment was most likely to be intermittent and invisible. Therefore, when using the census, which, although flawed, remains the best source for analysing women's employment patterns over time, the figures have to be handled both sensitively and critically.

In the following discussion the unrevised census statistics have been used as the raw data, rather than any of the plethora of standardized tables, all of which omit from the occupied population the wives and female relatives who had been included up until 1871. Although this approach creates problems of comparability and sacrifices the consistency of data, it does enable us to illustrate how changing social attitudes were incorporated into the construction of the statistics and the effects this had on the official pattern.

According to census figures, women as a proportion of the total labour force declined from 36.7 per cent in 1851 to 28.7 in 1911. However, the percentages from 1871 to 1911 remained relatively constant, the decline occurring between 1861 and 1871 when it was decided to exclude wives and female relatives of small business men and farmers from the occupied population (see Table 1.1). The proportion of economically active women to the total number of women followed a similar trend in that there was a decline from 32.83 per cent in 1861 to 25.5 per cent in 1871 with the percentage of economically active women hovering around this latter figure until 1911 (see Table 1.2).

A comparison of the growth rate of the female population between 1871 and 1911 and their participation rates suggests that the female population was increasing at a faster rate than

---

[13] See E. Higgs, 'Women, Occupations and Work in the Nineteenth Century Censuses', *History Workshop Journal*, 23 (Spring 1987), 59–80, for a discussion of this problem.

TABLE 1.2. *Economically active women as a percentage of the total number of women, 1851–1911*

	Scotland	Glasgow	Dundee	Edinburgh	Aberdeen
1851	32.22	37.1	37.98	33.16	32.1
1861	32.83	34.57	40.52	33.56	33.0
1871	25.50	30.80	40.68	29.40	27.47
1881	25.70	31.14	40.1	30.88	29.0
1891	26.70	30.04	43.0	31.43	28.50
1901	25.70	28.87	41.68	31.15	26.40
1911	24.20	27.68	40.14	31.16	25.70

Source: Census of Great Britain and Scotland, 1851–1911.

the numbers employed. However, this probably reflects the introduction and extension of compulsory education rather than the withdrawal of women from paid labour. The general trend and level of female employment in Scotland echoed the pattern in England, although in both countries there were significant regional variations. For example, in Scotland Dundee was exceptional in the extent of women's involvement in the economy, with women representing almost half the labour force and two-thirds of the population, earning it the nomenclature of 'a woman's town'.

It is not possible to chart the pattern of married women's employment over time, as they were listed separately for the first time in 1911. However, the shifting definitions of work outlined above and the increasing separation of home and work make it likely that there was a sharp decline in the numbers of married women working from the middle of the century until 1914. What is striking about this category is the low level of their participation rates, with only 4.1 per cent of married women recorded as working in Scotland in the 1911 census (Table 1.3), whilst the corresponding figure in England was almost 10 per cent.

The particularly low rates in Scotland might be interpreted as confirmation of the consolidation of the ideology of separate

TABLE 1.3. *Percentage of married women who worked, 1911*

Scotland	Glasgow	Dundee	Edinburgh	Great Britain
5.0	5.5	23.4	5.1	9.6

Source: Census of Great Britain and Scotland, 1911.

sexual spheres and the prevalence of a male family wage, that is, a wage which was sufficient to support a non-working wife and children. However, this seems an unconvincing interpretation, given that average wage levels in Scotland were, till the turn of the century, lower than in England, although there were a few sectors of the Scottish economy where earnings were above the English figure.[14]

The Victorian ideal of the non-working wife supported by her bread-winner husband seems to have been shared in Scotland. However, there is no evidence to suggest that the ideology of domesticity was more pervasive in Scotland than in England or that it was adhered to when the husband was unemployed or the male wage was insufficient to maintain his family. Where there was a demand for cheap female labour, restricted opportunities for male employment, or low wages for male workers, as in Dundee, there was no shortage of married women willing to work.

It is more likely that the explanation for the low rates recorded for married women lay in their under-representation in the official figures and the lack of opportunity for regular waged work for women in Scotland, although social and cultural attitudes to women's employment also provide part of the explanation. With the exception of Dundee, and small pockets of industry, there was not a high demand for female labour in the Scottish towns and cities. The west of Scotland was dominated by heavy industries and mining, which relied almost exclusively on male labour. Although Edinburgh's economy was more diversified, domestic service, which by its nature was more suitable for single women, dominated female employment. On the other hand, there was widespread employment for women, both single and married, in Scottish agriculture. However, this work often went unrecorded as it was performed on a seasonal basis or by the wives and daughters of farmers and farmworkers.[15]

As has been argued, the census is a particularly unreliable indicator of the extent of married women's work, much of

[14] R. H. Campbell, *The Rise and Fall of Scottish Industry 1707–1939* (Edinburgh: John Donald, 1980), 190.

[15] T. M. Devine, 'Women Workers 1850–1911', in T. M. Devine (ed.), *Farm Servants and Labour in Lowland Scotland 1770–1914* (Edinburgh: John Donald, 1984).

which was characterized by seasonality and casualness. The 'dark figure' of married women's employment is probably unknowable but some indication of its prevalence is contained in unofficial reports and investigations such as the survey of Dundee Social Union, which, in a sample of 3,039 households, found that, omitting 'irregular' earnings, more than half of the wives in the west district of the town were working or temporarily unemployed, whilst in the east district it was just under half.[16] This is considerably greater than the official figure of 23.4 per cent for married women's work in 1911.[17] In the Borders it seems to have been common practice for married women who appeared in the wages records of the woollen mills to be recorded simply as 'wives' in the census returns.[18]

The Dundee Social Union report also noted that many wives had irregular earnings which had been omitted from their survey and as an example of this they cited the practice of 'women taking in babies by the day', which they had found in 159 cases.[19] Further evidence of unrecorded women's work is contained in the Scottish Council for Women's Trades inquiry into the conditions of employment among charwomen, washerwomen, and cooks. Of a sample of 42 women interviewed, 32 were widows and 8 were married women.[20] The majority of the 40 married or widowed women were engaged in part-time or temporary work and a few carried out their work in the home. There were also complaints from many of the women about the scarcity of work in the summer months, indicating that there was a seasonal aspect to their employment. It was reported that the married women usually worked 'as and when the necessity arose and whenever work was available'; the wife of a labourer was 'glad to get a bit of work when she can from the neighbours' and it was reported that another labourer's wife 'does not work steadily but takes

[16] DSU, *Report on Housing, Industrial Conditions and the Medical Inspection of School Children* (Dundee: DSU, 1905), 24.   [17] Census of Scotland, 1911.
[18] J. C. Holley, 'The Two Family Economies of Industrialism: Factory Workers in Victorian Scotland', *Journal of Family History* (Spring 1981).
[19] DSU, *Report on Housing*, 24.
[20] M. H. Irwin, *Report of an Inquiry into the Conditions of Employment among Charwomen, Washerwomen, and Cooks* (Glasgow: SCWT, 1904).

a job from a neighbour sometimes when she needs it'; the wife of a coal porter was 'glad to take any work she can get around the doors'.[21]

The SCWT's investigation into homework revealed that it was pre-eminently a casual trade with the numbers engaged in it fluctuating constantly, the pattern often being determined by the state of the husband's employment.[22] Given that the census was concerned with 'regular' employment, it is likely that this kind of work never appeared in the official figures. This also applies to women's work in agriculture, which in the second half of the nineteenth century relied even more heavily on seasonal labour, particularly female labour. Indeed in the arable-farming districts of south-east Scotland, married male farm servants were often employed on condition that their female dependants would work on the farm whenever needed.[23] Evidence drawn from England corroborates the view that census figures reflected the prevailing belief that married women's domestic duties were their true occupation rather than accurately reflecting their participation in the economy.[24]

Developments in the Scottish economy between 1850 and 1914 obviously influenced the employment structure, particularly as these years spanned the culmination of Scotland's first wave of industrialization, based on textiles, and the crest of the second wave, based on the traditional heavy industries of coal, steel, engineering, and the relatively new industry of shipbuilding. Perhaps the most striking feature of these years in terms of the sectoral distribution of employment was the constancy of the proportion of those employed in manufacturing, which remained at about 43 to 44 per cent throughout the period, the shrinking of the primary sector, composed of agriculture, forestry, and fishing, from 28 per cent in 1851 to 11 per cent in 1911, and the expansion of the service sector.[25]

---

[21] M. H. Irwin, *Report of an Inquiry into the Conditions of Employment among Charwomen, Washerwomen, and Cooks* (Glasgow: SCWT, 1904).

[22] M. H. Irwin, *The Problem of Homework* (Glasgow: SCWT, 1903).

[23] Devine, 'Women Workers 1850–1911', 100.

[24] See Higgs, 'Women, Occupation and Work in the Nineteenth Century Census', 64.

[25] C. H. Lee, *British Regional Employment Statistics 1841–1971* (Cambridge University Press, 1979), 38.

Although the percentage of those employed in manufacture remained fairly steady, there were considerable shifts within this sector. For men the most significant of these shifts was the decline in the percentage of those engaged in the textile industry and the parallel increase of those engaged in the heavy industries. Between 1851 and 1911 the percentage of the occupied population engaged in textiles fell from 18.2 per cent to about 12 per cent.[26] This represented a shift within the distribution of the industrial workforce with the percentage of those employed in textiles falling from 44 per cent in 1851 to about 20 per cent in 1911, and a corresponding increase in the share of the industrial workforce engaged in heavy industries from 18 to 40 per cent.[27]

These changes in the sectoral distribution of employment as well as within sectors had a considerable impact on women's employment patterns. The census figures for the occupational distribution of women's work confirms the familiar interpretation of Scottish economic development outlined above: the decline of agriculture, the rise of the service sector, and the redistribution within the manufacturing sector. In the case of men, the heavy industries of coal, iron, and steel, and engineering and shipbuilding displaced textiles, whereas for women it was the consumer industries of food, drink, and tobacco (see Table 1.4).

Several important caveats have to be made before drawing conclusions from these figures. The number of women employed in agriculture was significantly higher than the census figure suggests, as the female relatives of small farmers and cottagers, and the larger number of, mainly female, seasonal workers are discounted from the calculations. Developments in Scottish agriculture in the second half of the nineteenth century, coupled with industrial demand for male labour, created a greater demand for seasonal labour, particularly cheap female labour, and might suggest a divergent trend from the official pattern.[28] The decline in female agricultural employment seems to have

[26] T. J. Byres, 'The Scottish Economy during the "Great Depression", 1873-1896: With Special Reference to the Heavy Industries of the South West', B. Litt. thesis, University of Glasgow, 1963, 23.

[27] Lee, *British Regional Employment Statistics*.

[28] Devine, 'Women Workers 1850-1911', 100-2.

TABLE 1.4. *Number and percentage of women in selected (principal) occupations, 1851–1911*

Occupation		1851	1861	1871	1881	1891	1901	1911
Domestic, indoor service	No.	114,751	135,423	122,064	134,069	164,855[a]	143,699	135,052
	%	22.88	25.51	25.28	26.90	29.62	24.28	22.76
Textile workers	No.	130,000	117,731	124,930	131,071	133,217	131,477	134,418
	%	25.92	22.88	25.87	26.30	23.93	22.22	22.65
Agricultural workers	No.	126,041	120,773	50,178	51,240	28,895	40,581[b]	32,423
	%	25.13	22.81	17.73	10.28	5.19	6.85	5.46
Clothing workers	No.	79,102	81,290	77,481	62,828	76,649	81,684	73,393
	%	15.77	15.35	16.04	12.60	13.77	13.80	12.37
Food/drink/tobacco workers[c]	No.	9,106	11,739	12,121	15,852	26,561	40,837	44,984
	%	1.82	2.22	2.71	3.18	4.77	6.90	7.58
Commercial clerks	No.	n/a	2	180	1,455	4,284	15,399	29,067
	%		0.0003	0.03	0.29	0.76	2.60	4.89
Teachers	No.	4,415	5,523	6,735	10,460	12,965	17,234	18,778
	%	0.88	1.043	1.39	2.09	2.32	2.91	3.16
Sick nurses, midwives	No.	2,358	1,866	2,149	2,698	3,772	8,197	10,629
	%	0.47	0.351	0.44	0.53	0.67	1.38	1.79

n/a = not available.

[a]Including the daughters of heads of households living in small cottages.

[b]Including 12,402 daughters and other relatives assisting in work on the farm. The 1871, 1881, and 1891 censuses did not include daughters, wives, and other female relatives of families in the occupied class.

[c]From C. H. Lee, *British Regional Employment Statistics 1841–1971* (Cambridge University Press, 1979).

Source: Census of Great Britain and Scotland, 1851–71.

occurred during the last decade of the century when, in spite of demand, there was a shortage of regular female farm labour as women increasingly sought alternative, better-paid employment off the land.[29]

In an attempt to remedy these difficulties in the census data for England, it has been suggested that the official number of women employed in agriculture in 1891 could conceivably be revised upwards by 14.7 per cent.[30] Given that Scottish agriculture employed a far higher proportion of the kind of female labour which was omitted from official calculations, it is possible that as late as 1891 as much as 20 per cent of the female labour force were employed in agriculture in Scotland, compared with the census figure of 5.1 per cent.

The numbers engaged in domestic service are almost certainly overestimated as it was common practice for enumerators to include unpaid female relatives and some categories of farm servant within the domestic service category, although the latter often worked on the farm.[31] A revised estimate of this category for England, which takes account of the vagaries of census practices, is less than half the official figure. Although the revisions are only crude estimates, they could considerably alter the pattern of the occupational distribution of women's work, with agriculture retaining an important role at least till the end of the century and domestic service no longer constituting the single most important source of employment for women.

Notwithstanding these caveats and revisions, the enduring feature of women's employment was that it was confined to relatively few occupations and was concentrated in certain well-defined areas of women's work. In 1851 domestic indoor service, agriculture, clothing, and textiles employed over 90 per cent of the female labour force, although by 1911 the four most important sources of employment for women accounted for 65 per cent of occupied women (see Table 1.4).

[29] Devine, 'Women Workers 1850–1911', 120.

[30] Higgs, 'Women, Occupation and Work in the Nineteenth Century Census', 74–5. He uses W. A. Armstrong's revised tables as his base and admits his upwards revision might be an overestimate.

[31] Devine, 'Women Workers 1850–1911', 109; Higgs, 'Women, Occupation and Work in the Nineteenth Century Census', 69.

Thus a discernible trend from the turn of the century was the increasing diversification of women's employment, although it was still the case that the bulk of female employment was confined to relatively few industries and occupations. Even in those expanding areas of employment such as commerce and the professions, the increase in women's employment is almost exclusively explained by the rise in the number of commercial clerks, who constituted approximately 86 per cent of women employed in this sector. In the professions the increase can be explained by the increase in the number of teachers, sick nurses, and midwives.

The degree of sex segregation of occupations was particularly pronounced in Scotland because of the predominance in the economy of the heavy industries, which employed almost exclusively male labour. Although these industries were concentrated in the central and west-central regions of the country, this pattern of occupational segregation and concentration was repeated throughout the major cities with the six major categories of employment accounting for over 80 per cent of employed women.

There were significant variations in the occupational distribution of women workers in the Scottish cities. For example, the major category in Glasgow throughout the period was textiles and clothing, with clothing assuming a more important role than textiles by 1911, a reflection of the contraction of Glasgow's cotton industry. The importance of the service sector in Edinburgh's economic structure and of the middle class in the social structure was reflected in the distribution of women's employment, with the domestic category occupying over 40 per cent of working women, and clothing, consumer industries, and professional services also employing significant numbers.

In contrast to the variegated economic structure of Edinburgh, Dundee's employment base was extremely narrow, with the jute and linen industries employing over 50 per cent of the working population throughout the period from 1851 until 1911. However, it was predominantly a women's industry. Of the total workforce 75 per cent were women and in 1851 three-quarters of all working women in the city were employed in jute whilst by 1911 this figure had fallen to

TABLE 1.5. *Major categories of female employment, 1901*

	Glasgow	Edinburgh	Aberdeen	Dundee
Domestic	21.61	42.53	25.63	8.00
Paper etc.	5.90	8.36	7.98	0.79
Textiles etc.	37.84	16.83	31.59	79.11
Food, tobacco, etc.	12.02	8.83	15.38	5.20
Professional services	5.15	7.77	6.90	2.79
Transport	2.94	1.36	1.79	0.55
TOTAL	85.46	85.68	89.27	96.44

Source: John Butt, 'The Changing Character of Urban Employment 1901–1981', in G. Gordon (ed.), *Perspectives of the Scottish City* (Aberdeen University Press, 1985).

two-thirds.[32] The dominance of the low-wage jute industry and the relatively small middle class in the city was reflected in the relative insignificance of the domestic service sector, which employed only 8 per cent of the female population in contrast to 25.63 per cent in Aberdeen and 42.53 per cent in Edinburgh (see Table 1.5).

The occupational distribution of Aberdeen's women workers was a little more evenly spread than the other cities, although no less segregated. Although the textile industry dominated it was not confined to one fibre, and the woollen, linen, and jute industries all provided employment for women.[33]

The structure of the labour market during this period suggests that there were in fact two labour markets, one for 'women's work' and one for 'men's work'. This is obviously an over-simplification as there were no industries and few occupations which were exclusively male or female. However, it is true to say that women were concentrated in a few occupations where there were relatively few men, such as domestic service, and, even when they were located in the same industry, there was a sexual division of labour.

In the textile industry the sexual division of labour was both vertical and horizontal. The supervisory positions were occupied almost exclusively by men, with the exception of shifting mistresses in the jute industry, who supervised young

---

[32] Census of Scotland, 1851 and 1911.
[33] J. Butt, 'The Changing Character of Urban Employment', in G. Gordon (ed.), *Perspectives of the Scottish City* (Aberdeen University Press, 1985), 214–15.

boys and girls. The tradesmen and the general labourers in textiles were all men. Although it is difficult to make generalizations about the textile industry as there were so many different branches with different work processes, there was a clear sexual division of labour. Even within those few tasks in which both men and women were engaged, such as weaving in the carpet industry, spinning in the Glasgow cotton industry, and preparing in the Dundee jute industry, a sexual division of labour emerged; in carpet-weaving the men worked on hand-looms, in spinning the men took over the larger mules and the finer counts of yarn, and in the preparing departments of the jute industry the men performed the heavier work.

Sexually segregated work also emerged in the skilled trades, which women began to enter towards the end of the century. In tailoring the men monopolized the first-class shops which catered for the 'bespoke trade' with women employed in the finishing processes such as button-holing. The third-class shops made extensive use of the sewing-machine and detailed division of labour, and employed mainly women. Even within the lower-class shops which produced for the ready-made market, women were excluded from pressing as it was argued that they were not physically strong enough to perform this task adequately.[34] In the bookbinding trades women were confined to 'stitching' and 'folding', and in printing the female compositors' jobs were restricted to typesetting, with the other processes involved in the trade remaining the preserve of men.[35]

Throughout the period between 1851 and 1911, the outstanding feature of women's employment pattern was not their exclusion from the labour market, but their concentration in a narrow range of occupations and in certain well-defined areas of 'women's work', resulting in a pronounced degree of occupational segregation on the basis of sex in the labour market. Notwithstanding this occupational segregation and concentration, an important feature of women's work was its diversity and the fluidity of the category 'women's work'.

[34] M. Nugent, 'Wages and Conditions in the Clothing Industry in Glasgow, *c.*1880–1914', undergraduate dissertation, University of Strathclyde, 1980, 4–5.
[35] Sian Reynolds, *Britannica's Typesetters* (Edinburgh University Press, 1989), 56–63.

Notions of what constituted 'women's work' varied over both time and place and the boundaries between men and women's work shifted. For example, the entry of women into male trades such as printing and tailoring and what has been termed the 'feminization' of clerical work, was a feature of late nineteenth-century and early twentieth-century occupational trends. Similarly, mule-spinning on the 'self-actor' was exclusively a male occupation in Lancashire, whereas in Glasgow this job fell increasingly to women because of alternative higher-paid employment which was available for men in the heavy industries. Women's work was also differentiated by status, skill, and earnings, despite the pervasive assumption in the historical and contemporary literature that women's work was a homogeneous category. In the hierarchy of women's work, shop work was highly regarded in comparison with factory work, which itself was internally differentiated. The women weavers of Glasgow and Dundee regarded themselves as a 'cut above' the spinners. On the other hand, some factory work, for example, spinning in cotton textiles, feeding in jute, block-printing in carpet-weaving, whilst lacking the status of office or shop work and denied a skilled classification, undoubtedly involved elements of genuine skill.

However, these important variations should not blind us to the overall pattern of women's work, which was segregated, concentrated, and low in status and earnings in comparison with men's work. A corollary of the phenomenon of 'women's work' was the notion of a women's wage, which was invariably set at a lower rate than men's. The average wage for women nationally was only 42 per cent of the male average,[36] and in textiles, one of the largest areas of women's employment, the annual average wage of women was 54 per cent of the male wage.[37] In agriculture, despite a growing scarcity of female labour, women's wages were so low that contemporaries believed that it was forcing women off the land. One commentator noted that 'At many branches of farm labour,

[36] B. Drake, *Women in Trade Unions* (London: Labour Research Department, 1921).

[37] *Return of the Rate of Wages in the Minor Textile Trades of the United Kingdom*, C. 6161 (London: HMSO, 1890), p. viii.

a good girl will do more than an average man, yet she still has to be content with half his wages . . .'.[38]

These averages, of course, masked considerable variations in women's earnings and the fact that some women earned more than some men. The highest average weekly wages recorded before 1886 by an official survey were 20s. per week for the women 'readers' in the Edinburgh printing trades, with the women 'self-acting' minders following a close second with 19s. 6d. per week. Their male equivalents earned 35s. to 40s. and 26s. respectively.[39] At the other end of the scale, the lowest wages recorded in the textile industry by the 1893 Royal Commission on Labour was from 4s. to 8s. per week for the women in the worsted spinning mills of Renfrewshire and Ayrshire. The Commission remarked that some of the women took out-of-door work during the harvest time in order to eke out their living.[40] The casual outwork of the clothing trade was notoriously badly paid and subject to interrupted earnings, which partly accounted for the low averages, but even in a complete week the homeworkers in shirt-finishing were lucky to earn 5s. 11d.[41]

Some women earned more than some men but this rarely happened within one trade or industry. For example, of the male workers in the cotton trade in Glasgow, only the nightwatchmen and lodge keepers earned less than the highest-earning women spinners.[42] The unskilled warehouse hands in Edinburgh's printing trade earned 15s. to 21s. per week, whilst the highest-paid skilled women earned 20s.[43]

The almost universal dividing line between men and women's work makes it difficult to make direct comparisons between male and female rates, but, in the few processes where men and women performed exactly the same tasks, the women's rate was usually lower than the men's. Margaret Irwin, of the

[38] Devine, 'Women Workers 1850–1911', 101.

[39] *Return of Wages 1830–1886*, C. 1572 (London: HMSO, 1887), 58 and 310.

[40] Royal Commission on Labour, *The Employment of Women*, C. 6894, vol. xxiii (London: HMSO, 1893), 183.

[41] Royal Commission on the Poor Laws, *William and Jones Report*, app. 1, C. 4690 (London: HMSO, 1909), 567.

[42] *Return of Wages*, 1830–1886, C. 1572 (London: HMSO, 1887), 58–9.

[43] Ibid. 310.

Scottish Council for Women's Trades, commented of the clothing industry that 'Where the women produce work of the same nature and efficiency as the men and are actually engaged side by side, the rate is much lower than the men.'[44]

The low pay received by most women was often justified by such statements as 'a woman's wage is always less than a man's' or 'it takes so much less to keep a woman than a man'.[45] These conventions appear to be related to the assumption that women were economic dependants rather than providers and yet the evidence suggests that not only were there substantial numbers of single unsupported women in the population, but that many women were themselves bread-winners with dependants. Although it is difficult to calculate the exact numbers of women who were sole bread-winners, the census does indicate that there were 561,745 working women in 1911 who were not dependent on the earnings of a husband.[46] Although some of these women would be supplementing the income of a father, a father and mother, or another relative, this would not be the case for the many widowed or deserted women in the population.

The 1911 census recorded that 12 per cent of the female population over 15 were widows, many of whom would have had families to support. The extent of wife desertion is impossible to quantify. However, the evidence of Poor Law records has led one historian to comment that 'this practice was one of more than marginal significance in Glasgow's working class society'.[47]

Given that the average female wage in Britain was less than half the average male wage, thousands of women were condemned to abject poverty as they were denied the right to earn a living wage. This is confirmed by the number of working women who had to apply for poor relief to supplement their wages. Margaret Irwin's investigation into the sweated trades found that 'many outworkers who are in receipt of wages too small to support them, though working full time, are aided

---

[44] M. H. Irwin, *Women's Work in Tailoring and Dressmaking* (Glasgow: SCWT, 1900), 11.   [45] Ibid. 11.

[46] Census of Scotland, 1911.

[47] J. H. Treble, 'The Characteristics of the Female Unskilled Labour Market in Glasgow 1891–1914', *Scottish Economic and Social History*, 6 (1986), 39.

from the rates'.[48] It has been estimated that almost one-quarter of all male occupations in the Scottish cities were susceptible to irregular employment. Therefore, the inability of most men to earn a wage which was sufficient to support a non-working wife and children, and the irregular nature of employment and hence earnings, forced many wives on to the labour market and often their earnings were central to the family's income.[49] A survey of 660 outworkers, by Glasgow's Chief Sanitary Inspector, included 300 wives who, it was claimed, consisted 'chiefly of the wives of labourers whose pay is small and whose employment is casual'.[50]

The SCWT's investigation into homework cited the case of Mrs. C., a trouser finisher, and noted that 'As her husband is unsteady in his habits, she seldom gets any help from him, and she and the eldest girl, who earns 7*s*. a week at the pottery, are practically the breadwinners of the household.'[51] However, it was not only the wives of the unskilled or the improvident and intemperate who worked, as even within the ranks of the skilled workers there was a wide range of economic experiences, with some trades more vulnerable to seasonal and cyclical unemployment than others. Therefore, often when financial circumstances dictated, the wives of tradesmen took up employment. A spinner whose mother was a weaver and father a tailor confirmed that the occasion for her mother seeking work was during a financial crisis: 'My mother went out to work for maybe a month or so in winter, but that was it finished. My father wouldn't allow her.'[52]

As women were relegated to the status of supplementary earners, whatever the reality of their status, this imposed considerable hardship on those families who had to rely intermittently on the earnings of the wife. The consequences

---

[48] Quoted in E. Cadbury *et al. Women's Work and Wages* (London: T. Fisher Unwin, 1907).

[49] R. Rodgers, 'Employment, Wages and Poverty, in Gordon (ed.), *Perspectives of the Scottish City*, 47.

[50] Royal Commission on the Poor Laws, *William and Jones Report*, app. 0(1), 657.

[51] Irwin, 'The Problem of Home Work', 13.

[52] Interview with Mrs. A., a former Dundee spinner (b. 1890).

were particularly severe for those women who were unsupported —single women, widows, deserted wives, many of whom were themselves bread-winners with dependants.

Although women's low rates of pay were related to social conventions and assumptions rather than the inherent skill of the job, women's work was usually designated as unskilled or semi-skilled. The explanation favoured by contemporary commentators was that women were not prepared to undertake the necessary training. However, this ignores the role of employers, trade unions, and the state in marginalizing women workers. Factory and workshop legislation often restricted the hours and location of women's work, and trade unions, often in collusion with employers, excluded women from apprenticeships or restricted their training to a limited number of processes to prevent them from acquiring the full panoply of skills required to qualify in the craft. For example, women compositors were denied training in the finishing processes and female tailors were never allowed to press garments they had sewn.[53] In the Alva tweed and Ayrshire shawl mills, women had displaced men in the warping departments but one man was still employed for every five women for the beaming and squaring of sections, which women were not thought capable of doing.[54]

Recent discussions of skill have highlighted the fact that many jobs have been socially constructed as skilled, and that the label bears little relation to the particular qualities required to perform a task but rather is a function of the ability of certain workers to get their work so defined.[55] Often trade union organization is seen as the means by which workers are able to retain their skilled label, with apprenticeships characterized as 'a period of virtual servitude designed to reinforce exclusive unionism'.[56] It has been commented of the printing trade that 'it was unofficially agreed by masters and men alike that no apprentice really needed seven years to learn

[53] Reynolds, *Britannica's Typesetters*; Irwin, *Women's Work in Tailoring and Dressmaking*.

[54] Royal Commission on Labour, *The Employment of Women*, 185.

[55] Charles More, *Skill and the English Working Class 1870–1914* (London: Croom Helm, 1980). Discusses in detail the various components and determinants of skill. [56] Quoted in ibid. 19.

the trade'.[57] On the other hand, the designation of some occupations as mere 'machine-minding' concealed the elements of genuine skill required to perform the task and often reflected the inflated claims of manufacturers regarding the efficiency of a machine as well as the interests and capacity of employers to label work as unskilled or semi-skilled in order to cheapen the cost of labour.[58]

Another strand in the social construction of skills is that it is also a category which is 'saturated with sexual bias'.[59] Few categories of women's work have been successfully designated as skilled, not only because women lack the trade union muscle required to impose the definition, but because of the pervasive belief that women's work is by definition unskilled. The male cotton spinners in Lancashire successfully retained their skilled status and the high earnings which differentiated them from unskilled groups and they assumed the position of an élite in the cotton industry. On the other hand, the women spinners in the Glasgow cotton industry had no such status and indeed were generally regarded as socially and morally inferior to the weavers.[60] Women's association with the domestic sphere, their consequent marginality to the labour market, and their status in society generally as dependent and subordinate individuals were the most powerful factors determining the value of the work they did, irrespective of the objective technical requirements of the job. Therefore, the concentration of women in low-status, unskilled work was as much related to the way skills were socially and ideologically constructed as to the exclusion of women from skilled work. In other words, work which women did was rarely recognized as skilled and constantly undervalued.

It is difficult to escape the conclusion that the overall pattern of women's employment was characterized by low pay, low status, and occupational segregation. Despite this bleak outline of women's employment and the fact that harsh economic

[57] Reynolds, *Britannica's Typesetters*, 51.
[58] M. Friefeld, 'Technological Change and the "Self-Acting" Mule: A Study of Skill and the Sexual Division of Labour', *Social History*, 2(3) (1986), and H. Catling, *The Spinning Mule* (Newton Abbot: David & Charles, 1970) makes a similar point.
[59] A. Phillips and B. Taylor, 'Sex and Skill: Notes towards a Feminist Economics', *Feminist Review*, 6 (1980).   [60] See Chs. 2 and 4.

realities forced most women into waged labour, it should not be assumed that work was invariably a negative experience devoid of intrinsic job satisfaction. The Edinburgh woman compositor who enthused that she 'would have worked weekends if they'd have let me . . . I loved my work, we all did' may not have been typical, but indicates that women may have positively evaluated their work, even when others did not.

The explanation for women's subordinate position in the labour market is far from simple. As has been illustrated, developments in the Scottish economy in the second half of the nineteenth century produced significant shifts in the sectoral distribution of employment as well as shifts within sectors, both of which had considerable implications for the pattern of women's employment. However, economic factors alone cannot explain why women's work was occupationally segregated from men's, generally defined as unskilled, and almost invariably lower paid than men's work.

Feminist writers in particular have argued that the sexual divisions which pervade waged work can only be explained by reference to the wider sexual division of labour in society. It has been argued that the sexual division of labour in the family with its emphasis on women's domestic responsibilities strongly influenced women's participation in the labour force. It has been pointed out that when women entered paid employment it was frequently in jobs which mirrored their domestic tasks and which were consistent with the Victorian ideal of womanhood as 'angel in the house'. Two of the three main sources of women's employment in mid- to late nineteenth-century Scotland can be viewed as extensions of women's domestic role, namely, domestic service and work in the clothing industry as seamstresses, milliners, shirtmakers, and dressmakers. The new opportunities in women's employment by the turn of the century were in the areas of teaching, nursing, and the manufacturing and retail of foodstuffs, again jobs which replicated women's domestic skills and tasks. However, there is clearly no simple equation between women's domestic responsibilities and the kind of work they did. Not all women's work reflected or extended their domestic responsibilities. One of the principal sources of women's employment in the mid-Victorian period was weaving in the textile industry, and in the early twentieth century clerical work, neither of which related to women's domestic role, and which previously had been dominated by men.

Alternative explanations of occupational segregation have developed which focus on the fact that women provided employers with a cheap and unskilled source of labour because it is assumed that women are dependants who do not require the same level of earnings as men. In this model employers are motivated to hire women as part of a strategy of deskilling and maximizing profitability. Although this approach helps explain women's work in areas such as tailoring, the boot and shoe industry, and some branches of textiles and engineering, it is not adequate as a general explanation of women's work as it only takes account of the employers' role and neglects the ways in which trade union practices have structured the sexual division of labour in the workplace. Nor does it explain why there was no universal and systematic strategy by employers to replace men with women, given their obvious advantage as a cheap source of labour. It also assumes that employers were motivated solely by economic considerations and that their practices were not shaped by social and ideological considerations, crucially, by prevailing notions about women's role in society, the nature of women's work, and its relationship to men's. It appears, therefore, that global explanations and general theoretical models are incapable of explaining the complex process of occupational segregation and differentiation in the labour process.

In recent years there has developed a mushrooming interest in the changing nature of workplace relations and work organization.[61] This rich vein of research has produced many useful insights into workplace organization, particularly the view that the evolution of the labour process is contingent on

---

[61] Much of this research was stimulated by H. Braverman's *Labour and Monopoly Capital: The Degradation of Work in the Twentieth Century* (New York: Monthly Review Press, 1974), although subsequent work has often taken issue with Braverman's central thesis. See e.g. Richard Edwards, *Contested Terrain: The Transformation of the Workplace in the Twentieth Century* (London: Heinemann, 1979); Craig Littler, *The Development of the Labour Process in Capitalist Societies* (London: Heinemann, 1982); Stephen Wood (ed.), *The Degradation of Work?* (London: Hutchinson, 1982); Paul Thompson, *The Nature of Work* (London: Macmillan, 1983).

the complex interaction between different sets of relationships, rather than being the product of the inexorable logic of capitalist development. One possible method of analysis suggested by this approach is that the fundamental relationships shaping the labour process are the relationships between capital and labour, among capitalists, and among groups of workers.[62] Whilst this perspective places primacy on economic relationships and focuses on the workplace to explain continuities and changes in work organization, inferentially it allows for the possibility that economic relationships can be mediated by relationships which may be shaped by non-economic variables and factors outside the workplace; for instance, those between capital and labour and between different groups of workers. A detailed empirical analysis of one particular industry which took account of these sets of relationships might shed light on the process of labour market segmentation and the emergence of sexually segregated work within the labour process itself.

The development of the cotton-spinning industry in Scotland in the nineteenth century provides a useful case-study to analyse the interweaving of economic, social, and ideological factors in the process by which certain tasks came to be defined as women's work. Most economic historians agree that the linen industry, which developed in eighteenth-century Scotland, formed the basis for the development of cotton textiles in that it provided a workforce already highly skilled in spinning and weaving.[63] What seems paradoxical is that the sexual division of labour in the domestic system of production was the reverse of the division of labour produced by the Industrial Revolution. In the domestic system the women were the spinners and the men the weavers, whereas, with the development of technology in the early stages of the Industrial Revolution, the spinning process was taken over by the men, whereas power-loom weaving became dominated by female labour. However, by the end of the century both the spinning and weaving sectors of the industry were dominated by women, with men virtually eliminated from the industry.

[62]   This method of analysis is suggested by B. Elbaum *et al.*, 'The Labour Process, Market Structure and Marxist Theory', *Cambridge Journal of Economics*, 3 (1979).
[63]   H. Hamilton, *The Industrial Revolution in Scotland* (Oxford University Press, 1932), 11.

Margaret Irwin in her report on the textile trade in the west of Scotland in 1895 claimed that a comparison between men's labour and women's labour in textiles was not possible 'as the chief branches of the textile trade are confined to women'.[64] She also noted that 'The great feature which differentiates the textile industries of Scotland from those of England is that, while in the latter country they are followed by both sexes, in this they are practically *women's* industries'.[65]

Weaving in both Scotland and England was dominated by women. However, in Scotland women also came to dominate spinning, which contrasted sharply with Lancashire—where mule spinning was carried on by men. Women engaged only in ring and throstle spinning, neither of which displaced mule spinning to any great extent before 1900. Margaret Irwin makes it clear how power-loom weaving was regarded very much as 'women's work' in Scotland and illustrates the rigidity of the sexual demarcation of occupations.

But a rooted prejudice exists among the working class of Scotland against the employment of men on the powerloom. A manager of a large factory told me that he had once made an effort to introduce male labour into his weaving department, and that, after a four week's trial, the men gave it up, being unable to stand the ridicule to which they were daily exposed for taking up 'women's work'.[66]

The crucial question to be asked is—why did the composition of the labour force and indeed the form of the labour process in cotton spinning in Scotland differ so markedly from England?

The Cotton Industry before 1837: The Spinner–Piecer System

By the 1830s, Glasgow was the centre of the cotton industry in Scotland, employing a workforce of about 10,000, over two-thirds of whom were female.[67] In the spinning sector of the

[64] Royal Commission on Labour, *The Employment of Women.*
[65] M. H. Irwin, 'Women's Industries in Scotland', *Proceedings of the Philosophical Society of Glasgow*, 27 (1895–6), 1.   [66] Ibid. 11.
[67] 'Statement of the Ages and Wages of Persons Employed in Cotton Mills in Glasgow and its Neighbourhood in April 1832', *Accounts and Papers relating to Revenue, Population Commerce etc.*, Session 19 Feb.–10 Sept. 1835, C. 693, vol. xlix, 412.

industry there were 3,987 females to 2,587 males. There were, however, only slightly more adult women to adult men.[68] Virtually all the mule spinners were men, who, operating an internal subcontract system, recruited and supervised three piecers, who were mainly boys and girls between the ages of 9 and 18, although some adult women were also employed as piecers.[69] The central concern of the Spinners' Association was to control entry into the trade in order to protect piece-rates. The object of the society was to limit the craft of mule spinning to members of the society and their male relatives. As one member of the Association commented: 'even a piecer would find it a very difficult matter to get any of the spinners to teach him the business unless he has relations or friends to help him on'.[70]

The union's policy seems to have had a considerable measure of success in that spinners' earnings in Glasgow compared favourably with those of other skilled craftsmen as well as the piece-rates paid to spinners in Lancashire.[71] Their control of entry into the trade was perhaps not as comprehensive as they would have liked, notwithstanding the observation of the Factory Commission that the Glasgow Association exercised 'a very inconvenient degree of control over their employers'.[72] In fact a special committee of the Association was set up in 1836, specifically to deal with the problem of the influx of strangers and 'illegal men' into the trade.[73]

Various attempts had been made by the employers to introduce female labour but they had met with only limited success and women's employment was confined to the smaller,

[68] 'Statement of the Ages and Wages of Persons Employed in Cotton Mills in Glasgow and its Neighbourhood in April 1832', *Accounts and Papers relating to Revenue, Population Commerce etc.*, Session 19 Feb.–10 Sept. 1835, C. 693, vol. xlix, 412.
[69] Factory Inquiry Commission, 1833, First Report, *Employment of Children in Factories with Minutes of Evidence and Reports by the District Commissioners*, in *Industrial Revolution: Children's Employment, 3*, Factories, xx (Shannon: Irish University Press, 1970), *passim*.   [70] Ibid. 82.
[71] W. H. Fraser, 'The Glasgow Cotton Spinners, 1837', in J. Butt and J. T. Ward (eds.), *Scottish Themes* (Edinburgh: Scottish Academic Press, 1976); J. Butt, 'Industrial Relations in the Cotton Industry', in J. Butt and K. Ponting, *Scottish Textile History* (Aberdeen University Press, 1987).
[72] Factory Inquiry Commission, 1833, First Report, *Employment of Children in Factories*, 83.   [73] Fraser, 'The Glasgow Cotton Spinners, 1837', 83.

lower-paying mules, which presumably the trade union disliked but which they would thole as long as women remained on the smallest and lowest-paying mules. A concerted effort had been made by the firm of John Dennistoun to introduce women into the Bridgeton mills at a rate one-third lower than the men,[74] but again to operate light wheels, which tended to be operated by young men. The employment of eleven female workers provoked a vehement response from the union, which sent a deputation to the manager arguing that 'if they could help it, they would not allow the women to be employed at all as spinners, but that at all events would fall on means to prevent their being employed for lower rates than those which they had fixed'.[75]

Faced with the intransigence of the employers, the Association resorted to harassing and haranguing the female spinners and their piecers, breaking the windows of their houses, and physically attacking them, with the aid of a crowd of some 7,000 to 8,000.[76] The company relented by offering to pay the women the same rates as men, and the union, much mollified, no doubt by the belief that they had staunched the flow of female labour into the industry, agreed to 'withdraw all further molestation', provided that the man accused of molesting one of the women was let off prosecution.[77]

Undoubtedly union strength was a major factor in limiting the introduction of women into mule spinning at this stage, although there were other considerations. Spinning on the larger hand mules with 300 or so spindles required considerable physical strength and stamina and probably encouraged employers to opt for male labour, generally considered physically stronger. However, there is a wealth of evidence suggesting that both the quality and the quantity of male spinners' work was widely variable and indeed there is the instance of Dennistoun's mill where one woman, employed on a large mule, earned 30s. a week, more than many of the men.[78] But women were not only cheap labour; they were perceived by some employers as being more docile. The

---

[74] Factory Inquiry Commission, 1833, First Report, *Employment of Children in Factories*, 84.　　[75] Ibid.　　[76] Ibid.　　[77] Ibid.　[78] Ibid.

manager of Dennistoun's mills avowed that, even if forced to pay the women spinners male rates, he would continue to employ them as they were 'less troublesome' than the men.[79]

Notwithstanding these advantages of employing female labour, they were not introduced into the Glasgow industry in any great numbers, although there were a number of women employed in rural mills. Fear of provoking a costly strike in a highly competitive market may have been a constraining factor. It has also been suggested that the use of internal subcontracting and the supervisory component involved in spinning meant that the jobs fell to men, whose patriarchal role made them the 'natural' recruiters and supervisors of labour.[80] The reluctance to recruit women may therefore have been related to the desire to avoid any disruption to established and effective systems of labour discipline. However, Glasgow employers were prevented from introducing other cost-cutting measures by a combination of union strength and the kind of yarn and machinery commonly used in the local industry. If long mules or coupled mules were introduced, as they had been in England, the union might have successfully maintained their piece-rates and therefore captured all the productivity gains for themselves.[81] In addition, the technical backwardness of the Scottish industry meant that inferior machinery was used in Glasgow, which made it difficult to use long mules or to couple together two mules with the coarse counts of yarn prevalent in the Glasgow industry (a 'count' is the number of 840-yard hanks per pound of yarn).[82]

Glasgow employers were therefore caught in a cleft stick, and the obvious alternative strategy, given that the Scottish industry was struggling against fierce competition from America and Lancashire, would have been to attempt to replace male

[79] Factory Inquiry Commission, 1833, First Report, *Employment of Children in Factories*, 84.

[80] W. Lazonick, 'The Division of Labour and Machinery: The Development of British and US Cotton Spinning', Discussion Papers Series, Harvard University, May 1978.

[81] W. Lazonick, 'Industrial Relations and Technical Change: The Case of the Self-Acting Mule', *Cambridge Journal of Economics*, 3 (1979).

[82] *Report from the Select Committee on Manufactures, Commerce and Shipping*, 1833, in *Industrial Revolution: Trade, 2* (Shannon: Irish University Press, 1970), 310, evidence of Mr H. Houldsworth.

labour with female labour, at least on the shorter and lighter mules of 200 spindles or less. Yet there is little evidence that employers made any systematic or sustained attempts to introduce women as spinners, directing their energies at reducing the piece-rates of the spinners. Employers' continued reliance on male labour and the established labour management system, which invested authority in a male spinner, can to some degree be explained by prevailing economic relationships in the industry. In the previous decade the industry had moved into coarser counts of yarn at the cheaper end of the market, which brought Glasgow into more direct competition with the larger and more robust Lancashire industry. Therefore, product market constraints may have discouraged employers from undertaking a wholesale reorganization of the labour process including the recruitment of women, preferring the less disruptive policy of retaining established production strategies. This policy was probably reinforced by the certainty that any attempt to rationalize would provoke a militant response from the spinners' union and a potentially damaging strike.

An additional constraint may have been employers' perceptions and sensitivity to culturally defined sexual boundaries and hierarchies. Employers' public utterances on female labour frequently reflected prevailing cultural prescriptions on women's role and were rarely restricted to observations about their advantage as cheap labour, as illustrated by the comments about women's docility by the manager of Dennistoun's mill. Employers' reconstitution of patriarchal household structures within the workplace, in the form of a male spinner having authority and control over children, young adults, and sometimes adult women, may have served their labour management needs, but it also reflected their acceptance of cultural definitions of sexual hierarchies of power and authority. Employers often shared societal definitions and concerns about suitable work for women, which may have led to a preference for men. The manager of the Bridgeton mills, which employed eleven women spinners, none the less expressed reservations about employing women in mills, commenting that a great many were 'loose in their morals' and that mule spinning even on light wheels was 'constant and rather severe work for women'.[83] Therefore, whilst employers' strategies for the recruitment and use of labour may have been rooted in market conditions, they were mediated by prevailing cultural definitions of suitable work for women.

1837–1880s: The Self-Actor and the Minder–Piecer System

What employers viewed as the stranglehold of the Spinners' Association was completely broken in 1837 after an unsuccessful strike, which almost certainly was provoked by the employers in a concerted effort to reduce piece-rates in the face of falling yarn prices[84] and of another increase in piece-rates for spinners. It is commonly supposed that the defeat of the union signalled the widespread and rapid introduction of the self-acting mule, which employers claimed was completely automatic and therefore dispensed with the need for skilled operators and enabled the adoption of a young female low-wage labour force.[85] This scenario was certainly predicted by some employers and used as a threat against the spinners' union in the 1830s if they persisted in maintaining their high piece-rates. William Graham, a cotton master extensively involved in cotton spinning and power-loom weaving in Glasgow, claimed in his evidence to the Select Committee on Manufactures, Commerce, and Shipping that his firms were introducing self-actors and the intention was to 'dismiss all the spinners, all the men that are making those exorbitant wages'.[86] Interestingly he still envisaged that it would be males who operated the machine, at least in the higher-paid work. When asked if some of the spinners would not be required to manage the self-acting mules he replied unequivocally: 'None; a spinner at present has two piecers under him, we shall still employ two piecers,

[83] Factory Inquiry Commission, 1833, First Report, *Employment of Children in Factories*, 85.

[84] Fraser, 'The Glasgow Cotton Spinners, 1837'.

[85] A. Slaven, *The Development of the West of Scotland, 1750–1960* (London: Routledge & Kegan Paul, 1975); Lazonick, 'Industrial Relations and Technical Change'; Fraser, 'The Glasgow Cotton Spinners, 1837'; WCE, sect. A, vol. 34, 381–413.

[86] *Report from the Select Committee on Manufactures, Commerce and Shipping*, 1833.

and to one of those piecers we may be obliged to give a couple of shillings more than the spinner gives him at present.'[87]

The immediate aftermath of the 1837 strike seemed to usher in a period of limited experimentation and reorganization of the labour process. By the time of the Select Committee on Combinations of Workmen's inquiry in 1838, between twenty and forty wheels had been coupled throwing the same number of spinners out of work from a total of 1,000 spinners. One cotton master claimed that coupling was spreading gradually throughout the town, although he also added the caveat that the system was only applicable to the finer counts of yarn.[88] There are also references to the introduction of self-acting mules in some mills and one employer claimed that in his own works they had dismissed their spinners and replaced them with 'little children' to keep the machines in order.[89]

The extent of coupling or doubling mules in Glasgow was limited; therefore, the number of male spinners displaced was obviously small and the system of introducing self-actors operated solely by young children seems to have been abandoned at a fairly early stage. Such evidence as exists suggests that the replacement of male labour and the introduction of women was in fact a very gradual process, which gained impetus mainly from the increasing availability of alternative higher-paid employment in the Clydeside's heavy industries, the natural wastage of the male labour force, and the contraction of the industry during and after the cotton famine of the 1860s. In other words, male spinners seem to have been pulled out of the industry as much as pushed out.

The Glasgow employers were particularly proprietorial about information relating to their firms, as both scholars and the Factory Inspectorate commented that they were unable to publish any details relating to the operation of Glasgow cotton

[87] *Report from the Select Committee on Manufactures, Commerce and Shipping*, 1833.
[88] *First Report of the Select Committee on Combination of Workmen*, 1837–8, C. 488, evidence of Mr H. Houldsworth.
[89] Ibid. 454.

mills.[90] This was probably a reflection of employers' fear of competition at a time when the Glasgow cotton industry was losing out in the competitive battle with Lancashire. In consequence, there are only snippets of information about the Glasgow trade in comparison with the voluminous outpourings produced by official, unofficial, and scholarly investigations of Lancashire's cotton industry.

The paucity of detailed information and the lack of disaggregated information on the cotton trade obviously prevents the possibility of any definitive statements about Glasgow cotton spinning and necessitates reliance on qualitative sources to supplement the dearth of hard facts. This material indicates that although the ratio of women to men in spinning increased from 3:1 to 4.25:1 between 1835 and 1856, much of the increase in female labour can be traced to the increasing reliance on women and young girls as piecers in spinning instead of boys.[91] Any reference to piecers in the post-1837 period suggests that they were female. A strike of male cotton spinners in 1861 claimed that their piecers' wages had risen by 25 per cent since 1837 and complained that 'as female labour is so much in demand, were we to propose any reductions to them they would convey their services elsewhere'.[92] Another strike of self-acting minders and their piecers in 1864 revolved around the employer's attempts to make 'one man and one woman do the same quantity and quality that was required by one man and two women formerly'.[93] The Return of Wages for 1830–86 noted that two of the three categories of piecers were 'girls chiefly'.[94]

From the Return of Wages it seems that men monopolized what was termed 'first-class' spinning, which probably means spinning on the common mules on fine counts.[95] There is no indication of the gender of those undertaking second-class and third-class spinning, or whether it involved the self-actor or

---

[90] D. Bremner, *Industries of Scotland* (Edinburgh: David & Charles, 1869); 'Half-Yearly Reports of the Inspectors of Factories with Appendices', in *Industrial Revolution*, Factories, vii (Shannon: Irish University Press, 1970), session 1842–7. Report by James Stewart for the quarter ending June 1844.

[91] *Accounts and Papers*, C. 693, vol. xlix.

[92] *Glasgow Sentinel*, 4 May 1861.　　　　　　　　[93] Ibid., 21 May 1864.

[94] *Return of Wages*, 1830–1886, 56.　　　　　　　[95] Ibid. 56–8.

the common mule, but, as women and young men had worked on short common mules before 1837, it seems likely that they retained this grade of work. According to the Return of Wages, both men and women worked as self-acting minders, although it is less certain in what proportions.[96] The Webbs claimed that in the 1860s as many women as men were minding; in other words, men still retained a prominent position in the trade, even on self-actors, which were thought to have displaced them.[97]

The sparse information about the Glasgow cotton trade makes it difficult to reconstruct the details of the labour process. From what can be inferred from the qualitatively and quantitatively limited sources, internal subcontracting and piece-work seems to have been the norm for spinning both on the larger common mules and on the self-actors. On the long mules one male spinner would recruit and supervise three piecers, who would be mainly women and girls paid on time wages.[98] The term 'minder' was applied to spinners operating the self-actors. Both men and women held this position, supervising usually two piecers, again predominantly females paid on time wages.[99] There emerged a sexually segregated division of labour among those working on the self-actor, with men capturing the work on the higher-paying finer counts and women minders confined to the lower counts.[100]

Spinners managed to retain reasonable earnings, despite the precarious position of the Glasgow trade. Throughout the 1850s and until the early 1860s, first-class spinners (men) earned between 5s. 4d. and 6s. 6d. per day, second-class spinners between 4s. 6d. and 5s. 6d., and third-class spinners on short wheels between 3s. and 3s. 6d. per day, earnings which compared favourably with crafts such as printing.[101] By 1866 the male self-acting minders on the higher counts were earning 26s. per week and the women minders 19s. to 19s. 6d. per week, but this was in 1866 when the cotton trade had been crippled by the American Civil War and earnings had presumably been reduced.[102]

[96] *Return of Wages*, 1830–1886, 56–8.
[97] WCE, sect. A, vol. 34, p. 413.   [98] Ibid.
[99] Ibid.; *Return of Wages*, 1835–1886.
[100] *Return of Wages*, 1835–1886.   [101] Ibid.   [102] Ibid.

It appears, then, that men maintained a sizeable if diminishing presence in Glasgow cotton spinning until the 1860s when the industry went into rapid decline. Given the highly competitive and precarious nature of the Glasgow cotton industry this scenario runs counter to what might have been expected, and was indeed threatened, once the employers had broken the union. Male trade union exclusionary practices cannot account for men's retention of the position of minder on the self-actor as the union after 1837 was a spent force, organizationally and financially. The employment profile of men in cotton spinning suggests that women may have been recruited because of the shortage of male labour, indicating a drift out of the industry by men rather than forcible expulsion by employers. Margaret Irwin seemed to have no doubt that this was the significant factor: 'One obvious reason for the textile industries being abandoned to women in the northern and western districts is that the men are attracted by the highly skilled and highly paid mineral, metal, and building trades.'[103]

The pull of more stable and lucrative employment certainly applied to the years after the American Civil War, which had such a crippling effect on the industry and sealed Glasgow's fate in the competition with Lancashire's cotton industry. According to one interpretation, 'many fortunes were lost; resources were diverted to the developing heavy industries and skilled operatives were attracted to the better paying and more stable engineering industries'.[104]

It has been persuasively argued that the occupation of minder on the self-actor required genuine skill and was not simply a skill socially constructed or contrived in order to preserve the privileges and earnings of a group of élite male workers.[105] It is argued that the reason the self-actor was dominated by men in America and Britain was that women had been squeezed out of the trade at an earlier stage of production by the introduction of long or coupled mules, which required strength and stamina and hence male labour. This entailed a breakdown

[103] Irwin, 'Women's Industries in Scotland', 17.
[104] J. Cunnison and J. B. S. Gilfillan (eds.), *Third Statistical Account of Scotland: Glasgow* (Glasgow: Collins, 1955), ch. 8.
[105] Friefeld, 'Technological Change and the "Self-Acting" Mule'.

in the intergenerational transmission of this female craft skill and, in conjunction with the exclusionary practice of the union in refusing to accept female piecers, accounted for male dominance of the trade.[106]

Whether or not the loss of the craft of mule spinning to a generation of women explains their exclusion from the Lancashire trade, it has little relevance for the Scottish situation. Admittedly before 1837 there were few women spinners and piecers, but after the strike female piecers were widely recruited, ensuring a plentiful supply of women who had acquired a training in the craft of spinning. Whether or not women were specifically trained as spinners, they seemed to pick up the skill. A firm which dismissed its male workforce in the 1830s and hired women to operate the short mules claimed that 'Most of the women had been formerly piecers, and had thus learned the business of spinning'.[107] From the 1840s in Glasgow there would have been no shortage of trained women with the requisite skills, and yet men continued to dominate spinning for twenty years after this.

Yet another explanation advanced for male dominance of spinning in Lancashire was that physical stamina was still an important element of work on the self-actor, although this varied with the size and speed of the machine and the quality of yarn. Consequently, piecing, which was the main task of the spinner as well as the piecer, tended to be done by adult males.[108] Again the Scottish evidence illustrates the folly of generalizing on the basis of the Lancashire experience and the dangers of a posteriori reasoning. Women's work as spinners may have been restricted to the coarser numbers and the smaller mules, but in Glasgow women worked as piecers on all classes of spinning, that is, all sizes and speeds of common mules and self-actors, and on all counts of yarn, with the same number of piecers per self-actor as the Lancashire system, namely, two piecers to one spinner. This undermines the argument that physical factors partly explain the dominance of men and

---

[106] Friefeld, 'Technological Change and the "Self-Acting" Mule'.

[107] Factory Inquiry Commission, 1833, First Report, *Employment of Children in Factories*.

[108] Lazonick, 'Industrial Relations and Technical Change'.

suggests that a more convincing explanation for their confine-
ment as spinners to smaller self-actors was related to the lower
rates of pay on this class of work.

The development of Glasgow's cotton-spinning industry in
the period provides clear evidence that, even in a situation
where employers had a free hand to recruit whomsoever they
wanted, and where there were strong pressures to lower costs
and achieve greater control over the production process, their
strategy was not automatically to recruit women workers.

The 1880s: The Multi-Pair System

By the 1880s, the total workforce in cotton spinning and
weaving in Scotland was reduced to 5,974 from a peak of about
40,000 with only 34 adult men and 471 women employed in
both mule and throstle spinning in Glasgow and a completely
reorganized division of labour. The new system, which was
first introduced in 1880 'purely out of economy', involved one
man, a 'doffer', supervising five and a half pairs of mules with
three women each on weft. A variation of this system was
introduced by the Glasgow Spinning Company in the new
works it established in 1884. This firm specialized in medium
counts of yarn and paid the male 'doffers' 34s. 6d. per
week.[109]

In the Glasgow system women piecers were variously
described as 'spinners', 'piecers', and 'guides', and, whilst the
exact nature of their task is unclear, it is doubtful that they
were analogous to the piecers in the Lancashire system. Their
different titles probably denote the fact that this new system
of work had created new categories of workers whose
tasks involved the piecing and spinning which constituted
the old minder–piecer system. In the much reduced and
reorganized industry of the 1880s, the supervisory grades
were occupied exclusively by men, with women reduced to
subordinate roles and stripped of the supervisory function and
technical skills they had exercised on the old minder–piecer
system.

[109] WCE, sect. A, vol. 34, p. 413.

The radically different organization of work in Glasgow cotton spinning illustrates that how technology is used is less dependent upon the inherent nature of the technology than on the web of economic and social relations within which it is to be deployed. Moreover, the divergent experience of the Glasgow industry suggests that the sex composition of the labour force can influence both the form of the labour process and employers' strategies, and patriarchal ideology can influence which sex gets which job. It is noteworthy that it was only when the industry was abandoned to women that reorganization was introduced and the old hierarchical system of production was scrapped.

How then are we to disentangle the various forces which interacted to produce the particular sexual division of labour and labour process which characterized Glasgow's cotton-spinning industry? Can the set of relationships identified earlier as those between capital and labour, among capitalists, and among workers satisfactorily explain these developments?

The conflict of interest between capital and labour and the recurrent clashes over piece-rates in the 1820s and 1830s obviously lay at the heart of many of the developments in the earlier period. The wider market conditions of cotton textiles and the intense competition between capitalists made it imperative that employers cheapen labour costs, but the strength of trade union organization and militancy constrained employers. However, the exclusion of women from the craft of spinning during this period was only partly the product of trade union resistance. Cotton masters did not display great eagerness to displace men and there were only sporadic and isolated attempts actively to recruit women. Piece-rates were a much more bitterly contested issue and one which was a constant preoccupation for employers.

Although employers successfully crushed the union in 1837, men continued to monpolize spinning. Glasgow's weak position in the competitive race and the need for skilled labour may have imposed limitations on employers' ability to restructure the division of labour, to introduce new technology, or to displace male with female labour. All of these strategies may have had long-term benefits, but would have been disruptive, costly, and perhaps damaging in the short term if undertaken

by any individual firm. Alternatively, it may have been the case
that men were retained because employers, having retrieved
the initiative in 1837 and broken the Gordian knot of high
piece-rates, no longer had the incentive to replace men with
cheaper female labour and to restructure the division of labour.
However, given the fiercely competitive battle in cotton textiles,
which Scotland was rapidly losing, cost-cutting measures might
have been expected. Investment in new and up-to-date
technology was a costly and risky option, and in fact the
Scottish cotton industry has frequently been criticized for its
failure to invest in this area.[110] Therefore, restructuring the
division of labour and replacing men with cheaper female
labour, which would have had the necessary training by the
mid-1840s, would have been the most obvious strategy, given
that union opposition had been crushed. In fact the nature of
the local labour market was probably more significant in
explaining the drift of men out of the industry and confirming
it as a woman's industry than the exclusionary strategies of
employers.

   Conflicts between capital and labour, the structure of local
labour markets, and product market constraints to some degree
influenced the sexual composition of the labour force and the
form of the labour process in spinning. Employers' strategies
were clearly contingent on the shifting combination and balance
of these relationships. However, economic rationale has
limitations as an explanatory variable. It might just explain
the retention of men in spinning, but it cannot satisfactorily
explain men's monopoly of the higher-grade and higher-paid
work on self-actors. Nor can it explain why in the 1880s when
the remnants of the industry were reorganized, including the
restructuring of the division of labour, it was men who captured
the supervisory positions, making a more rigid demarcation
between men and women's work than had previously existed.

   The development of the division of labour, the organization
of work, and authority structures in the industry seem to
indicate that employers' practices were based on more than
purely economic considerations and were influenced by the

[110] A. J. Robertson, 'The Decline of the Scottish Cotton Industry', *Business History*, 12(2) (1970).

wider social relations of production and the social division of labour, crucially the relations between men and women and their cultural role in society. Women workers were perceived differently by employers. Not only were they viewed as cheap labour, they were generally assumed to be more docile and less troublesome. They were also clearly identified as occupying a distinct and subordinate position in the social division of labour and this means that employers saw them as a distinct and different category of worker from men.

This was not only reflected in the lower wages women were paid, but also in the ways work was organized. Authority structures took a different form, technology was used differently, and the labour process generally took a different shape when women were the majority of the labour force. Employers seemed to unquestioningly assume that men were the natural inheritors of supervisory, skilled, and higher-paid jobs. No matter how the boundaries of the sexual division were drawn or redrawn, women were inevitably assigned, with the compliance and the sanction of employers, to the lower rungs of the status, skill, and earnings hierarchy. Men's virtual monopoly both of genuine skill and socially constructed skill, again with the support of employers, is illustrated by the fact that, although women minders supervised piecers and executed skilled work, albeit on the lower-class work, they were never accorded the same status as men in the industry. In the Glasgow cotton trade the women spinners were generally regarded as an inferior class to the weavers, whose work was certainly no more skilled than spinning. The contention by Friefeld that, if women had not been squeezed out of work on the common mule and had been employed as minders on the self-actor, 'British women would have held the position of highly skilled workers during the formation of the industrial working class'[111] seems highly questionable in the light of the Scottish experience, and indicates how persistent and impenetrable the gendered definitions of skilled work are.

Employers cannot be viewed simply as profit maximizers whose Gradgrind-like behaviour was subverted by the struggles of labour to maintain skill, status, and earnings, or constrained

[111] Friefeld, 'Technological Change and the "Self-Acting" Mule'.

by an intensely competitive market environment. Individual capitalists' practices were suffused with assumptions and values about the sexual division of labour which meant that they clearly differentiated between 'men's work' and 'women's work'. Decisions relating to technology and economics were taken within a particular ideological framework, and, if we are to understand decisions relating to the organization of work, crucially decisions about when and how to employ female labour, then it is necessary to analyse social relations outside the workplace as well as those within.

The different pattern of development of Scottish and English cotton spinning illustrates that any explanation for the pattern of women's employment and its salient characteristics has to address both economic and ideological factors. Women's status as cheap labour could be used to great effect by employers. However, this status was itself premised on ideological assumptions about the role of women which profoundly affected both the pattern of their employment and their experience of employment. The ideology of separate sexual spheres, the assumption that woman's primary role was as wife and mother, and the ideology of domesticity did not exclude women from the labour force, but it dictated the terms of their entry. Therefore, if we are to understand the way work was organized, the sexual division of labour, and the social construction of skill, we must take account of the pervasiveness and immanence of gender ideologies in the process, and the ways in which they mediated economic relationships.

It was not only employers' practices which incorporated the ideologies, but also trade union practices, and these have to be examined in order to determine their significance in shaping the pattern of women's employment.

2. The Trade Union Movement in Scotland

DISCUSSIONS of working-class organizations in the second half of the nineteenth century have tended to focus on the history of formal organizations, usually on the history of the trade union movement. There are obviously methodological reasons for this which arise from the availability of sources and the existence of record books, trade journals, newspaper accounts, etc. In other words, it is easier to acquire information about organizations which leave written records of their activities. This concentration and preoccupation with those sections of the working class which were involved in formal organizations not only obscures this history of the 'unorganized', but leads us to define organization and struggle in a particular way and consequently to ignore or deem irrelevant other forms of struggle which may take place outwith these formal organizations.

However, any study of the 'unorganized' or those who have been marginal to the trade union movement in Scotland is only understandable in the broader context of Scottish unionism and the particular forms which it assumed. The problem is therefore to view the unorganized in a way which does not involve adopting the perspectives, concerns, and prejudices of the formally organized sections, yet takes into account the impact which the trade union movement exerted on the entire working class, the influence and pervasiveness of the values to which it was committed, and the relevance those values had for the unorganized sections.

Although the weakness of Scottish working-class organizations and resistance has often been stressed to the exclusion of the more combative episodes in working-class history in the first half of the nineteenth century, there were undoubtedly economic, political, and cultural factors in Scotland which facilitated class collaboration and contained the sharpest expressions of class conflict.

Massive immigration from Ireland in the late eighteenth century and the first half of the nineteenth century, and internal migration from the Highlands and rural areas coupled with a high birth-rate, produced a superabundance of labour. This provided Scottish capitalists with a plentiful source of cheap labour, which rendered it potentially more docile and tractable. The unevenness of industrialization and the coexistence of difference forms of manufacture endowed class relations with a fluidity which further impelled class co-operation and blurred the boundaries of class divisions. The prevalence of handicraft manufacture and the flourishing of small-workshop production continued to provide the possibility of the artisan making the transition to small-master status and thus creating an identity of interests between master and workers. It has been argued that it was these kinds of factors which contributed to Scottish Chartism being a predominantly moral force and revealing only muted forms of class consciousness.[1]

The continued exclusion of significant sections of the middle class from the franchise, because of the difficulties of applying the conditions of the Reform Act to Scotland, provided an additional impetus to class co-operation.[2] The tenets of Calvinism, with their emphasis on thrift, temperance, and self-help, may not have subordinated the working class completely to the bourgeois philosophy of economic liberalism. However, they did infuse the working class with a distinctive ideology which had significant consciousness.

The development of trade-unionism in Scotland seems to have followed the national pattern, in that growth was neither steady nor linear, but fluctuated according to a number of factors such as changes in the trade cycle and the state of industrial relations within particular industries. The defeat of the Glasgow Cotton Spinners in 1837 and the harsh sentences imposed on the defendants not only broke the confidence of the Spinners' Union but had considerable ramifications in that other workers were discouraged from forming unions. This

[1] T. Dickson and T. Clarke, 'Class and Class Consciousness in Early Industrial Capitalism', in T. Dickson (ed.), *Capital and Class in Scotland* (Edinburgh: John Donald, 1982), 29–30.

[2] K. Burgess, 'Client Capitalism at its Zenith', in T. Dickson (ed.), *Scottish Capitalism* (London: Lawrence & Wishart, 1980), 211.

was compounded by the depression of the early 1840s, which dealt another hammer-blow and further inhibited the development of the unions.[3] When conditions were favourable to growth in the early 1850s, this legacy of weakness, which arose from the particular economic development of Scotland with its large reserve army of labour and relatively low wages, resulted in Scottish unions trailing behind their English counterparts, the revived unions tending to be localized and small.

It could be argued that the stress on local union autonomy, which arose largely from the structure of the Scottish economy with its concentration of industry in the west-central belt, was an additional impediment. Although it allowed the various unions to flourish independently, it did inhibit a major source of strength, the development of national unions with strong links, capable of acting in a unified and concerted fashion. The relative weakness of Scottish unionism and its federal structure meant that trades councils assumed a position of prominence unequalled in England, although it should be made clear that the trades councils at no time included all the organized sections within their ranks.

In the mid-Victorian period, the Scottish trade union movement had an extremely narrow base, and, though the core of its membership was the male skilled classes, it by no means encompassed the entire skilled workforce and of course largely excluded unskilled male and female workers. There is certainly evidence that unskilled workers organized during this period; harbour labourers and causeway labourers in Glasgow were at one time affiliated to the Glasgow Trades Council and agricultural workers formed a Farm Servants' Protection Society in Midlothian in 1865.[4] However, the unions of the unskilled were ephemeral and rarely survived unfavourable economic conditions and they certainly did not occupy a central role in the organized labour movement of the third quarter of the nineteenth century.

---

[3] W. H. Fraser, 'Trades Councils in the Labour Movement in 19th Century Scotland', in I. MacDougall (ed.), *Essays in Scottish Labour History* (Edinburgh: John Donald, 1978), 1.

[4] T. Johnston, *The History of the Working Classes in Scotland* (Wakefield: E. P. Publishing, 1974), 355.

The effects of declining profits and prices and foreign competition in the last quarter of the century, aggravated in Scotland by the collapse of the City of Glasgow Bank, had a catastrophic effect on the business community and consequently on trade union organization throughout Scotland. It is doubtful, as the Webbs claim, that only half a dozen Scottish trade unions survived the blow,[5] but certainly the number of societies affiliating to the Glasgow Trades Council had declined to 32 by 1886. The general picture of trade union development until 1855 is a relatively dismal one but not uniformly so, and from the mid-1880s there was an unprecedented boom in membership which is associated with the development of 'New Unionism'. The traditional account of New Unionism centres on the rise of a militant new organization committed to the recruitment of all grades of workers and inspired by more radical if not socialist ideology.[6] However, this account has been subjected to a critique by a number of historians who argue that the extension of trade-unionism involved the unions of craft and skilled workers as much as the previously unorganized and that the traditionally unionized sectors such as building, mining, and metals were as involved in the upsurge in industrial conflict as the newly emerging unions.[7] Events in Scotland would tend to support the interpretation that the years 1888–92 were a period of general increase in both union membership and collective struggle and were not confined to newly emerging unions. Although the boom of the late 1880s resulted in an extension of unionism to the previously unorganized and the re-emergence of the organizations of unskilled groups which had been wiped out by the years of depression and slumps, the growth in skilled unions and craft organizations was a more significant feature and affiliations to the Glasgow Trades Council were swelled by the increasing numbers of engineers, boilermakers, and those in the traditional

---

    [5] S. and B. Webb, *History of Trade Unionism* (London: Longmans, Green, 1920), 349.

    [6] E. J. Hobsbawm, *Labouring Men* (London: Weidenfeld and Nicolson, 1968); S. and B. Webb, *History of Trade Unionism*.

    [7] A. E. Duffy, 'New Unionism in Britain 1889–1890: A Reappraisal', *Economic History Review*, 2nd ser., 14(2) (1961–2); J. Lovell, *British Trade Unions 1875–1933* (London: Macmillan, 1977), ch. 2.

craft trades who were re-forming unions or establishing them for the first time. Workers in the heavy industries were prominent in the revival of 1888–92, although the traditional artisan trades also played an important role, even in Glasgow where the heavy industries dominated. Similarly, the mushrooming of industrial struggles and the concomitant militancy involved the unions of skilled and craft workers as much as the unskilled.

If the term 'New Unionism' is interpreted as embodying a new spirit or attitude in trade unions, or as being inspired by socialist ideology, again in Scotland these developments were more likely to be located amongst craft unions. For example, in Aberdeen the leading socialist trade-unionists were almost exclusively craft workers and in the Aberdeen Trades Council the socialist members included tailors, plumbers, shoemakers, bakers, and compositors.[8]

The mid-Victorian years are often characterized as a period of social stability and political and industrial quiescence, particularly when contrasted with the political and industrial strife of the 1830s and 1840s. It is generally argued that the labour movement appeared to become integrated into the capitalist system in the third quarter of the nineteenth century, divested of its revolutionary potential and its agitations designed to promote only limited and specific reforms. Similarly, it is argued that its organizations no longer advocated collective class action, but instead became committed to defensive actions based on a narrow economism which stressed sectionalist and exclusivist craft principles.[9]

There have been several explanations offered for what has been perceived as the transformation of the robust combative labour movement of the Chartist era into the quiescent one of the mid-Victorian period. However, the explanation which has gained the most currency and engendered the greatest

[8] K. D. Buckley, *Trade Unionism in Aberdeen, 1878–1900* (Edinburgh: Oliver and Boyd, 1955), 22.

[9] E. J. Hobsbawm, 'The Labour Aristocracy in Nineteenth Century Britain', in Hobsbawm, *Labouring Men*; G. S. Jones, 'Class and Class Struggle in the Industrial Revolution', *New Left Review*, 90 (1975); P. Joyce, *Work, Society and Politics* (London: Methuen, 1982); K. Burgess, *The Challenge of Labour* (London: Croom Helm, 1980), ch. 1; J. Foster, *Class Struggle and the Industrial Revolution* (London: Methuen, 1974).

controversy is the concept of the labour aristocracy;[10] that is, the emergence of a stratum of workers, privileged in comparison with the mass of semi-skilled and unskilled, and who exhibited distinctive forms of political and cultural behaviour. The debate ranges over a whole series of issues which deal with the composition of the labour aristocracy; its values and norms; its impact on the working-class movement, and the development of class consciousness; its role in explaining the roots of reformism and the failure to develop a mass revolutionary movement in Britain. More recent contributions to the debate have questioned the usefulness of the concept as an explanatory tool, the validity of such contrasts between the early and mid-Victorian labour movement, and whether it can be argued that such a stratum of the working class did exist. Whatever the merits of the labour aristocracy thesis the debate has drawn attention to the divisions within the working class and the social and political consequences of these divisions. Whilst the labour aristocracy is not synonymous with trade-unionism an important aspect of the argument is the dominance of this stratum and its ideology within the labour and trade union movement of the period.

The leading role of the heavy industries in Scotland's industrial structure ensured that the unions of the 'new' skilled workers dominated trade union organization. However, their influence was concentrated in the west of Scotland and therefore the organizations of the traditional craft trades were still of considerable importance and played a leading role in the institutions of the organized working class. The defence of sectional rights and privileges was certainly the pivot of trade union policies and for most of the period their concern was to protect the bargaining position of their trades by restricting entry.

The relatively advantaged position of those workers in the heavy industries who were able to secure gains by virtue of their strategic position in the economy was reflected in the

[10] Hobsbawm, 'The Labour Aristocracy in Nineteenth Century Britain'; Foster, *Class Struggle and the Industrial Revolution*; R. Q. Gray, *The Labour Aristocracy in Victorian Edinburgh* (Oxford: Clarendon Press, 1976); J. Field, 'British Historians and the Concept of the Labour Aristocracy', *Radical History Review*, 19 (Winter 1978–9), 61–85, has a full discussion of the historiography of the concept.

commitment of these unions to sectionalist trade policies which relied on their own bargaining strength for success. This produced an ideology which emphasized the solidarity and interest of their particular craft rather than the common interests of the wider working-class movement. This commitment to policies which entailed the confirmation and defence of craft privileges was certainly instrumental in consolidating many of the gains which had been won and in obtaining others, but in terms of the development of the entire working-class movement it arguably had a stultifying influence and on occasions was counter-productive for the craft groups themselves. During a four-month lock-out in the Clyde shipyards in 1866, the ASE and other unions paid the unorganized labourers a pittance of 2s. 6d. per week whilst their own members received 10s. per week. Starvation drove the labourers back to work and the organized trades were easily broken after this and the demand for shorter hours defeated.[11] Similarly, the iron moulders had succeeded in 1872 in obtaining a fifty-one-hour week but, as they were the only group in the industry to win this concession, the employers' hand was strengthened to retract the agreement when market conditions were unfavourable, as they did not have to confront the combined forces of all the trades in the industry.[12]

The working class has never been an undifferentiated mass and the organizations which it has espoused, in order to defend and improve its position at the point of production, have always reflected the fissures and schisms within the class. Therefore, the sectional character of unionism in the post-Chartist period was not a new phenomenon and frequently its policies and concerns were indistinguishable from those pursued by the unions of the earlier period. The different economic and political context of the mid-Victorian era may have strengthened craft sectionalism and reconciled the working class to industrial capitalism but this does not mean that it was divested of any awareness of class divisions and the sense of a separate class identity. Discussions of how to improve the wages and conditions of the working class rarely revealed a

[11] Johnston, *The History of the Working Classes in Scotland*, 372.
[12] Ibid. 369.

wholesale acceptance of orthodox economic principles and always contained a recognition that labour was the source of all wealth and that the fortunes of capital were created by the toil of the working masses. The perception of an inherent conflict of interest between capital and labour permeated trade union discussions, and the awareness of the divide between the two classes was frequently articulated even by those union officials who advocated conciliation and co-operation if not class collaboration. Thus the attempts of the Edinburgh Trades Council to reduce the working week referred to the need for workers to 'influence the Labour Market in their favour' as the best means by which the working class could secure a more equitable share of the wealth which 'their labour produces'.[13]

James McNeal, Secretary of the Clyde Boilermakers and Shipbuilders, unequivocally demonstrated a keen sense of class oppression when he wrote that 'While labour lives in hovels and starves in rags and capital lives in palaces and feasts in robes, speak no more of the castes of the tribes of India'.[14] The article illustrates that the radical tradition of the earlier period had not completely disappeared even if it was not shared by all trade-unionists. His claim that 'the only pure and free labour that can exist is that system wherein the products of labour are exchanged between producers and no party in the shape of prince, lord or master, to stand between the actual producers and exchangers directly or indirectly to claim the lion's share'[15] is reminiscent of the radical political tradition which sprung from the erosion of the independence of the artisan, and demonstrates the longevity of the political legacy of the Chartist period.

Although the focus of trade union energies was directed at maintaining craft privileges and distinctions, the movement was also capable of sponsoring class action rather than craft action. Trade unions were instrumental in promoting the short-time movement which cut across occupational sectionalism and achieved a limited degree of success in uniting the skilled and the unskilled in a common cause.[16]

[13] MacDougall (ed.), *Essays in Scottish Labour History*, 246.
[14] *Glasgow Herald*, 9 Dec. 1857, quoted in Johnston, *The History of the Working Classes in Scotland*, 370.
[15] Ibid. 320.
[16] See Ch. 5 for an illustration of these limitations.

In Scotland the organized labour movement was committed from an early stage to extending trade-unionism to the unskilled. The Glasgow Trades Council from its inception displayed a willingness to help the unorganized, usually lacing their advice with homilies on the improvement to their moral welfare which trade-unionism would bring. In 1859, the bleachers embarked on a long campaign to shorten their hours and were given every assistance by the Glasgow Trades Council, including the establishment of a select committee to investigate the conditions of the bleachworkers in Glasgow.[17]

Throughout the period the Glasgow Trades Council received a constant stream of deputations from groups of workers seeking advice or financial aid, or even asking the Council to exercise their influence to resolve particular disputes. This was not a policy peculiar to Glasgow but seems to have been adopted by the majority of the trades councils in Scotland. The establishment of an agricultural union in Midlothian in 1865 was assisted by the Edinburgh Trades Council and a demonstration by the union was addressed by an official of the Edinburgh masons' union.[18] In 1875, the Dundee Trades Council gave financial and organizational assistance to the Dundee millworkers, who had been on strike for several weeks and were also involved in the inauguration of the Dundee Mill and Factory Workers' Association in September 1875.

The involvement of the Scottish movement in the extension of trade-unionism to previously unorganized sections was largely a consequence of the greater influence in the labour movement of trades councils, whose very basis committed them to a form of action that dissolved occupational boundaries and forced them to address issues which had a wider significance than the fate of a particular craft group or trade. However, this commitment was perhaps given additional impetus by the emphasis placed on self-improvement and self-advancement in Scottish society that in part derived from the precepts of Calvinism, which provided a code of personal conduct bound up with diligence, thrift, and self-help. Because economic and spiritual immiserization were inextricably linked in the

---

[17] *Glasgow Sentinel*, 9 July 1859.
[18] Johnston, *The History of the Working Classes in Scotland*, 355.

Calvinistic ethic, trade unions saw their organizations not simply as the means of improving wages and conditions, but also as the way for the working classes to achieve moral dignity and self-respect.

At a general meeting of miners at Maryhill in Glasgow, which was addressed by leading trade-unionists of the district, and whose purpose was to attempt to organize the miners, the chairman remarked that 'They would try some means to bring about a rise of wages, so as to enable them to rise from that social and moral status to which they had sunk'.[19] Organized sections, to some extent, saw themselves in the role of moral entrepreneurs and were therefore concerned to 'rescue' those sections of the working class whom they considered morally and socially degenerate by bringing them within the pale of the trade union movement.

The trade unions of this period have been frequently associated with industrial pacifism and advocating a conciliatory approach to industrial relations. The reports of the Glasgow Trades Council clearly indicates that they favoured negotiation, arbitration, and conciliation and desired to avoid strikes at all costs and in this respect they saw their methods as sharply differentiated from the earlier unionists. The 'evils' of strikes was a recurrent theme in Trades Council discussion and although there were divergencies of opinion on the best remedies there was a unanimity in the belief that strikes were evils which should be avoided. A member of the Glasgow Trades Council opined that he 'never liked strikes, perhaps it might be said he was prejudiced on that subject, as even when strikes were considered successful, they were often injurious by pressing too hard on the employers of labour and driving away certain kinds of employment from particular localities'.[20]

This attitude to strikes and the grip of popular political economy was perhaps a product of both objective economic conditions in Scotland and the influence of Calvinistic ideology. The relative abundance of the labour supply in Scotland contributed to the enfeeblement of the trade union movement,

---

[19] *Sentinel*, 21 Aug. 1859.
[20] *Sentinel*, 2 Aug. 1862, report of a meeting of the GTC.

and may have acted to dissuade workers from going on strike as they were keenly aware that they could readily be replaced. The influence of popular political economy on trade-unionists may also have been related to the increasing involvement of the Scottish economy in the export market, for which free trade was a *sine qua non* for prosperity. However, there were also close links between Calvinist ideology and the tenets of popular political economy and the former was almost certainly a potent force for the dissemination of belief in thrift, self-help, and possessive individualism.

However, the organized labour movement never abandoned the strike weapon and the mid-Victorian era in Scotland could not justifiably be described as a period of industrial harmony. The struggle to obtain a shorter working week generated a number of strikes throughout industry and, at various periods, joiners, engineers, tailors, shipbuilders, and iron- and steelworkers were engaged in bitter and protracted struggles for a shorter week. Similarly, appeals to the state of trade by employers made little impression on unions when they felt an improvement in their wages was merited, and the law of supply and demand could similarly be ignored if its operation proved to be unfavourable to the unions. The principle of a 'fair wage', which was frequently invoked, although implying a belief in the possibility of economic justice within capitalist society, also provided a potential area of conflict and was often inconsistent with acceptance of the 'state of trade' argument in wage bargaining. Therefore, trade-unionists clearly believed that there were limits to the rule of political economy.

Although certain sections of the workforce enjoyed relative economic prosperity, it was generally precariously based, being contingent on the fluctuations in the trade cycle. Therefore, it is possible to exaggerate the degree to which sections of the working class were economically distinct from the rest.[21] The hierarchy of the working class was relatively fluid, particularly in terms of downward mobility, and there was a wide range of economic experience even within the ranks of the skilled. Some trades may have achieved a *modus vivendi* with employers

---

[21] See Gray, *The Labour Aristocracy in Victorian Edinburgh*, ch. 9, for a discussion of the range of economic experiences within the skilled stratum.

whereby conflict could be minimized because gains could be
achieved by playing the capitalist rules of the game, but others
had to contend with bitter opposition from employers. In 1868
the Master Iron Founders locked out members of the moulders'
union throughout Scotland in a concerted effort to smash their
organization and declared that the 'obnoxious union must be
crushed'.[22] After nine weeks the men returned to work utterly
defeated and only managed to salvage one condition: they did
not have to renounce their union membership. In Edinburgh
in 1862 the iron trades struck against a reduction in the
meal hour, and in one workshop the men were threatened
with imprisonment if they continued to resist.[23] Although the
rhetoric of the trade union movement included acceptance of
many economic orthodoxies, in practice they were often
breached and the *détente* which many unions reached with
employers was of a fragile and unstable nature.

The preoccupation of Scottish trade-unionism with self-
improvement, providence, temperance, and to some extent
Sabbatarianism derived from the moral code of Calvinism,
which was deeply instilled in the Scottish labour movement.
Temperance, in particular, was a central issue and one
constantly urged by trades councils, who affirmed their
commitment by meeting in coffee houses or temperance halls.
Yet commitment to temperance did not necessarily cut across
class differences and weaken working-class action, for usually
it was combined with a strong sense of class interest and class
differences. In Edinburgh, overtures made by the Temperance
Electoral Association to the Trades Council to co-operate over
the question of the municipal elections met with a lukewarm
reception as it was argued that 'we consider that the right men
for Councillors are those who will represent the rights of
labour, whether temperance men or not'.[24]

Support for temperance was a feature of the early Scottish
Chartist movement largely because of the widespread problem
of drunkenness amongst the Scottish working class. But it was
not so much a mark of the pervasiveness of ruling-class ideology
as a desire for their politics to be taken seriously. As one leading

---

[22] Johnston, *The History of the Working Classes in Scotland*, 369.
[23] Ibid.   [24] MacDougall (ed.), *Essays in Scottish Labour History*, 285.

Scottish Chartist remarked: 'Radicalism has been made a laughing stock throughout the country by reason of the drinking habits of many of its advocates; pot house politicians hiccuping for liberty [are] a revolting spectacle.'[25]

The concern of the mid-Victorian labour movement with acceptance and recognition of their organizations led them to embrace temperance as part of that struggle and was not simply a reflection of wholesale subscription to bourgeois values. Gray's work on the Edinburgh artisan class suggests that the values of thrift and self-help and the goals of self-improvement and respectability were usually articulated in the language of the working class and defined within the framework of working-class life, and should not be seen as an attempt to mimic the bourgeoisie or surmount the divide between manual and non-manual occupations.[26] Bourgeois ideology was not unambiguously imposed on the working class, but was subjected to transformation, adaptation, and reformulation through the filter of working-class life and experience. Therefore, 'respectability' as aspired to by the mid-Victorian trade-unionist often had a collective and class connotation and the emphasis on self-help which distinguished Scottish unionism could be interpreted as part of the process of weaning working-class organizations away from the patronage of the benevolent middle classes.

For most of the second half of the nineteenth century the politics of organized labour were contained with the radical wing of liberalism. However, increasingly the labour movement became disenchanted with Scottish liberalism and its failure to endorse working-class parliamentary representation. This culminated in the decision of Keir Hardie and others to sever organizational links with liberalism and sink their efforts into establishing an independent working-class party. The decision of Scottish trade-unionists to break with the British Trades Union Congress over their resentment at the formation of the Scottish Trades Union Congress in 1897 gave a further fillip to independent labour politics. The STUC played a pivotal

---

[25] Quoted in I. Donnachie, 'Drink and Society 1750–1850: Some Aspects of the Scottish Experience', *Journal of the Scottish Labour History Society*, 13 (May 1979), 19.   [26] Gray, *The Labour Aristocracy in Victorian Edinburgh*.

role at national level in co-ordinating and organizing the movement for independent working-class representation.[27] Therefore, the political ambitions of the trade union movement in the 1890s and early twentieth century became geared to gaining independent labour representation at both local and national level. By 1896 the Workers' Municipal Committee, an alliance of the Independent Labour Party, the co-operative societies, the Irish National League, and various trade unions, was already in existence to facilitate the election of representatives of labour to municipal councils.[28] At the national level the Scottish Workers' Parliamentary Elections Committee held its first annual conference in the Co-operation Halls in Glasgow in 1900, with the aim of 'securing a full measure of Labour representation in the House of Commons'.[29]

However, the demand for independent working-class representation was not equated with socialism. Although the programme of the SWPEC included nationalization of railways and mines, and the fixing of a minimum wage by law, the emphasis was firmly placed on the election of working-class representatives to the House of Commons, and the question of formulating an alternative political programme was of secondary importance. The proud boast of the Glasgow Trades Council during the elections of 1901 was that 'men of widely divergent views' were involved in promoting the election of Robert Smillie to the North-East Lanark seat and that this indicated 'the growing opinion among the thoughtful and intelligent in favour of labour representation'.[30]

The rhetoric of the labour movement became increasingly couched in the language of socialism and directed at establishing the public ownership of the means of production. In concluding the 1907 Annual Report of the Glasgow Trades Council, John Howden, the President, argued that 'So long as the present industrial conditions are allowed to continue so long will there

[27] W. Knox, 'The Political and Workplace Culture of the Scottish Working Class 1832–1914', in W. H. Fraser and R. J. Morris (eds.), *People and Society in Scotland 1830–1914*, iii (Edinburgh: John Donald, 1990).

[28] STUC, *Annual Report, 1896–1897*, NLS.

[29] STUC, *Annual Report, 1900–1901*.

[30] Ibid.

be depression in trade with its consequent unemployment and the suffering and misery and poverty this entails, and the only cure to prevent these results is an entire reconstruction of our industrial system'.[31]

Although the labour movement increasingly became disengaged from its ties with the Liberals, it expressed a consciousness which was more in the tradition of popular radicalism than socialism, with the targets of reform and vilification being the landed aristocracy, the Church, and the monarchy. The Aberdeen Trades Council in 1885 favoured the disestablishment and disendowment of the Church of Scotland[32] and the Glasgow Trades Council refused to celebrate the Queen's jubilee in 1887, as a protest against poverty and distress.[33] The trade union movement's conception of socialism was sufficiently muted to allow a degree of overlap between its philosophy and that of progressive liberal thought. Indeed it has been argued that the dominant conception of socialism in the early twentieth-century union movement was hardly distinguishable from the most radical stands within the liberal tradition.[34]

A central plank of the labour movement's political programme was municipal collectivism, a policy which had been introduced to a limited extent in Glasgow long before it became associated with socialist ideology and indeed which found support from a wide spectrum of political opinion. It was, however, a notion which was sufficiently vague to provide scope for a variety of interpretations and gain adherents whose political and social philosophies were widely divergent. Professor William Smart of Glasgow University, who was a luminary of the social reform movement in the city and, for a time, President of the Women's Protection and Provident League, espoused a version of the municipal idea which he took pains to dissociate from socialism or advocation of the public ownership of the means of production.

[31] STUC, *Annual Report, 1907–1908*.
[32] Buckley, *Trade Unionism in Aberdeen*, 95.
[33] GTC, *Annual Report, 1886–1887*.
[34] Gray, *The Labour Aristocracy in Victorian Edinburgh*, ch. 9; J. Smith, 'Labour Traditions in Glasgow and Liverpool', *History Workshop Journal*, 17 (Spring 1984), 35.

As government action can never supersede, and is not intended to
rival private enterprise for the innumerable things it brings, it should
never be the enemy of private enterprise, nor be represented as public
beneficence over against private greed . . . . as is carelessly done when
production for the public good is contrasted with 'production
for Profit'. Under government I include both Central and local
government, the latter being a branch of the former, and the functions
being the same in both cases.[35]

Although even progressive middle-class opinion was implacably opposed to the political aspirations of organized labour
in its more radical postures, there was still some common
ground between their ideologies. The precepts of Victorian
evangelical social reformism were being called into question
and reformulated so that physical rather than spiritual reform
came to be emphasized, or more correctly the former was
defined as logically prior to the latter. The contrast between
the newly emerging thinking and what was regarded as the
outmoded approach of the mid-Victorian era was aptly
summed up by Robert Bremner of the Faculty of Procurators,
in an article published by the SCWT: 'Physical existence comes
before moral existence: and physical reform must precede
moral and spiritual reform.'[36]

This shift in policy towards more material solutions
did not replace the concern with moral and spiritual
enrichment, but was to be a more effective means of
achieving them. The literature of the various organizations
involved with social policy reflected a community of shared
assumptions about the causes of poverty, prescriptive action,
and the need to differentiate between the 'deserving' and
'undeserving' poor in order to eliminate the corrupting
influence of the latter. Although labour representatives
on the parish councils professed to treat applicants for
relief in a more generous fashion, they still continued
to distinguish between 'deserving' and 'undeserving' poor
and to extol the virtues of thrift and self-help. Thus it
was claimed that the system of relief penalized the provident

worker, 'who is in receipt of superannuation . . . [and] has no more consideration paid to him than to his more improvident neighbour'.[37]

None the less, resolutions passed in trades councils, union branches, and the Scottish Trades Union Congress increasingly emphasized the structural causes of poverty and traced its roots in the inequalities of power and wealth. Thus at the ninth Annual Conference of the STUC a motion calling for the prohibition of alcohol was defeated by an amendment which dismissed such legislative action as a mere palliative to the problems of poverty and misery and offered as an alternative solution the more equitable distribution of wealth so that 'conditions are so altered as to secure to every one a healthy life amidst healthy surroundings'.[38]

It has been argued that the restructuring of the labour process on an industry-wide basis which began in the late nineteenth century, from the introduction of labour-saving machinery, piece-rates, and bonus systems to the emergence of new divisions of labour, created the potential for united working-class action. It is argued that all sections of the workforce responded to assaults on their conditions of work, and that the process of deskilling contributed to a heightened sense of class solidarity by creating a more homogeneous working class, less differentiated by skill, conditions, and wages.[39] It would appear that contemporary trade-unionists perceived a change, for the rhetoric of unionism revolved around the celebration of a new era which signalled the demise of the old sectionalist and exclusivist policies. The literature and meetings of associations such as trades councils had a 'winds of change' flavour which welcomed the new unity of the working class and was critical of the divisiveness and selfishness of the 'old' unions. This view was the theme of the presidential address to the third Annual Congress of the STUC:

[37] GTC, *Annual Report, 1902–1903.*
[38] STUC, *Report of the Ninth Annual Congress, 1905.*
[39] R. Price, 'The New Unionism and the Labour Process, 1888–1920', in W. Mommsen and G. H. G. Hubung (eds.), *The Development of Trade Unionism in Great Britain and Germany, 1880–1914* (London: Allen and Unwin, 1985); Gray, *The Labour Aristocracy in Victorian Edinburgh*, ch. 9.

The industrial conditions which surrounded their life in the workshops were pretty much dependent upon the introduction of labour-saving machinery, which was ever changing . . . Working in sections the labour army presented a broken front to the organised forces of capital and the result was they were beaten in detail, conditions of labour being forced upon their acceptance which, if labour spoke with a single voice, would be rejected with scorn. . . . When speaking on this question it was oftentimes overlooked that there were thousands of working men whose wages never amounted to 20s. a week and whose daily life was haunted by the ever present spectre of absolute want. If in extending the hand of federation friendship they failed to reach that class, then no matter how perfect their scheme might be, it would be written down as a delusion and a snare by every man who had an intelligent grasp of the facts of existence . . . The cry of the unemployed heard in the past as in a desert required that they should break down the barriers which had hitherto separated union from union, and demanded that united action should be taken to secure the workers a fair share of the profits which naturally spring from labour. The days of labour aristocracy had been swept away by the introduction of labour saving machinery . . .[40]

However, the received view of this period as involving the constant erosion of craft skills as a result of the introduction of machinery is an inadequate interpretation of developments in the industrial arena. Extensive introduction of new technology was not the preferred method of dealing with the problem of labour productivity by British employers. Indeed entrepreneurial failure and the lack of investment in new technologies has often been blamed for the erosion of Britain's industrial hegemony and in Scotland there was even greater reluctance on the part of employers to renew their industrial base.[41] Therefore, the extent to which skills had been eroded before 1914 has probably been exaggerated, for many skilled workers managed to retain vestiges of autonomy and control even when

[40] STUC, *Report of the Third Annual Congress, 1899.*
[41] A. Reid 'Labour, Capital and the State in Britain, 1880-1920' in Mommsen and Hubung (eds.), *The Development of Trade Unionism in Great Britain and Germany.* Reid argues that employers' response to foreign competition was to shift either into the production of more specialized products or into the more protected markets of the formal empire, rather than engage in wholesale introduction of new technology; R. H. Campbell, *The Rise and Fall of Scottish Industry 1707-1939* (Edinburgh: John Donald, 1980).

new machinery was introduced.[42] This, therefore, calls into
question the thesis that the restructuring of the labour process
created an increasingly homogeneous category of worker and
laid the basis for a heightened sense of class solidarity. There
may have been non-economic factors and changes in the wider
society which radicalized the working class and cemented
disparate sections;[43] however, at the point of production,
there were still divisions of authority, skill, status, and earnings
within the workforce.

A typical response of employers to the relatively shrinking
world market was to reduce labour costs by introducing cheap
labour and increasing the employment of apprentices, and often
the response of the union movement was a sectional one.[44]
Indeed the years leading up to the First World War were
littered with disputes over preserving craft control against the
encroachment of 'cheap' labour substitutes.

There were, therefore, many continuities in the form and
content of trade-unionism from the middle of the nineteenth
century until the First World War. Many of the changes which
have often been presented as sharp breaks in fact descended
directly from the mid-Victorian movements whose political
subordination to liberalism and industrial moderation have
always been exaggerated.

Domestic Ideology

One aspect of trade union ideology which has received scant
attention and where one can also trace continuities was its
conception of the family and the role of women in society.

[42] J. Zeitlin, 'Craft Control and the Division of Labour: Engineers and Compositors in Britain, 1890–1930', *Cambridge Journal of Economics*, 3(3) (1979); Sian
Reynolds, *Britannica's Typesetters* (Edinburgh University Press, 1989), ch. 5.
[43] G. Dangerfield, *The Strange Death of Liberal England* (London: MacGibbon
and Kee, 1966); S. Meacham, 'The Sense of an Impending Clash: English Working
Class Unrest before the First World War', *American Historical Review*, 77(5) (1972).
Both writers argue that the industrial unrest of the pre-war years was symptomatic
of and compounded by increasing class polarization and a growing awareness of
political and social divisions in society.
[44] William Knox, 'Apprenticeship and De-skilling in Britain, 1850–1914',
International Review of Social History, 31 (1986), pt. 2.

Historical debate about divisions within the working class has largely centred on the divisions between skilled and unskilled workers, which have usually been perceived as the most significant divisions. However, an analysis of the domestic ideology of trade-unionism highlights the ways in which Scottish trade-union practices were influenced by the dominant ideologies of gender and the significance this form of sectionalism had for both trade-unionism and women.

A central plank of trade union policy was the demand for a family wage, and a hallmark of working-class respectability became the family where the man was the financial provider who could afford to maintain a non-working wife, whose task in turn was the creation of a domestic environment where the spiritual, emotional, and material needs of all the family members would be catered for. Trade union discussions were liberally peppered with reference to the 'proper place' of women being the home, whilst industrial work was deemed to be the province of men. This view was clearly expressed by a delegate to the Scottish Tailors' Conference who was arguing in favour of the union helping to organize female labour in the trade:

It was well known that the vast majority of the females who go into tailoring, or any other trade, do so merely with the view of temporary employment during the period between girlhood and the time they hope to take their proper place as the wife of someone, and it should be impressed upon them that by working at low wages during this period of temporary employment they are keeping down wages of those that in after life may have to support them.[45]

It is important to stress that the demand for a family wage and the conception of women's role which it implied were new developments which were only incorporated into the trade union canons during the second half of the nineteenth century. The notion of women being associated with the domestic sphere was not a new departure, as long before the Industrial Revolution women had responsibility for the management of

[45] SNAOT, *Fourteenth Annual Conference, 1881*, NLS.

household tasks.[46] However, in the pre-industrial period women were expected to contribute to the family economy, albeit as supplementary earners whose work was often supervised by the male head of the family, who had absolute authority over the household. Therefore, the assumption that the adult male wage should be enough to support a non-working wife and children was a significant departure from pre-industrial practices.

Although the precise origin of the family wage has not yet been satisfactorily explained, there is broad agreement that it emerged as a product of working-class struggle and was not an inevitable consequence of the development of industrial capitalism. There is little evidence to suggest that the demand was fully formulated in the early years of industrialization, although the view that the husband was the primary bread-winner was already entrenched, as was women's primary responsibility for the home and domestic work. In the first decades of the century it seems to have been widely accepted that the male bread-winner's earnings could be supplemented by the earnings of children but that married women should not enter the factory. A master calico printer in Belfast who attempted to hire women from Scotland into his works was asked by a member of the Select Committee on Combinations of Workmen if he would 'think it a misfortune if a mother, in consequence of the scanty wages which her husband was receiving, should be under the necessity of entrusting the care of her infant children to other hands, and should entirely forsake her house, and go to a manufactory'.[47]

Although the notion of 'the angel in the house' was very much a middle-class conception of the role of married women, the working classes appear to have shared the view that a married woman's place was not the factory floor unless she was driven there by harsh economic realities. The manager of the Adelphi cotton-spinning works in Glasgow claimed that 'women do not generally work much in factories after they get

[46] A. Clarke, *Working Life of Women in the Seventeenth Century* (Routledge & Kegan Paul, 1982); M. Chaytor, 'Household and Kinship: Ryton in the Late 16th and Early 17th Centuries', *History Workshop Journal*, 10 (Autumn 1980).
[47] First Report of the Select Committee on Combinations of Workmen 1837–38, C. 488 (London: HMSO, 1838), evidence of Mr. T. Grimshaw, Q3160.

married',[48] and added that only seven of the women in his works had husbands who were alive, five of whom had no children and the remaining two having husbands who lived elsewhere. The evidence of two foremen confirms the view that it was acceptable to put one's children to work in the factory, but not one's wife. One had nine children, the other eleven, and all had worked in mills, the girls 'till their marriage'. However, their wives were 'never in a factory'.[49]

The division between home and work and the creation for women of the new role of housewife was noted as early as 1828 by Dr G. J. M. Ritchie, in an article on 'The Medical Topography of Neilston':

In the families in which all the members are so far advanced as to be fit for labour the aggregate amount of their earnings is very considerable, and is in general placed at the disposal of the eldest female whose sole employment consists in making purchases, and attending to the household duties.[50]

It is interesting that the role of housewife was associated with a greater amount of leisure and lack of supervision, which might make women more vulnerable to the vices of drunkenness and dissoluteness. Dr Ritchie observed that many of the women, unlike the male members of their family, who were presumably engaged in waged labour outside the home, often 'acquired habits of dram drinking', which 'probably depends on the comparatively little restraint imposed on these females, on their greater leisure, and on the seducing attentions of retail dealers anxious to cultivate their custom . . .'.[51] This observation probably reflected fear of the consequences of the removal of patriarchal supervision of women in the household, just as many of the objections to women's labour in the early factory system were based on the undermining of patriarchal authority which it might entail.

[48] Factory Inquiry Commission, 1833, First Report, *Employment of Children in Factories with Minutes of Evidence and Reports by the District Commissioners*, in *Industrial Revolution: Children's Employment, 3*, Factories, xx (Shannon: Irish University Press, 1970), evidence of John Stephen, Manager, Adelphi Works.
[49] Ibid., miscellaneous evidence.
[50] G. M. Ritchie, 'The Medical Topography of Neilston', *Glasgow Medical Journal*, (1828), 26. I am grateful to Alan Steele for this reference.
[51] Ibid.

Female labour was generally employed for lower wages than male labour, a continuation of pre-industrial practices which assumed that the subsistence needs of women and children were less than men's. Women were viewed, therefore, as a source of cheap competition by male workers, who saw them as a threat to their status, skill, and earnings. Consequently, the response of male labour was to organize against cheap female labour by seeking to exclude women from competition in the same labour market. The Glasgow cotton spinners' union epitomized this response when they claimed that they would 'render any woman's life miserable who would attempt to become a spinner for the first time'.[52]

Although there is an instance of the cotton spinners' union demanding equal pay for women who had displaced men, it was for work on short mules, which were generally operated by young men. Therefore, they may not have been viewed as such a serious threat to adult male labour, which tended to operate the larger mules. Despite the claim by a leading member of the Spinners' Association that its object was not to prevent women from working but to ensure that they were paid established rates, his statement that 'women do not throw off the quantity, neither is the quality of their work so good and where the master has not it in his power to rob them of their regular rates of wages he is inclined to employ men'[53] implies a conviction that men's work was inherently superior to women's and that this was recognized by employers. Although it was not fully articulated in public debate at this stage, there was an unstated assumption that industrial work was the property of men, and the industrial world unnatural territory for women. This belief was fuelled by the shared concerns of the working class about the moral and social effects of female factory labour which pervaded the parliamentary reports. Middle-class representatives framed their objections in terms of the difficulties of factory women acquiring the skills and habits of domestic economy and the attendant danger of the breakdown of the family, whilst working-class representatives

[52] Factory Inquiry Commission, 1833, First Report, *Employment of Children in Factories*, 82.
[53] *First Report of the Select Committee on Combinations of Workmen*, evidence of James McNish.

focused more on morality, particularly sexual morality. James McNish, a spinner and a member of the Short-Time Committee, voiced a common sentiment amongst the working-class witnesses to the Children's Employment Commission in 1833 when he complained that:

> It is the tendency of bringing so many young women together to such an establishment as this, to render them vicious and dissolute and to demoralise them; that the system of employing them for so many hours at work, separately from other classes of the community altogether, and in general from their parents, renders it impossible for them to have morals or education attended to.[54]

Another male spinner directly addressed the question of sexual morality claiming that 'The want of education of the factory girls makes them looser and more dissolute in their manners than they otherwise would be; that there is a great deal of promiscuous intercourse of the sexes at these works; that illegitimate children are not uncommon.'[55]

The intention of these comments was to provide ammunition and evidence for the case for limiting child labour, which it was hoped would ultimately lead to a reduction in hours for adult labour. Although there was obviously political capital to be made by playing on middle-class concerns about the disintegration of social control and the decline in the moral standards of the working class, it is telling that both working-class and middle-class anxieties about the deleterious moral consequences of factory employment focused on young females rather than young males.

Regulation of female sexuality was a recurrent theme in the debates as was the erosion of patriarchal supervision of family labour. Industrialization decomposed without completely destroying the family economy whereby wages were earned by the family unit rather than the individual, and at the same time it stripped men of their role as supervisors and organizers of family labour and hence of the source of their patriarchal power.

---

[54] Factory Inquiry Commission, 1833, First Report, *Employment of Children in Factories*, evidence of James McNish, spinner.
[55] Ibid., evidence of John Harley, spinner.

Although the family system of labour persisted in some occupations until the late nineteenth century, either through internal subcontracting or through more informal systems of family recruitment, in the course of the century it became increasingly rare. This was related to two separate, although sometimes overlapping, developments: on the one hand, the introduction of state legislation to regulate female and child labour, and, on the other, the attempts of employers to gain more control over the labour process by usurping the power of key male workers to hire, fire, and supervise labour.[56] The demise of the family labour system may have given additional impetus to the formulation of the demand for a family wage. Men had always assumed that their labour should be higher paid than women's, but in the first half of the century male workers seldom resorted to arguments about their family responsibilities as economic providers to justify their higher earnings. Women's subsistence needs were generally believed to be less than men's and this assumption, coupled with an assertion of their superior worth and value to employers, was usually considered sufficient grounds to pay men more. With the collapse of the family system of labour which had invested control over labour and the allocation of rewards to the male head of household, and the consequent undermining of patriarchal authority, working-class family ideology was reformulated to emphasize the bread-winning role of men. This gave greater leverage to male workers' wage claims, as well as to their claim to prior rights to work, and restructured patriarchal authority in the home and in the workplace around the notion of the male provider.

The belief in the prior right of men to work, which had not been articulated in terms of the male bread-winner in public discourse in the first decades of the century, was enshrined in the demand for a family wage, which was consolidated in the second half of the century. To some extent this represented a reconstruction of gender relations and a redrawing of the boundaries of women's sphere in that, whilst it could include waged work, it was within carefully delineated areas of 'suitable

---

[56] See James Mark-Lawson and Anne Witz, 'From "Family Labour" to "Family Wages"', *Social History*, 13(2) (1988).

work for women'. The family wage strategy incorporated and adapted pre-existing ideologies of gender divisions to the changed context of industrialization, and not only preserved woman's 'natural' domestic role, and her role as dependant, but confirmed industrial work as the property of men and reconstituted patriarchal authority around the notion of the male provider and bread-winner rather than as supervisor and organizer of family labour.

Fears of undercutting from cheap female labour, concerns about the morals of young female factory labour, which was unregulated by family supervision and control, and the belief that the ultimate destination of all women was marriage and motherhood combined to produce an exclusionary trade union strategy towards female labour by the second half of the century which served to marginalize women's position in the labour market.

The ideology of domesticity and separate sexual spheres involved an array of roles for women, and in the context of working-class culture was imbued with values and meanings which were quite distinct from the formulation of that ideology in the bourgeois family. The image of the angel in the house, as aspired to by the middle classes, ascribed to women the role of overseer of the household. However, essentially their womanhood, and ultimately the status of the bourgeois family, derived from women's role as ladies of leisure who possessed gentility and were the embodiment of Christian purity.

The symbol of the non-working wife was central to both middle-class and working-class conceptions of the domestic ideal but domesticity was constructed differently in the working-class home. Domesticity and respectability were closely associated in working-class life and it was viewed as the woman's role to acquire the necessary domestic skills required to provide a good and comfortable home life for her husband thereby diverting him from temptation into a life of crime, drunkenness, and impropriety. Therefore, working-class women's role as moral guardians involved domestic labour and proficiency in household tasks such as cooking, baking, cleaning, sewing, washing, etc. Part of the opposition to women working was based on fear of the consequence that these domestic skills would atrophy when women were engaged in waged labour outside the home. This was the view expressed by one of the contributors at a meeting of Dundee's Working Men's Club on the establishment of infant nurseries. The speaker criticized those 'tradesmen' whose wives went out to work when they should be at home looking after their children and claimed that 'many men took to bad habits because of their wives not being able to keep house, and therefore it would be a boon if some means were adopted to train operative females in housekeeping'.[57]

The meaning of domesticity in working-class culture was therefore more concerned with the acquisition and application of practical skills in contradistinction to its formulation in the middle-class home where it was associated with household management as well as manners, etiquette, gentility, and 'the lady of leisure'. The same speaker illustrated that working-class concern with respectability and the domestic ideal did not necessarily involve the total subordination of the working class to middle-class cultural values, but could be combined with a sense of class pride. On the question of domestic training for working women, he added:

that others than the daughters of gentlemen would require to be instructors, as they had more need to learn themselves than they should learn others. (*Laughter and Applause.*) Those ladies who went about and lectured on politics could do far more good if they applied themselves to the improvement of their class in domestic work. (*Applause.*)[58]

The trade union movement's policy of a family wage and its commitment to the domestic ideal powerfully influenced its attitude to women once they were drawn into the labour market. As women workers were regarded as out of place, they were viewed primarily as a 'problem'; however, the nature of the problem took different forms in different contexts. The view that trade unions' opposition to women workers stemmed solely from the fact that women were viewed as a source of cheap competition is only a partial explanation for men's opposition to women working. Trade-unionists expressed concern about the atrophying of domestic skills, the threat to

[57] *Dundee Advertiser*, 8 Jan. 1875.   [58] Ibid.

the spiritual and material well-being of the family, and the
morals of working women, when there was no direct threat
from female labour. Thus young female piecers in Glasgow,
the women spinners in Dundee's jute industry, and the
young women coalpickers in Lanarkshire offended the moral
sensibilities of male labour even when they were not competing
for their jobs.

The concerns expressed by trade unions in relation to
protective legislation for women centred on the protection of
female morality as much as excessive hours of work or appalling
conditions. Indeed feminist historians have commented that
the trade union movement remained silent on hours and
conditions of work when it involved trades where only women
were employed.[59] However, working men seemed particularly
concerned to regulate women's labour when it involved them
working alongside men at close quarters, or in a state less than
fully clothed.

In 1859 bleachworkers and finishers in the Glasgow area
began agitations to reduce their hours of work and to extend
the provisions of the Factory Act to bleaching and finishing
works. The bleachers enlisted the support of the Glasgow
Trades Council in their campaign, and they in turn set up a
select committee of the Council to investigate conditions in the
trade. In highlighting the plight of women and children in the
bleachfields, there was clearly an element of hiding behind
the petticoats of women to facilitate legislation in which men also
had a vested interest. Unlike men, women were not regarded
as free agents but as defenceless creatures who required the
protection of others, such as the male trade union movement
or the state. Therefore, support for protective legislation was
justified on the basis that it was 'the duty of the Legislature
to protect those who cannot protect themselves'.[60] However,
the report of the Trades Council's select committee dwelled
on the damage to the moral as well as the physical health of
the women and children in bleachfields:

[59] See S. Alexander, 'Women's Work in Nineteenth Century London: A Study of
the Years 1820–1850', in J. Mitchell and A. Oakley (eds.), *The Rights and Wrongs
of Women* (Harmondsworth: Penguin, 1976).
[60] *Sentinel*, 9 July 1859.

It appears that the temperature of these works is in general very high, rising in some cases to 120 degrees. In such cases females are under the necessity of divesting themselves of their articles of clothing, not infrequently almost to a state of nudity, otherwise they could not go about their work in such unreasonable heat . . . To the question if women had ever been observed in an indecent position through the undue exposure of their persons in the divestment of their clothing, the answer had invariably been 'yes' and that the general effect is injurious to morality.[61]

Given the excessive hours worked in the bleachfields, the lack of regularity of hours, and the intolerable heat, the Trades Council's report and the comments of the bleachworkers' Short-Time Committee displayed an almost obsessive concern with the effects of such conditions on the health of the women and children. Even when expressing concern over the long hours, and the excessive amount of overtime demanded by the employers, the question of morals intruded into the discussion. The Short-Time Committee commented that:

Several of the witnesses stated that they had known women and children work for 36 hours consecutively, in a heat varying from 120 to 140 degrees. This, of course, caused the females to divest themselves of nearly all their clothes, therefore exposing themselves in an improper manner. Indeed one witness stated that he had seen them almost naked, only those parts which any female would hide remained covered.[62]

Similar concerns were expressed by the radical *Glasgow Sentinel*. When the Society for Promoting the Employment of Women held a meeting in Glasgow with a view to setting up a similar society there, the *Sentinel* carried a lengthy article condemning the scheme to introduce women compositors. The article stressed that they were not against the scheme in principle, acknowledging that 'there are many employments suited for women to which they might be more largely introduced than they are—service in the general run of shops we take to be one of those'.[63]

However, the work of a compositor was deemed to be eminently unsuitable for women and, whilst the point was

---

[61] *Sentinel*, 17 Mar. 1860, Report of a bleachers' meeting in the City Halls.
[62] Ibid., 3 Nov. 1859. [63] Ibid., 13 Oct. 1860.

made that women's labour would be used to undercut men's wages, the bulk of the article concentrated on the immorality of such work. The primary concern seemed to be that women worked alongside men, but the fact that the work involved going out on the streets at night was also cause for concern:

The employment of women at occupations where it is necessary they should be mixed up with men is not desirable, and, although the means of living comfortably are increased by such a practice, there is certainly no moral gain in it. We do not wish to cast any reflection on women who work in factories, seeing that in those places they work very much in groups and, therefore the compositor is that which we take to be, perhaps above all others, the least suitable for women. A very large proportion of this work is carried on in connection with the newspaper press of this country, and it may be remarked that a great deal of this work is night work, not only unhealthy in its character, but unsuited for women by the necessity it would impose them by walking the streets by night.[64]

The views expressed in the article indicate a tolerance of women's work on the condition that it did not threaten the prior rights of men to work, that it arose from necessity, that is, where no other means of support was available, and crucially that the chastity and modesty of women were preserved. Clearly the question of female morality was a dominant concern which preoccupied both bourgeois commentators and the male trade union movement. However, working women themselves were anxious to redeem their reputations and refute suggestions of immorality. The *Sentinel* published two letters from factory workers about the morals of women cotton workers. The first letter from 'a spinster' who had worked for forty-five years as a weaver in a power-loom factory maintained 'that this class was above all others who worked as cotton mill operatives, as they were the daughters of managers, foremen, clerks, engineers, mechanics etc. where the others were recruited from the class of common labourers'.[65] The second letter was from a female cotton mill operative who clearly interpreted the weaver's remarks as casting aspersions on the morality of millworkers. She was anxious to display the fact that respectability defined by the possession of moral propriety

[64] *Sentinel*, 13 Oct. 1860.   [65] Ibid., 5 June 1875.

was not the monopoly of skilled workers: 'the work is not so healthy or clean as what it is in a powerloom factory [but] the morals of cotton factory workers are just as good as others of the working classes not excepting the children of purity [the weavers]'.[66]

Certainly trade-unionists' instrumental and self-interested motives for regulating female labour could be camouflaged by appeals to morality, but the frequency of references to this question suggests that it was not a cynically manufactured concern but a very real one. Indeed the issue of the protection of female morals was used by the Secretary of the Scottish National Association of Operative Tailors to argue for a less sectional policy towards female labour. The report of the conference stated that:

He condemned the practice of mixing the sexes in workshops more especially as our trade is carried on in a state of undress of semi-nudity, but he cautioned the delegates that they must not forget the wider aspect of the question by which the morality of our large towns was affected. He went on to say that if we legislated with the view of keeping females out of our trade and other classes of the community did likewise, we would be responsible for keeping the surplus female population out of honest employment and leaving them no resort but prostitution or starvation. If suitable workshops were provided, and the provisions of the Workshop Act duly enforced, he for one was prepared to admit that equal right of the opposite sex as to gain their living at our trade was one that in many ways was suited to them.[67]

It would appear that concern over the virtue of women was an important strand in the trade union movement's opposition to female labour even when the more pressing and immediate concern was fear of cheap competition. It should perhaps not be surprising that female morality was a primary concern of the trade union movement, for in the Victorian period the quintessential female virtues were modesty and chastity. As ignorance was regarded as the best protective shield from sexual impurity, the means of regulating female sexuality frequently involved avoiding situations which might make women aware

[66] *Sentinel*, 5 June 1875.
[67] SNAOT, *Fourteenth Annual Conference, 1881*.

of their sexuality or where they might fall prey to seduction,[68] hence the anxiety of male trade-unionists to segregate working women and men, or at least ensure that the conditions in which they worked together were closely supervised and did not involve any loss of female modesty.

In part concerns about working women's morals had an objective basis in the dangers confronting women in the nineteenth-century factory environment. Sexual harassment, rape, and illegitimacy were not unknown, and young female children were particularly vulnerable.[69] Working-class men's anxieties to protect women's virtue cannot simply be viewed as the product of the cultural diffusion of bourgeois morality, but may have reflected genuine concerns for the fate of women factory workers. Therefore, on one level working men's many public utterances about female morality expressed a paternalistic concern to protect women, who were assumed to be incapable of protecting themselves. However, underlying the veneer of paternalism it is possible to detect patriarchal concerns. For instance, the solution proffered to avoid these moral dangers was either to exclude women or to regulate their behaviour, rather than to focus on male behaviour as the problem. In addition, the dangers which women workers were said to be exposed to were usually directly attributed to the erosion of patriarchal control of family labour, and as such male workers' concerns about female morality could be construed as an attempt to reassert patriarchal regulation of women's sexuality either by excluding female workers from the workplace or by segregating their work from men's.

Although trade unions have often been depicted as hostile to women's trade-unionism, this preoccupation with women's sexual morality and concern that they conform to their prescribed gender roles could actually fuel a desire to organize

---

[68] See L. Bland, ' "Guardians of the Race" or "Vampires upon the Nation's Health": Female Sexuality and its Regulation in Early 20th Century Britain', in E. Whitelegg *et al.* (eds.), *The Changing Experience of Women* (Oxford: Robertson, 1982); D. Gorham, *The Victorian Girl and the Feminine Ideal* (London: Croom Helm, 1982).

[69] Factory Inquiry Commission, 1833, First Report, *Employment of Children in Factories, passim*, for references to rape illegitimacy; Ian Lamberty, 'Sexual Harassment in the Nineteenth Century English Cotton Industry', *History Workshop Journal*, 19 (Spring 1985).

women into trade unions. At a meeting of female power-loom weavers and other female operatives in 1863 the topic for discussion was 'The Past and Present Moral and Social Conditions of the Female Sex'. The gathering was addressed by leading trade-unionists and members of the clergy, and the contributions of Mr Cunningham and Mr Matthew Cullen of the Glasgow Trades Council stressed the importance of combination as a means of social elevation and a way of maintaining dignity and respectability. Women's unionization was encouraged and sanctioned as a means of improving their material conditions and thus safeguarding their health particularly for the purposes of reproduction. Mr Cunningham expressed the fear that 'there was at present far too little attention paid to the well-being of the female operatives of the country, that there was too little remembrance of the fact that on their condition depended that of the male portion of the community'.[70]

This conception of women and the notion of the potential moralizing influence of trade-unionism could encourage trade-unionists to co-operate with philanthropic elements in order to organize women workers. In addition to working in conjunction with these organizations, trades councils throughout Scotland and individual trade-unionists periodically took initiatives themselves to set up trade unions for women. The tailors' union (the SNAOT), which adopted an exclusionary strategy towards female labour in its own trade, was instrumental in setting up a Benefit Society for Glasgow Working Women in 1876.[71]

This kind of evidence signals the need for a more nuanced portrayal of trade-unionists' attitudes to women workers than the portrayal of outright hostility which is based on the pronouncements and proclamations of craft unions in the throes of campaigning against substitution by cheap female labour. The degree of sexually segregated work in the Scottish labour market at this time, with approximately 80 per cent of women concentrated in female-dominated occupations, to some extent side-stepped the issue of competition and provided

[70] *Sentinel*, 17 Oct. 1863.
[71] WPPL, *Second Annual Report* (June 1876), 10, British Library.

the foundation for less sectional policy. Although trade unions may have encouraged organizations amongst women, it was relegated to a separate sphere and usually involved women who represented no competition or threat to men's work. However, even absence of competition was not always a guarantee of a sympathetic stance as there were certain unions and a small number of trades councils which, if not obstructive, did little to encourage organization amongst women. A Glasgow correspondent in the *Women's Trade Union Review* noted that 'the Greenock Trades Council have been true to their stick in the mud policy by refusing to take part in any organising of the women of that town'.[72]

There were many strands to trade-unionists' opposition to female labour, and they meshed to produce a powerful exclusionary idiom. It has sometimes been argued that, as male workers organized not only to keep women out of their trades, but to resist all unskilled cheap labour, male or female, their strategy sprang from economic self-interest rather than patriarchal concerns. Certainly the most immediate problem posed by female labour was its status as cheap labour and this was the issue around which trade-unionists organized. However, the strategy of exclusion was more complex in its constitution than simple economics. Controlling entry into the trade through regulation of apprenticeship and other devices was a central element of craft strategies, but as Walby has observed this does not explain why women were excluded from apprenticeship.[73] Nor does the logic of craft control explain why the demand for equal pay was cynically adopted as an exclusionary device by some trade unions when faced with competition from female labour, rather than pursued as a genuine alternative strategy to exclusion. Nor can economic self-interest explain why trade-unionists expressed moral outrage at certain kinds of women's work which threatened neither their wages nor their jobs.

Resistance to cheap female labour was fired and reinforced by ideological motives which further inhibited the development of a strategy which was less sectional and more likely to lead

[72] WTUR, Apr. 1892, 12.
[73] S. Walby, *Patriarchy at Work* (Oxford: Blackwell, 1986).

to a united working-class response to the employers' offensive. By the turn of the century the rhetoric of the trade union movement condemned the sectionalist practices of the 'old' unions. However, it wholeheartedly gave its support to the exclusionary policies pursued by most of the skilled unions which sought to eliminate women from their trades. Admittedly sectionalist strategies were adopted towards all forms of cheap labour, but there were instances of inclusionary policies and conciliatory attitudes towards unskilled or semi-skilled grades of male workers in an attempt to eradicate what was regarded as the greater evil of cheap female labour.

Thus the fourteenth Annual Congress of the STUC completely endorsed the attempts of the Scottish Typographical Association to exclude women and unanimously adopted the position:

That this congress condemns the pernicious system of employing females as cheap labour to compete against adult male labour and heartily sympathises with the Scottish Typographical Association in its efforts to eliminate it from their trade in Edinburgh, and pledges itself to all that lies in its powers to support the Typographical Association.[74]

The arguments that opposition to female labour stemmed from opposition to their economic exploitation, and the ramifications this had throughout the labour market, were buttressed by reference to women's 'natural' role and the unsexing influence of work. In 1905 the STUC expressed unanimous opposition to female labour in mines and supported a motion from the miners which argued that:

the conversation which went on at a pitbank was not fitted for the drawing room, as most of the gentlemen at the Congress would understand, neither was it fitted for the ears of females employed there, and it unsexed and degraded them. When female labour was abolished underground he thought the law should have applied to females above ground too, for the degradation which accompanied the employment of women upon the pitbanks was a scandal to any civilised community.[75]

[74] STUC, *Report of the Fourteenth Annual Congress, 1910*.
[75] STUC, *Report of the Ninth Annual Congress, 1905*.

In this instance the union movement's concern to protect women from work which was degrading and unsexing smacks of hypocrisy and seems motivated more by self-interest and patriarchal control than charitable concern for fellow workers. Miners' real opposition to women's labour was their belief that it undercut male labour and deprived men of jobs.[76] However, they cloaked their arguments in moral terms in order to deflect attention from their self-interested motives, and, by capturing the moral high ground, the intention was to broaden the base of their support by appealing to middle-class elements who would be responsive to arguments about the physical and moral unsuitability of women's work.

The first time the question of female labour was discussed at the SNAOT's annual conference, an uncompromising stance was argued and the following motion adopted: 'That in any branch where female labour is introduced into a shop among the workmen, against the wish of the men, and they refuse to work beside them such men will be held justifiable in so doing, but in no case shall any of our members be justified in teaching females'.[77]

Female labour was again a focal point of debate at the fourteenth Annual Conference of the SNAOT and the contribution of a Glasgow delegate indicates the strength of the assumption that women were dependants and men providers:

it is a well known fact that for various reasons, females are able to work for less wages than men. They look upon their connection with the trade as being of only a temporary nature, and in many instances are not entirely dependent on their own labour for their support. They never contemplate having to labour for their whole life for the support of themselves and others as the male portion of the trade have to do.[78]

Although there were branches within the union which argued for a less sectional policy and suggested the union should help organize the women in their own society as a means of

[76] A. V. John, *By the Sweat of their Brow: Women Workers at Victorian Coal Mines* (London: Croom Helm, 1980).
[77] SNAOT, *Report of the Ninth Annual Conference, 1876.*
[78] SNAOT, *Report of the Fourteenth Annual Conference, 1881.*

increasing their wages, the more hard-line policy prevailed until the 1890s, with various conferences confirming the rule that expelled men for teaching women the trade. By 1892 the Scottish tailors had decided to modify their policy, as their outright opposition to female labour had been ineffectual, and women were entering the trade in increasing numbers. A debate on what form official union policy should take produced a number of contributions which advocated organizing the women and agitating for higher wages. A delegate from Edinburgh argued:

we could not eradicate the evil, so far as the abolition of work is concerned, and in his opinion the only alternative was to make a determined effort to organise the females with a view to ultimately raising their wages to the same rate as men. He was aware of the difficulties, for example, their looking forward to getting married which no doubt made them indifferent or apathetic in this matter.[79]

The question was never finally resolved or incorporated into official union policy and the union tended to respond to the introduction of female labour on an *ad hoc* basis. The prevailing consensus by the end of the century seemed to favour the recognition of female labour so long as the standard rate was paid and to organize them in a separate society. However, the basis of this policy was expediency and opportunism rather than recognition of the right of women to work for equal wages. A conference debate on a particular dispute involving the introduction of female labour was concluded by unanimously agreeing to take the position that they did not object to female labour provided it was paid at the same rate as men's: 'these were the only lines to fight this question, as no women's work was the same value as a man's.'[80]

The bookbinding trades were experiencing the same pressures, particularly in Glasgow where the extension of female labour had taken place on a greater scale than elsewhere in Scotland, although it tended to be concentrated in the Glasgow firm of Collins and Company. The initial policy of the union to the introduction of women had been to insist on the complete

---

[79] SNAOT, *Report of the Nineteenth Annual Conference, 1892.*
[80] SNAOT, *Report of the Twenty-First Annual Conference, 1896.*

abolition of female labour. However, as this became increasingly impracticable, they resorted to a policy which sought to control female labour, restrict its numbers to those already in the trade, and ensure that as 'unskilled' women left they would be replaced by skilled men. In October 1895, the Glasgow branch issued a memorial to the master binders and rulers of Glasgow which set out fairly stringent limitations on women's work including the following demands:

That females be restricted to quarter bound flush work (stationery) all sizes. In ruling that females be restricted to straight through work. Stripping and setting of pens to be done by journeymen or apprentices.

In Letterpress, that females be allowed to make all cases, except those in which leather is used . . .

That all machinery used in conjunction with bookbinding be worked by journeymen or apprentices.

That in the event of females being preferred to do such forms of work as are thereby claimed to be the legitimate work of skilled tradesmen, the Trade Union conditions be strictly adhered to . . .[81]

In order to strengthen its resistance to female labour, the union discarded its sectional recruitment policy in relation to other men in the trade and adopted a more open policy which encouraged minor trades and the semi-skilled to enlist in the union. Amongst the inducements offered were the lowering of subscription rates and the promise to fight for parity for the non-union men. The central committee of the union encouraged the Glasgow men in their campaign and made further recommendations to facilitate the recruitment of non-society men and strengthen organization, including the appointment of a special organizer for six weeks.[82]

Although the thrust of their arguments was directed against the cheapness of women's work, they also couched their opposition in terms which linked the defence of their skills to the defence of manly virtues. To encourage non-associated members of the trade to join the union, they appealed to a common conception of manhood, which they saw as the unifying bond in the fight against female labour: 'We therefore

---

[81] Bookbinders' and Machine Rulers' Consolidated Union, Trade Circulars and Reports, 1896–1900, 59, MLG.   [82] Ibid. 67.

ask you to join our ranks and help in the noble work of maintaining the rights of skilled workmen which undoubtedly are your rights as well as ours. . . . Our appeal is not to purely selfish considerations, but to nobler and more manly motives by which we hope you will be activated in becoming members of our society.'[83]

Their arguments were heavily overlaid by references to the immorality of cheap labour and they portrayed their battle as one of justice and righteousness struggling against the greed and selfishness of employers. Part of that struggle was to restore women to their rightful place and to reassert the role of the man as bread-winner and provider in the face of attempts by employers to violate the prescribed roles of men and women and undermine the Christian institution of the family. They saw themselves as the guardians of a moral code which was endangered by the untrammelled and unregulated march of industrialization and the unrestricted competition of capitalism. In a letter to the Editor of the *Daily News* concerning the lock-out of about 100 men from the Glasgow firm of Collins, the General Secretary of the Bookbinders' and Machine Rulers' Consolidated Union complained that:

The substitution of female labour for men's work in factories and workshops is no advantage to women generally, for though it may suit the women who displace men, this is no advantage to the wives, daughters, sisters and mothers of the displaced workmen. If there is one branch of industry in which Christian principles should prevail, and from which 'sweating' should be entirely absent, it is surely that which has to do with the manufacture and production of Bibles. Christmastide suggests thoughts of Christ and those thoughts suggest a Divine Fatherhood with an idea of human brotherhood immeasurably above the sordid and selfish spirit now prevalent in the commercial world. A gluttonous desire to accumulate wealth now afflicts the country. It is destroying true patriotism and causing the word 'religion', even in Bible loving Scotland, to stink the nostrils of thousands of working men . . . Before lauding the cheapness of Bibles, the officials of bible societies should make sure that they have been produced by labour for which fair and proper wages have been paid.[84]

[83] Bookbinders' and Machine Rulers' Consolidated Union, Trade Circulars and Reports, 1896–1900, Dec. 1897, 182. [84] Ibid. Dec. 1897, 249.

In another letter to the *Glasgow Herald* he charged the employers with violating Christian principles and the teachings of the Bible by stripping men of their role as bread-winners and making them dependent on the earnings of women.[85] The definition of men as bread-winners and women as dependants seems particularly inappropriate in this case as almost two-thirds of the men were unmarried.[86] At the heart of their opposition to women working lay the deeply embedded belief that men had a prior right to work, and therefore the crux of their policy centred on sectionalist policies to exclude women, rather than fighting to establish a *living* wage for women and men. The Scottish bookbinders eventually had to come to terms with the painful reality of women's increasing presence in the trade and face the fact that organization rather than elimination might be the best long-term solution. However, opinion remained divided about this thorny issue. At a General Council meeting of the National Union of Printing, Bookbinding and Paper Workers in 1903, a motion was moved proposing the organization of a female section of the union. This was supported by an Edinburgh representative who argued: 'We are between two alternatives that we get the girls in our power or leave them disregarded for employers to use them against us.'[87] Although the motion succeeded by one vote the membership later reversed the decision, reflecting not only the divisions within the union, but the persistence of deep-seated prejudices towards women workers.

The fragility of the union movement's commitment to organizing women is highlighted by the refusal of the Glasgow branch of the Glasgow Typographical Society to continue contributing to the funds of the SCWT 'as this body are advising women to keep themselves in touch with the printing trade as line and mono machines is work that might come within the scope of women's work'.[88] The Scottish Typographical Association had for years wrestled with the question of female

---

[85] Bookbinders' and Machine Rulers' Consolidated Union, Trade Circulars and Reports 1896–1900, Mar. 1898, 310.   [86] Ibid, June 1895, 356.

[87] C. J. Bundack, *The Story of the National Union of Printing, Bookbinding, and Paper Workers* (Oxford University Press, 1959), 69.

[88] Glasgow Typographical Society, Board of Management Minute Books, T-GTSI/1/6, 14 Mar. 1903, SUA.

labour and the union's literature is crammed with articles, correspondence, debates, and letters on the issue. There was a consensus within the union that the further introduction of female labour into the trade should be controlled. However, the areas where there was little or no female labour took a more hard-line approach to the question, advocating their complete exclusion. This was the policy of the Glasgow Society, which proposed a resolution at a special delegate meeting on the female question, conferring power on the STA to expel every member employed in offices where women were employed.[89] Glasgow eventually withdrew the resolution but argued vehemently against an Aberdeen resolution that 'female labour be allowed in all offices; girls being reckoned in the ratio of apprentices to journeymen'.[90]

A further area of contention was how to relate to the women who were already in the trade: should they encourage trade union organization amongst them, and, if so, should it be in a separate society or by incorporation into the STA, or should they refrain from organizing and pursue a policy of non-co-operation? The hard-line approach was advocated by an Edinburgh printer ('JTY'), who argued in a letter to the union journal against organizing women as he felt this would be the thin end of the wedge and perpetuate what they were all agreed should be eliminated:

And not only will the organising of females be of no benefit whatever to the Association but such organising would be fraught with the gravest possible danger to the trade as a whole. There is a women's movement coming along which will seize upon and use any organised body of women to serve its own immediate ends and purposes, and no matter upon which footing *we* may have organised female compositors; the organised female compositors will, in their own good time, then take their stand as to them seemeth best. And while I have every possible sympathy with the women's movement, I cannot agree that success to that movement lies in the way of open competition with men in the industrial field, but rather . . . should our, and their, energies be directed to endeavouring to emancipate and banish women from the industrial field entirely and forever.[91]

[89] *Scottish Typographical Circular*, 523 (Mar. 1905), NLS.
[90] Ibid.
[91] *Scottish Typographical Journal* (1911), 172.

The more enlightened approach which argued in favour of organizing the women eventually won the day, and in 1911 the Edinburgh Female Compositors' Society was established. However, they had no vote on the policies of the STA and could not be represented at the unions' delegate meetings.[92] Again the more progressive view was not an indication of a sincere commitment to the right of women to work, and support for equal pay was simply a tactic employed to ensure that more women were not taken on. As one correspondent to the *Scottish Typographical Journal* noted:

Those who advocate the organization of the females in Edinburgh are strongly opposed to the 'recognition' of cheap labour anywhere. They do not urge organisations to perpetuate that conditions of things. But . . . we do say that given no further introduction the men and women in the trade may well work for the mutual improvement of their conditions of labour. This position the women themselves understand and accept. If the Edinburgh men are called upon to resist the introduction of cheap labour (again) surely we will be ever so much stronger if we have the sympathy and support of the women presently employed.[93]

Perhaps the most convincing evidence of the entrenched resistance of the STA to women workers was their stance in 1909 when they issued a memorial to the employers on the dual issue of female labour and new machines. The demand was 'That from the first of January 1910, there shall be no further introduction of females into our trade in Edinburgh, nor any importation of female compositors from other centres, and that in future, machine composition be solely undertaken by male union labour'.[94] There were various negotiations conducted between the union and the employers over the following months, which failed to resolve the issue fully. In the late summer of 1910 there was a confrontation between the two sides which was resolved in the union's favour, with no women being recruited into composing for six years and all new keyboard composing machines to be operated by

[92] S. Gillespie, *One Hundred Years of Progress: The Scottish Typographical Association, 1853–1952* (Glasgow: Maclehose, 1953), 205.
[93] *Scottish Typographical Journal* (1911).
[94] See Reynolds, *Britannica's Typesetters*, for a detailed and finely balanced study of Edinburgh's women compositors.

male union labour. The quid pro quo was the agreement by the union to maintain peace on all questions of wages and hours for three years. The union itself later admitted that the settlement had done little to improve the position of the existing women compositors in the industry.[95] Given that this question was as much about the machine question and new technology as about female labour, and given the strong position the union was in, the union could conceivably have argued that employers should give equal pay to anyone, male or female, working the monotype machines, which were completely new machines requiring completely new skills. They were, after all, prepared to accept new male labour into the trade. This appears to cast some doubt on the protestations of the union that the dispute was 'not a sex question, but a wages question, wholly and solely'.[96]

Craft workers' exclusionary strategies pivoted around the question of skill. The struggles around definitions of skill and the tenacity with which such definitions were defended, indicate its importance as a means of maintaining sectional advantages for strengthening bargaining positions. However, there was also an ideological dimension to the question of skill. Its primary function may have been as a bargaining device, but it also provided status and was a badge of superiority which differentiated skilled workers from the mass of the unskilled. An important component of this status was the opportunity it afforded for men to be the providers and to maintain their wife and children at home without their being forced to work for wages in factory, mine, or mill. A non-working wife was a measure of respectability and one of the hallmarks of masculinity.

The encroachment of male unskilled labour threatened the material interests of skilled workers but female labour substitution posed an ideological threat. Women's work could be tolerated so long as it remained within a separate sphere and did not encroach on the territory of men. In Scotland the rigid sex segregation of jobs meant that the categories of men's and women's work were distinct and therefore reinforced

---

[95] Reynolds, *Britannica's Typesetters*.　　[96] Ibid.

rather than undermined gender divisions. When women began to invade the territory of men, this posed a threat to male material interests and provoked a sectional response. However, this sectionalism was overlaid and reinforced by an ideology of gender and sexual roles which women's penetration of male occupational preserves threatened to undermine. Male workers articulated their opposition in the standard trade union terms of defence of jobs and earnings, but their language indicates that they also perceived women's entry into certain areas of work as a threat to the important categories of masculinity and femininity.

Therefore, the strategy generally adopted by the trade union movement was not to fight for equal pay for women or to improve their wages, or to establish a minimum wage, but to concentrate their energies on eliminating female competition from their trades. The tactics employed by different sections of skilled workers to female labour substitution usually varied in relation to the degree to which women had already gained a foothold in the trade. Those trades which had already experienced the introduction of women as an accompaniment to the introduction of new technology tended to favour a more enlightened approach which involved extending some recognition to women workers. However, those groups of workers who by means of formal and informal workshop organization still exercised a fair amount of control of the work process advocated the most exclusionary policies.

Given that opposition to female labour was underpinned by an ideology of gender and a particular conception of the family, it is a moot point whether the unions of the unskilled could have exhibited a more egalitarian approach. The introduction of labour-saving machinery or cheaper grades of workers may not have been the central threat posed to the ranks of the unskilled, who had never organized on the basis of their technical indispensability, but, when confronted with large-scale redundancies or an overstocked labour market, it is possible that they may have resorted to arguments which stressed that waged work was the 'natural' province of men and domestic responsibilities and home the 'natural' sphere of women. It is certainly the case that, within the unions of the unskilled or semi-skilled, the interest of women workers could have been better served. Indeed the Dundee Mill and Factory Operatives' Union was formed in 1885 specifically for women in the jute industry because of the failure of the existing textile union adequately to represent the interests of the lower-paid women. The Glasgow male cotton spinners' union allowed men operating self-actors to join their society but not women, and, when the male self-actor minders formed their own union, they too excluded women, although they eventually helped to organize a separate society for them.[97]

Whatever the transformations undergone by the trade union movement from the last decade of the nineteenth century, one aspect of its ideology which remained unrevised was its perception of women's role in society. The sexual division of labour and the association of women with the home were viewed by trade unions as part of the natural order of things which had been violated by the rapacity of unrestrained capitalism. For the trade union movement, the notion of separate sexual spheres was not an ideology to be challenged, but a goal to be realized.

As with the bourgeoisie, respectability and domesticity were intertwined in the Victorian and Edwardian working-class value system. Just as these notions had different meanings for the two classes the ideology of separate spheres could be differently interpreted within the working class. The dominant or loudest working-class discourse was that of the organized minority who perhaps could achieve the ideal of the male breadwinner wage. However, the reality of working-class life was such that economic necessity forced many women into the labour market. Therefore, the meaning of separate sexual spheres in working-class discourse was not always narrowly conceived in terms of the domestic realm counterpoised to the public realm. Women's sphere could include waged work, under certain conditions and in certain circumstances, particularly if it conformed to conventionally defined areas of suitable work for women, which of course varied over time and place. Working-class accommodation to the dominant ideology of gender divisions was shaped by the material reality of working-class life; therefore, the boundaries between men

[97] *Sentinel*, 6 Apr. 1867.

and women's domain may have been accepted, but they were often drawn in different places. Thus the concerns of the working class about women's work were focused as much on the location of their work as on their exclusion from work, that is, regulating where women worked and with whom. Working-class attempts to achieve both respectability and the domestic ideal were often combined with and fuelled class consciousness and combativeness. The struggle to achieve them could often bring trade unions into conflict with employers who would be reluctant to provide the material basis necessary for their realization, that is, a wage sufficient to provide domestic comforts for a man and his family. The domestic ideal could be interpreted as part of the attempt by the working class to obtain the best possible conditions under capitalism, as part of its 'accommodation' to capitalism.[98] Women, as homemakers, were to create a domestic environment governed by love, affection, and harmony, and the home was conceived of as a shelter and refuge from the ill winds of commercial capitalism where the cash nexus, competition, and the laws of the market-place ruled. However, this was an aspiration which was ideological in the sense that it embodied a conception of gender divisions presented as 'natural' which confined women to a status dependent and subordinate to men.

Trade unions did not bear sole responsibility for the degree of sex segregation in the workplace; indeed the demand for a family wage was predicated on a pre-existing ideology of gender divisions rather than causing it. Trade unions in Scotland were neither large enough nor strong enough to impose their will on capital. More importantly they were not continually faced with attempts by employers to replace male workers with cheap female labour, despite the obvious advantages to capital, indicating the pervasiveness of the assumptions about women's proper sphere. However, if trade unions cannot be blamed for women's subordinate status in the labour market and their lower earnings, neither can they

[98] See H. F. Moorhouse, 'The Marxist Theory of the Labour Aristocracy', *Social History*, 3(1)(1978). This article interprets working-class attitudes as a form of 'non-committed compliance' to capitalism, engendered by structural constraints and the need to adjust in order to survive.

be exculpated. Trade-unionists were certainly constrained in their choice of strategy, particularly by the balance of forces between capital and labour, but to portray their actions as 'realistic', and as the inevitable response to the logic of the capitalist labour market, ignores the role of ideology as an important constraint on their choice of strategy. Trade union practices reproduced and reinforced the sexual divisions of labour in both the home and the workplace by pursuing exclusionary policies and failing to challenge the ideological basis of women's status as cheap labour. By continuing to press for a family wage based on the earnings of a male provider, and invoking their prior claim to work, trade unions contributed to the persistence of women's cheap labour and therefore encouraged the substitution of men by women. Adherence to the policy of a family wage with its inherent conception of women's dependence was ultimately divisive. It benefited the material interests of a small section of the working class at the expense of consigning large numbers of unsupported women to the status of supplementary earners and hence condemning them to poverty.

As opposition to female labour was ideologically reinforced and not simply a pragmatic response to attempts at undercutting, it inhibited a strategy of fighting for equal pay and encouraged a policy of eliminating female competition from trades, or controlling its entry when inroads had already been made. Sectional exclusiveness was essentially a short-sighted policy which was successful when the balance of forces favoured labour. In the long term it merely accentuated the problem and weakened the capacity of the union movement to mount a united attack on employers by incorporating gender divisions which further aggravated the fragmentation of the working class.

3. Women, Trade-Unionism, and Industrial Militancy, 1850-c.1890

TRADE unionism was not a new phenomenon for Scottish women, for they had been involved in the embryonic trade union movement of the eighteenth century and the early nineteenth century, as well as taking an active part in popular disturbances, for example, in food riots, protests against machinery, and anti-militia riots. Women also played an active although usually secondary part in the general unions of the 1830s and the Chartist Movement, even forming their own female lodges.[1] It is difficult, however, to gauge the extent of their participation in trade unions in the period after 1850, as the official records of governments and trade unions are of little help, being both incomplete and unreliable.

It has already been demonstrated that Scottish trade-unionism was weak, hardly spreading beyond the traditional craft boundaries and indeed excluding much of the skilled labour force. Therefore, any failure to combine by unskilled women and men must be seen in this context.

The majority of the half million Scottish working women were confined to a limited range of jobs. The four leading occupations—agriculture, textiles, domestic service, and clothing—before the mid-1870s accounted for 90 per cent of the female labour force. Given the nature of agriculture work and the organization of domestic service and dressmaking into small scattered and isolated groups, it was likely that only in textiles would there have been any real potential to develop trade union muscle, although at a mass meeting of domestic servants in Dundee in March 1872 a Dundee and District Domestic Servants' Association was formed. Before the mid-1870s, there is evidence of a number of women's trade unions

---

[1] D. Thompson, *The Early Chartists* (London: Macmillan, 1971); K. T. Logue, *Popular Disturbances in Scotland 1780-1815* (Edinburgh: John Donald, 1979); S. Lewenhak, *Women and Trade Unions* (London: Benn, 1977).

being formed. They were not, however, characterized by their longevity and frequently they emerged during or immediately after a dispute, only to disappear quickly. There are frequent references to meetings of female workers, either to discuss a particular grievance or to discuss the possibility of forming a union, but rarely were these reports followed through; therefore, we can only conclude that the meetings proved fruitless or the results did not provide interesting copy for the newspaper.

As early as 1833 the women power-loom weavers in Glasgow had formed an association which was 'countenanced by the overseers or tenters'.[2] It is unlikely that this union maintained a continuous existence throughout the century as in 1863 the *Sentinel* newspaper reported that at a meeting of female power-loom weavers and other female operatives one contributor: 'expressed his gratification that they had organised themselves into a society for the protection of the industry'.[3]

In 1849 an Edinburgh Society of Women in the Printing Trades was established but the hostility between the sexes and the opposition of the typographical societies, which had no intention of supporting a women's society, ensured its rapid demise.[4] One of the most notoriously difficult occupations to organize was homework, which became a focus for agitation and reform for various groups towards the end of the century. It has generally been assumed that, because of their isolated position, homeworkers had made little attempt to improve their wages, and yet as early as 1866 there is evidence to indicate that they saw the necessity of collective action and made attempts, however unsuccessful, to improve their position. In December 1866 a meeting of homeworkers was held at New Pitsligo, Aberdeenshire, to discuss the question of prices for knitting. The patronizing tone of the newspaper report of the meeting illustrates an attitude to women which casts aspersions on their ability to organize in a disciplined fashion:

[2] Factory Inquiry Commission, 1833. First Report, *Employment of Children in Factories with Minutes of Evidence and Reports by the District Commissioners*, in *Industrial Revolution: Children's Employment, 3*, Factories, xx (Shannon, Irish University Press, 1970).   [3] *Glasgow Sentinel*, 17 Oct. 1863.
[4] B. Drake, *Women in Trade Unions* (London: Labour Research Department, 1921), 8.

A meeting of quite an unusual kind was held at New Pitsligo, Aberdeenshire on the evening of Wednesday last, in Miss Whyte's school. It was verily a meeting of women more or less connected with stocking knitting, and although the evening was pitchy dark and rain was falling in torrents, the meeting was attended by about forty. Some of the party were over four score and had seen and helped to nurse several grandchildren. Mrs Thompson, mid-wife, one of the best knitters in the county was called on to preside and discharged the duties of the chair with great ability. She explained that the object of the meeting was to talk over the absurdly low price paid per cut for knitting, and to endeavour, if possible, to get an advance, the present rate of wages being only from 1d. to 1¾d. per cut for Wheeling and 2d. per cut for fingering worsted. After some general conversation, which by the way, was carried on with astonishing quietness and order, it was finally resolved that the best knitters could not earn above 1½d. to 2d. per day of 16 hours at the present scale . . . the chairwoman expressed a desire that the knitters in other places would move in the matter, and do all they could with a view to getting better wages for their essential work . . . After resolving to communicate with the manufacturers thanks was passed to the 'worthy chairwoman' and the meeting separated.[5]

Another example of the awareness of the necessity for organization was an attempt by the 'peakies'[6] of Ayrshire to improve both their conditions and pay in 1867:

A general meeting of the Peakies of Ayrshire will take place on Irvine Moor on Wednesday, 15th May at 11 o'clock, when it is expected that a large gathering will be there as much is needed to be done to prevent a threatened reduction that is hanging over us at present. Sisters to the wires when we hear others reading (for we have no time to read ourselves) about all other trades adopting short time— even the miners have done it, and have reaped a fair day's wage for a fair day's work—it is time we were doing something and I apprehend that short time is the only thing that will prevent this threatened reduction amongst the Peakies of Ayrshire.[7]

The article was signed 'A Peakie' but, as there is no further report of the activities of the 'peakies' in the newspaper, we have no way of knowing the outcome of the meeting or whether any lasting organization emerged.

---

[5] *Sentinel*, 1 Dec. 1866.   [6] Those involved in knitting Ayrshire bonnets.
[7] *Sentinel*, 27 Apr. 1867.

Whatever the outcome, it is certain that these unions, however short-lived, were rarely incorporated into the official and established trade union movement as there is no reference to delegates from women's unions being represented at the various trades councils.

However, the general upsurge in trade union activity of the early 1870s also affected women. In 1872, the Edinburgh Upholsterers' and Sewers' Society was founded and included women in its membership.[8] The Dundee Mill and Factory Workers' Association was inaugurated in September 1875, as the result of a protracted general strike of millworkers in the city and, although the majority were men, women were also included in the ranks. By December 1875, the Secretary of the Association reported that there were already 3,000 paying members.[9] There were a number of attempts to form a Society of Glasgow Tailoresses by the tailors, the Glasgow Trades Council, and the Women's Protection and Provident League (WPPL), which was formed in 1874 and whose leadership comprised middle-class and upper-class philanthropists. Although the meetings were initially well attended, the tailoresses' societies tended to be short-lived.

Many of the east coast unions were very much influenced by the Reverend Henry Williamson, who founded the Dundee and District Mill and Factory Workers' Union in 1885. Williamson was virulently anti-strike and often intervened in disputes in order to persuade the strikers to return to work and seek to have their demand met 'without having to resort to the desperate effort of a strike'.[10] There were a number of other unions in the east of Scotland, either including a substantial number of women in their ranks or comprised solely of women, which were not so directly influenced by Williamson, although they usually involved the participation of middle-class philanthropists or members of the clergy. In April 1887, a mass meeting of millworkers at Hawick voted to form a union and agreed to nominate a provisional committee of twenty-four to draw up rules and make arrangements for

---

[8] N. Soldon, *Women in British Trade Unions, 1874–1976* (Dublin: Gill and Macmillan, 1978), 10.   [9] *Sentinel*, 4 Dec. 1875.
[10] *Glasgow Weekly Herald*, 16 Feb. 1889.

the formal inauguration of the union,[11] and, in 1888, a meeting of bleachfield workers presided over by the Reverend David Macrae voted to form a union to promote the interests of the bleachfield workers in Forfarshire.

Any statement about the extent of women's trade union organization in this period must necessarily be tentative. However, certain conclusions might be drawn from the admittedly patchy evidence. Women's unions exhibited the same tendencies as the unions of unskilled men, forming either during or after a dispute or in a favourable economic climate, but often failing to survive the onset of economic recession. There is also evidence to indicate that women attempted to organize before the advent of 'New Unionism', often with the intervention of the philanthropic middle-class men and women who were so active in establishing unions for women, and on some occasions with the aid of male trade-unionists. However, it could not be argued that the extent of women's involvement in formal organization can be seen as a beacon in the relatively bleak landscape of Scottish unionism but, if situated in this context, it can be concluded that women's trade-unionism was more extensive and vigorous than has been generally assumed, although not enduring. This is not to ignore the question of the lesser trade union organization of women, but rather to question the validity of contemporary attitudes to the problems of organizing women.

The literature of trades councils, individual unions, the WPPL, and other interested bodies abounds with references to the difficulties and problems of organizing women. A variety of explanations were suggested which ranged from those which located the problem in the 'inherent feminine nature' to explanations which attempted to take account of the circumstances of female employment and its transitory nature.

A correspondent of the *Trade Unionist* writing on the question of women at work commented that 'the short sentence, "organise the women workers", simply bristles with difficulties. Many of them have been pointed out again and again. The lack of qualities in women of self-reliance,

---

[11] *Glasgow Weekly Herald*, 16 Apr. 1887.

independence and self-government, through miseducation, their greater timidity, home cares, and many like objections.'[12] A Scottish correspondent writing in the *Women's Trade Union Review* argued that the difficult task of organizing women was made more onerous in Scotland by the absence of a good organizer who would be capable of 'rousing the women workers out of their lethargy' and went on to note that 'It is hoped the Scottish Mill and Factory Workers' Federal Union will in the near future appoint an agent to keep reactionary workers from injuring their organisation.'[13] This view of women as apathetic and reactionary was shared by many Scottish trade-unionists. The 1890 Annual Report of the Aberdeen Trades Council devoted a special section to women's organization but took an extremely pessimistic view of the possibilities of women combining in any significant way:

The great need for better organisation among our female workers has been of late admitted all round. The Council has endeavoured to bring this about, but the result has been very disappointing. In the month of March under the auspices of the Council, Lady Dilke paid a visit to Aberdeen for this purpose. Lady Dilke, along with her private secretary, Miss Abraham, has been very successful in other towns in forming Unions among the Female Workers but, in Aberdeen, there is apparently an apathy, through some unknown cause, that they do not come forward in any number to join.[14]

Perhaps the most pessimistic view on organizing women workers was expressed by a Glasgow delegate to the General Council of the Bookbinders' Union who argued that: 'all attempts to organise the women would be a miserable failure, and if organised they would be a stumbling-block in the long run'.[15]

The rather one-dimensional view of women workers as apathetic and reactionary has been somewhat modified by the application of what is imagined to be scholarly vigilance by labour historians. In other words, they have attempted to take into account the objective conditions which made it more

[12] Quoted in *WTUR*, July 1897, 17.   [13] *WTUR*, 1 July 1892, 6.
[14] WCE, sect. D, Aberdeen Trades Council, *Annual Report 1890*.
[15] C. J. Bundock, *The National Unions of Printing and Bookbinding and Paper Workers* (Oxford University Press, 1959), 69.

difficult for women to organize into unions. This has included a discussion of low wages and how this created difficulties in paying union contributions on a regular basis. It has also been argued that the dependent status of most women as either wives or daughters might mean that they were not at liberty to dispose of their incomes as they wished. The long hours which women worked, coupled with their domestic role, afforded them few opportunities of attending meetings, which were usually held in the evenings, and were therefore further impediments to unionization. However, most women, and particularly married women, were involved in employment which was casual, temporary, or seasonal. They were therefore not a permanent part of the workforce and thus lacked the continuity of employment necessary for the development of organizations in institutional forms.

These attempts to grapple with the problems of the lesser trade union organization of women have some validity, but, despite the variety of explanations offered, they share one common feature, which is to approach the question in terms of solving a problem created by women. Women come to be viewed as deviants, as aberrations from the norm, and thus the framework of the analyses is so constructed that we do not question the role of the trade union movement in creating the problems; rather, we take it as given. If the problem is reconstructed so that we come to question that which we have taken for granted, then a different set of questions has to be asked and different criteria applied. For example, what was the relevance of the trade union movement to women? An organization must in some way relate to the needs of the people which it hopes to recruit to membership. To what extent was the form and character of unionism in tune with the experience of women?

Trade-unionists' wage demands frequently hinged on sectional claims to possess essential skills or to perform strategically important tasks in the labour process. Whilst this sectionalism also excluded male workers, it was particularly antithetical to the interests of women workers. As has been argued, the notion of skill was suffused with masculine connotations and the category was by definition virtually a male one. The demand for a family wage, based on the assumption of a male provider,

which was used as a lever to give both moral and material force
to wage claims, was not only an inappropriate strategy for
women workers, but was made explicitly at their expense.
Therefore, the centrality of skill and differentiation in the
bargaining repertoire of trade unions was not only inherently
sectional and exclusionary, but was clearly not a useful model
of bargaining strategy for those on the lowest rungs of the
hierarchy of skills and status. Although unionists may have
encouraged organization amongst non-union labour, the nature
of organization was always defined in terms of the existing
organization amongst skilled men and was therefore more
relevant to their needs and interests. Few concessions were
made for the different or particular circumstances of some
groups who may not have found established policies and
practices concordant with their needs or experience.

Thrift, self-reliance, and self-help were not only constantly
urged by the trade union movement, but unions were often
associated with co-operative societies and savings institutions,
urging their members to invest in these bodies. The concern
with intemperance and improvidence led unions to frown upon
what they considered small, 'unsound', local savings societies
and credit, both of which were necessary to workers of irregular
and low income. It is clear that this pattern of economic
behavour was only available to those sections of workers who
had a regular, if not high, income and whose economic
circumstances enabled them to plan for the future and envisage
an improvement in their personal situation. As women were
amongst the most vulnerable sections of workers, partly
because of the casual nature of their work and partly by being
concentrated in industries such as textiles which were subject
to frequent bouts of unemployment, this policy held little
attraction for them and was unlikely to entice them into the
ranks of trade-unionism. It also assumes that women were at
liberty to dispose of their income as they wished and, given
the dependent status of many women, this is an assumption
which cannot readily be made.

Sound and stable organization was also an integral element
of trade-unionism and this involved not only regular financial
contributions but attendance at meetings and active participation
in trade union affairs. The discussions of the Glasgow Trades

Council frequently centred on the need to involve more members and often condemned the lamentable attendance of delegates. If it proved a difficult task to involve men then it is understandable that women would find it even more difficult, given the household tasks they were expected to perform, whether married or not. If ordinary membership posed difficulties, participation in the leadership of unions by women was even more unlikely and explains why unions which had a majority of women in their membership, such as the cotton unions in England, rarely included women in the upper echelons or in directing and formulating policy.

The explanation for male domination of union hierarchies was more than simply a practical problem. Although women may have been encouraged to take office when they formed a substantial part of the workforce, there seems to have been an in-built resistance to women representing men. The Secretary of Liverpool's Anti-Sweating League commented of the executive of the clerks' union: 'the idea is to have equal numbers of the sexes but as the men so greatly outnumber the women, this would not be fair at present'.[16] No such questions of equity surfaced in the many unions where men took over the leadership of largely female unions, such as in the textile industry.

The trade union movement was not only dominated by men, but the language of negotiation and agitation was couched in terms which related to men, and arguably the style of meetings was conducted in a masculine mode which was alien to women. The arcane procedures of minute-taking and formulating resolutions and the formal mode of address at trade union meetings would be quite unfamiliar to women, who may have found them intimidating and daunting, particularly when the gender of the language was not neuter but masculine, as in terms such as 'chairman'. However, women were left with little choice but to adopt this form of meeting, which was so much part of the ritual of trade-unionism. The women's section of the Scottish Typographical Association assiduously adopted the rituals and vocabulary of the men's union, although,

---

[16] WCE, sect. A, vol. xlvi.

interestingly, they used the term 'chumship' rather than 'companionship' at their meetings.[17]

For these reasons some of those involved in organizing women workers questioned the strategy of women joining men's unions and suggested that 'women only' organizations were of more benefit to the women as 'they are then obliged to come forward and are not overpowered by the business methods of the men'.[18] A letter from Sarah Dickinson, the Secretary of the Manchester Trades and Labour Council, echoed this view and argued that in a union formed for and by women they would acquire experience in organizing as well as having a voice in the management of the unions, whereas, if included in the men's union, 'they are effaced and take no part'.[19] In her view men tried to control women 'more than they should'.[20]

Trade-unionists frequently expressed patronizing and even contemptuous attitudes to women workers. Constant references were made to the need for their moral and social elevation. Moreover, women were usually seen as apathetic, helpless creatures who were unable to drag themselves out of the mire of indifference into which they had sunk, and required the assistance of those to 'whom the women naturally look to for protection and support' (namely, men).[21] This condescension towards women workers is evident in the views expressed in the *Scottish Typographical Journal* towards the separate women's section of the union:

If she [woman] is a difficult subject to educate in the ways of social organization, the more the pity, the harder the struggle and all the more need . . . for training her to honestly take her place and stand—where her heart and inclinations lie—at your side as a helpmeet, not against you as a tool in the hands of that class that lives by bleeding both.[22]

[17] I am grateful to Sian Reynolds for drawing these points to my attention.

[18] WCE, sect. A, vol. xlvi, letter from the organizing secretary of the Liverpool Anti-Sweating League, 1914.

[19] Ibid., letter from Sarah Dickinson, Secretary of Manchester Trades and Labour Committee, 27 Jan. 1914.

[20] Ibid.

[21] *WTUR*, Apr. 1892, 12.

[22] Sian Reynolds, *Britannica's Typesetters* (Edinburgh University Press, 1989), 117.

Trade unions were a product and very much a part of the period in which they emerged and as such reflected rather than challenged the inequality of relations between the sexes. They never took up issues which related specifically to women, either as women workers, or simply as women. The Glasgow Trades Council's initial stance on enfranchisement was to demand household suffrage. Only later did they adopt manhood suffrage as their goal, but never before the turn of the century did they seriously contemplate the question of female suffrage. The trade union movement tended to be hostile to votes for women on the same basis as men, regarding it as a way of enfranchising more of the middle classes, who were likely to be out of sympathy with the goals of the labour movement.

Sarah Dickinson's attempts to organize the women ring spinners of Manchester was an episode redolent with all that was negative in trade-unionist's attitudes to women. In 1913 the ring spinners, who were not unionized, had gone on strike and, according to Dickinson, had not received support from the Card and Blowing Room Operatives' Union. Dickinson, in her capacity as Secretary of the Manchester Trades and Labour Council, organized the women herself, thereby incurring the wrath of the male Secretary of the union, who, arguing that his union was the right one for the ring spinners to join, dismissed Sarah Dickinson as 'an office seeker' and a 'suffragette'.[23]

Although lip-sevice was paid to the rights of women to work, it was generally assumed that women were capable of performing only a limited number of jobs, which were preferably in tune with their prescribed gender roles, but which crucially did not threaten men's prior claims. Therefore, few efforts were made to campaign for demands which would facilitate women's employment other than in a narrow range of usually low-paid occupations. Even where work was an economic necessity for women and when they were unsupported, or bread-winners themselves, little was done to assist them. For example, crèches were available in the Dundee textile industry, but they were initiated by philanthropic organizations, sometimes with the assistance of the employers

---

[23] WCE, sect. E, letter from Sarah Dickinson.

who were so anxious for women's labour. In Dundee, trade-unionists were more interested in campaigning for classes in domestic economy for female workers than crèches or some other system of child care.

The organization, structure, and character of the official trade union movement did not accommodate the heterogeneity of the Scottish working classes and the different needs, experiences, and circumstances of the various strata. Trade-unionists certainly saw themselves as the spokesmen and representatives of their class, but, in order to become integrated into the movement, all groups of workers would have had to surrender their specific concerns and embrace those of that movement. In effect the concerns of the labour movement, their bargaining strategies, and their adherence to a specific set of values isolated them from the majority of working people, whilst their commitment to an ideology of domesticity further impelled the isolation of women workers, who were viewed primarily as an anomaly or a problem.

The foregoing discussion has revolved around the question of women's lesser trade union organization, and, although we have dispensed with some of the more simplistic explanations, it is still an approach which concentrates on women's failure to organize and diverts our attention away from those areas where women did organize. I would argue that this approach is partly a product of our adoption of the nineteenth-century trade union movement's perspectives and leads us to view non-union labour through the eyes of the official movement. The primacy placed on continuous, stable organization, the preference for negotiation and conciliation, and the desire for public acceptance and respectability meant that organization was defined in a particular way, and any struggle which took place outside this narrow and partial definition was not deemed to be organization. Consequently, ephemeral action by 'unorganized' workers was regarded unfavourably by contemporaries and has been largely ignored by labour historians.

More recent analyses of women's paid labour, including much research by feminist historians, has given new legitimacy to the notion of the passive woman worker. Feminist historians have argued that women's entry into the labour market was mediated by their subordination as a gender, and that this accounts for women's segregation into low-paid, low-status jobs. Whilst this approach has provided useful insights into women's paid work and underlined the importance of linkages between the home, community, and work for understanding the development of the labour process, the argument has often been taken a stage further and women's subordinate labour market position posited as an explanation for their industrial behaviour or more precisely their quiescence and passivity in the workplace. By substituting women's subordinate position in the labour market for innate psychological traits or biological facts, as an explanation for women's docility, these accounts have reinforced conventional views and shibboleths about women's workplace behaviour, rather than questioned them.[24]

There has also been a related tendency to see the concept of gender as relevant only to the analysis of women's work and, moreover, to see it as the decisive influence on women's experience.[25] Women's attitudes and responses to work have been assumed to be derived from their primary identification with the home and the family whereas, in explaining men's responses, more weight has been given to their work situations. It has also been assumed that there was a congruity between domesticity and passivity and that women's association with the domestic sphere acted as a brake on the development of trade union organization and collective action. The outcome has been to emphasize the distinctiveness and separateness of men and women's experiences of work, and to assume that work for women was a peripheral experience and marginal to their identities. Therefore, the pervasiveness and persistence of the view that women workers were unorganized, passive, and submissive has not been based on systematic investigations of the historical reality of women's working lives but on general

[24] Recent examples of this approach are M. Barrett and M. MacIntosh, 'The "Family Wage": Some Problems for Socialists and Feminists', *Capital and Class*, 11 (Summer 1980), and Leonora Davidoff and Belinda Westover, 'From Queen Victoria to the Jazz Age: Women's World in England, 1880–1939', in Leonora Davidoff and Belinda Westover (eds.), *Our Work, Our Lives, Our Words* (London: Macmillan, 1986).
[25] This point is developed by R. Feldberg and E. N. Glenn in ' "Male and female" Job versus Gender Models in the Sociology of Work', in J. Siltanen and M. Stanworth (eds.), *Women and the Public Sphere* (London: Hutchinson, 1984).

theories of gender differences whether sociologically constructed or psychologically and biologically based. In fact the many references to the apathy of women towards trade union organization in the pronouncements of nineteenth-century trade-unionists and philanthropists are matched by the equally numerous references to women's impatience and propensity to strike. The Reverend Henry Williamson's Dundee and District Mill and Factory Workers' Union was aimed specifically at organizing women and girls 'because women and girls were the only kind of workers who came out on strike and threw a whole town out of employment';[26] whilst Sir Charles Dilke found that women's unionism was feeble outside Lancashire and thought the reason was that 'Women wanted too rapidly to see a direct and immediate return for their money.'[27]

The fact that women were less conspicuous in the traditional areas of labour organization has led to the assumption that they were intrinsically more conservative and less disposed to struggle, and yet the available evidence suggests not a lack of militancy but rather an impatience with the negotiating process associated with formal trade union organization. The reports of the secretaries (usually male) of the various English cotton unions substantiate this view as they often commented that women would not take part in the proceedings of the unions and therefore had not grasped the idea of trade-unionism. The Secretary of the Bolton and District Card and Ring Room Operatives' Provincial Association, which had 10,000 women members of a total membership of 12,000, complained that 'they only become interested when they have a particular grievance to be removed'.[28]

It could be argued that on occasions the impetus behind the organization of women workers was to avoid the spontaneous action they engaged in and to channel and contain their grievances within the formal union structure. The first Annual Report of the Women's Trade Union Association, which was founded to promote trade unions amongst the women of the East End of London, commented that:

[26] Soldon, *Women in British Trade Unions*, 29.
[27] *WTUR*, Oct. 1892, 8.   [28] WCE, sect. A, vol. xlvii, 250.

It is our firm conviction that organisation among women is absolutely necessary for the prevention of those frequent and futile strikes which at present occur where women and girls are employed. Among the factories in various industries with which we have had to go in the course of the year, we have hardly met one in which there has not been one small strike or more.[29]

Although the mid-Victorian labour movement did not abandon the strike weapon, they prided themselves on the conduct of the strike, believing it was legitimate and justifiable action which was resorted to when all other channels of resolving their grievance had been exhausted. This sharply contrasts with their views of strikes involving non-union labour, which they saw as the product of improvidence and impatience. It was not strikes *per se* that trade union leaders opposed, but strikes without the presence of a union, which would imply planning, forethought, and due process. There is evidence to indicate that action by women workers was regarded simply as the product of capriciousness and wilfulness and was thus not endowed with any respectability or legitimacy.

The entrenched assumptions about working women's passivity can be challenged by reference to the experience of largely non-unionized Scottish women workers from around 1850 until 1890, at which point there were a number of organizations established to recruit women into the broader labour movement.

Women's Strikes

As a result of the structure of women's employment, most of the evidence is drawn from the textile trade, although not all. In 1851 the textile industry employed almost all women in the manufacturing sector, although this figure had fallen to about 80 per cent by 1891. Throughout the period about one-quarter of the female labour force worked in textiles. There were many branches of the textile industry in Scotland: the woollen industry of the borders, lace in Ayrshire, linen on the east coast, and many minor branches such as silk and hosiery. It is

---

[29] WCE, sect. D, Women's Trade Union Association, *Annual Report 1889–90*.

important to stress the heterogeneity of these textile industries in terms of technology, the composition of the labour force, the sexual division of labour, and the labour process, and that in effect they were virtually different industries. The two most significant branches in terms of women's employment were the cotton industry in Glasgow and the Dundee jute industry. At its peak in 1861 Glasgow's cotton industry employed almost 23,000 women, whilst jute employed about 19,000 women in 1891.

As women were not involved to any great degree in the organized labour movement, it is a difficult task to gather information about their activities and their attitudes towards industrial relations. We therefore have to rely on newspapers as a major source of information as strike statistics were not compiled until 1889. These too are unsatisfactory as they were more interested in the activities of the trade union movement and long dramatic strikes. Women's strikes tended to be spontaneous and of relatively short duration; therefore, there are few detailed references to strikes by women in newspapers and often the accounts which do exist are fragmentary and incomplete, rarely being followed through to the conclusion of a dispute. In spite of these drawbacks, it is still possible to glean from the scattered reports a picture of working women which substantiates a view of them as not only militant but capable of self-organization and independent action.

The following survey of strikes is based on reports in mainly national rather than local newspapers and is therefore not a complete or exhaustive account of women's industrial action. The intention is to highlight the incidence of disputes, the range of issues involved, and, where possible, the outcomes, rather than to provide explanations of the specific causes or circumstances of particular disputes.

Between the mid-1850s and 1890 there were approximately 108 disputes involving women in the textile industry. Just under half of the strikes were in the Glasgow cotton industry and the Dundee jute industry, reflecting the importance of these industries as centres of female employment. However, what is also significant is the geographical spread of the strikes and their incidence across the range of textile industries. Of the 90 disputes where the issue is known, just over 75 per cent concerned wages, 52 per cent were for increases, and 25 per cent were against reductions. In only 23 of the 47 strikes for increases is the outcome known. In 13 cases the strike was successful and in 10 it was unsuccessful. Of the 23 disputes against reductions, the outcome is known in 8 cases and either the action was completely successful or a compromise was reached. There were 11 strikes against changed working conditions and, of the 5 known outcomes, 4 were successful. There were also 7 strikes reported of non-textile workers, including matchgirls in Govan, pottery workers in Bo'ness, and dynamite workers in Ardeer.

It is difficult to make general assessments about the pattern of strike activity, given the fragmentary nature of the sources, but the evidence suggests that there was some degree of correlation between strikes and cyclical fluctuations. For example, in Dundee there were a particularly large number of disputes during periods of violent downturn in trade such as occurred in 1874, 1875, and 1885. This was also the case in periods of upturn such as between 1888 and 1890. The usual form of action was spontaneous and short-lived, although this general trend was punctuated by a number of protracted disputes. The issues involved encompassed the whole gamut of industrial relations questions, including conditions of work,

TABLE 3.1. *Strikes in the Scottish textile trades, c.1850–1890*

Issue	No.	Outcome		
		Successful	Unsuccessful	Unknown
For increased wages	47	13	10	24
Against reduced wages	23	8	—	15
Against changed working conditions	11	4	1	6
For trade union representation	1	—	—	1
Against victimization	2	—	—	2
Against bad materials	3	1	—	2
For improved conditions	3	—	—	3
Unknown	18	—	—	18
TOTAL	108	26	11	53
Total Glasgow cotton strikes	26			
Total Dundee jute strikes	24			
Others	58			

solidarity issues, and disputes about speed-ups and general efficiency measures. However, most disputes were either directly or indirectly related to wages.

The accepted view of women in Scottish textiles, principally the cotton and jute industries, was that the latter half of the nineteenth century saw a gradual but inevitable grinding down of their living standards, with little resistance from the women. The corollary of this view was that they were low paid because they were women and had failed to combine effectively to oppose reductions also because they were women. Lenman, referring to the various attempts at organization by the Dundee jute workers during the century, commented that 'real help for and by working people did not come until the organization of the Jute and Flax Workers' Union in 1906'.[30]

Wages and union organizations in the Scottish textile industry were often unfavourably compared with those in Lancashire. Their inferiority was attributed to the Scottish textile industry's heavy reliance on female labour, and its consequent failure to develop a strong trade union system because of the absence of skilled men capable of organizing the unskilled majority. With regard to the cotton industry in Glasgow this simplistic formulation cannot be applied. The wages of cotton workers were certainly lower than in Lancashire but this ignores the fact that women were customarily expected to work for less money. The comparison becomes increasingly meaningless if no account is taken of the fact that Glasgow was engaged in a losing battle with the Lancashire cotton industry. The history of the Glasgow cotton industry in the last half of the century was a dismal story of decline, the competition from Lancashire being compounded by the internal weaknesses of the industry in Scotland and the failure to invest. The fortunes of the jute industry were equally mixed, although it was more successful, and it too had to endure competition from abroad and the fluctuations of the trade cycle.

According to G. H. Wood, the trend of wages in the cotton industry in Scotland was not so dismal as has been generally

---

[30] B. Lenman *et al.*, *Dundee and its Textile Industry 1850–1914* (Dundee: Abertay Historical Association, 1969), 71.

assumed and he claimed that, until 1886, the advances in Scotland kept pace with Lancashire.[31] The higher wages in Lancashire cannot simply be attributed to the existence of a highly organized male craft union which set the standards for others. The depressed state of the Glasgow cotton industry and the generally lower level of wages in Scotland have to be taken into account. Similarly, the jute trade was precarious and plagued by Indian competition, which provoked employers to over-expand and over-produce. The explanation for the relatively low wages of Scotland's textile workers cannot simply be attributed to incapacity to organize by the workforce and must take account of the objective constraints on attempts to improve earnings and the powerful social and ideological factors which determined women's earnings.

No matter how weak trade-unionism was amongst the women textile workers or how low their earnings, it is clear that they did not supinely submit to employers' demands. As early as 1853 power-loom and hand-loom weavers in Arbroath were on strike for an increase. Although there is no information on the outcome of the dispute, the determination of the strikers could not be doubted.

These working people still continue on strike for an advance of wages. Yesterday and Saturday and Friday, they paraded the streets with banners upon which were inscribed the following mottoes:
'Ninepence and no surrender'
'Threepence and no surrender'
'United we stand, divided we fall'.[32]

In 1861 male and female cotton spinners struck at Lochwinnoch over a reduction of 5 per cent whilst male cotton spinners in Glasgow who had been threatened with a 7½ per cent reduction agreed to accept it because of the 'unsatisfactory state of the trade' and the fact that 'the masters have no control over the present depression'.[33] The Glasgow spinners complained that wages of the female piecers had advanced by 25 per cent at the expense of the spinners in the previous twenty years,

---

[31] G. H. Wood, 'The Statistics of Wages in the UK during the 19th Century: The Cotton Industry', *Journal of the Royal Statistical Society*, 73 (June 1910), 588.
[32] *Sentinel*, 8 Oct. 1853.   [33] Ibid., 2 Mar. 1861.

but female labour was so much in demand, the piecers would countenance no reduction in their wages.[34]

The American Civil War created widespread distress amongst the cotton operatives, to the extent that by the end of 1862 only 6,000 of the 24,800 workers in and around Glasgow were in full employment.[35] As there were on average 100 females for every 10 men in spinning departments and 100 women for every 5 men in weaving, there was obviously a large proportion of women unemployed. The distress caused by the American war and the precarious nature of employment, with a large reserve army of unemployed ready to replace them, did not seem to deter the workers from taking action to redress grievances over either pay or conditions. This is even more remarkable when we take into account the fact that the majority of women in the cotton industry were labelled as unskilled and could therefore in theory be easily replaced.

In February 1863, there was a strike of 180 female power-loom weavers and 80 hand-loom weavers in the employment of Ebenezer Hendry and Sons, Bridgeton. Their complaint was the refusal of their employer to receive a deputation to present their grievances and the refusal of arbitration in cases of dispute: 'So unbearable had such treatment become, that, without any organisation, the whole of the hands had left work on Friday afternoon, leaving cloth on their looms averaging £30 value in wages, due to them, but payment of which had been refused.'[36] Unfortunately, the outcome of the dispute is not known, as there are no other references to it in the *Sentinel* or any of the other leading Glasgow newspapers, and no mention of it at the Glasgow Trades Council.

In the same month that the Glasgow Trades Council was discussing the state of the cotton spinners and power-loom weavers and the depression in the cotton industry, the female power-loom weavers at ex-Lord Provost Galbraith's mill at St Rollox were refusing to work the looms because they claimed that the cotton imported from China was of poor quality and they should therefore get an advance on their wages to make up for the loss they sustained by working bad materials.[37]

---

[34] *Sentinel*, 4 May 1861.   [35] Ibid., 29 Nov. 1862.
[36] Ibid., 7 Feb. 1863.   [37] Ibid., 30 Jan. 1864.

A series of disputes plagued the industry for the following six months and in July a report of a meeting of the Glasgow Trades Council noted that 'from various causes, disputes existed between the operatives and Messrs Walker, Robertson and Scott, at their respective factories—which were now in a state of blockade'.[38]

It was not only in Glasgow that textile workers took action to defend or improve their living standards. Between May 1865 and December 1866, strikes were reported at Forfar, Musselburgh, Greenock, Hawick, and Kelso. The female spinners in the flax mill at Greenock struck for an increase of 2s. per week[39] whilst the female power-frame workers in the hosiery trade at Hawick successfully struck for an increase of 1s. per week. In this instance it seems to have been the women who led the way, as the newspaper noted that 'in the same week Mr Laing [the employer] gave the male powerframe workers an advance unasked'.[40]

In the same month girls at the net factory in Musselburgh presented a petition resolving to strike unless they were granted an increase of 8d. per net. Despite the entreaties of the manager to wait until the proprietor returned from the Continent, the women left the factory in a body, refusing to work another day at the old prices. The dispute was terminated about three weeks later when a compromise was reached and the women granted half the increase they had demanded.[41]

Throughout the 1870s and the 1880s there were a number of occasions when women took successful action for increases, often the dispute being resolved in one day. In May 1870, the women employed at Airdrie Cotton Mills struck work at breakfast for an increase of 6d. per cut on their warps and by dinner time their demand was granted and work resumed.[42] In January 1883, 300 millworkers in Ward Works, Dundee, refused to resume work after breakfast till an increase was granted.[43] In the course of the afternoon, an intimation was made that the demand had been acceded to and most of the strikers returned. In July and August of 1883, there was a

[38] *Sentinel*, 30 July 1864.   [39] Ibid., 21 Apr. 1866.
[40] Ibid., 5 May 1866.   [41] Ibid., 19 May 1866.
[42] Ibid., 7 May 1870.   [43] *Glasgow Weekly Herald*, 20 Jan. 1883.

spate of strikes in Dundee mills for an advance of wages. Although the workers had already gained a 5 per cent increase they did not consider this sufficient and demanded more.

The depressed state of the Glasgow cotton trade meant that many of the disputes in the 1880s were against reductions and to protect existing working conditions but, despite this, the frequency of disputes indicates tenacity and a determination to resist any deterioration in their standard of pay and conditions. There were, however, a small number of strikes for increased wages. In 1887, 900 weavers at Grant's Mill in Mill End struck for an advance of 10 per cent because of complaints about bad yarn. The issue was resolved by a compromise solution which involved an increase of ½*d.* on certain fabrics and the substitution of better-quality yarn.[44]

Women workers often seemed less persuaded by the arguments of orthodox economics than the official trade union movement, and displayed a willingness to take action whatever the state of trade. They were constantly urged to be more cautious and often the role of trade unions and trades councils was seen to be to contain discontent and persuade the women to return to work.

In January 1875, over 2,000 workers at the Baltic Jute Works in Bridgeton, principally female, went on strike over a reduction which had been imposed three months previously and had been accepted because the workers had been led to believe that the wages of the jute workers in other areas would also be reduced. This had not happened,

and the consequence had been that a few of the men and boys and all the women and girls employed at the Glasgow Jute Co have resolved to get their pay raised to its former rate. Twenty or thirty men employed as calenders and lappers continue working, those who are on strike being the spinners, weavers, winders and warpers. The reduction of wages, according to the statements of the workers, represents a loss to the weavers of ½d per cut and also of a bounty amounting to 1d of every cut beyond 9. The spinners by the reduction lose 6d per day each.[45]

[44] *North British Daily Mail*, 21 May 1887.   [45] Ibid., 28 Jan. 1875.

A deputation of the workers attended a meeting of the Glasgow Trades Council and 'After some discussion, a committee was appointed to meet the workers' committee, for the purpose of endeavouring to get the dispute settled by arbitration'.[46] In the face of the intransigence of the employers, the majority of the workers acted on the advice of the trades council, although the return to work was reluctant and protracted.

In April 1870, the mill girls at T. & J. Ferguson's, Kilmarnock, struck against a reduction of wages. The employers claimed that they had been paying more than the price paid in Glasgow and therefore intended to give only the average price paid in Glasgow, less ½d. per piece for carriage. A deputation of the girls visited Glasgow and found that not only were wages higher there, but the charge for carriage was too high. Delegates from the Trades Council met with the girls and promised to give them financial support. The dispute lasted about three weeks and the final report in the newspaper, which had previously been sympathetic, reminded the workers that the average experience of the weavers in Glasgow was greater than in Kilmarnock and that this probably accounted for their lower earnings. At a meeting between the girls and the trades council delegates, it was agreed that 'a deputation of the girls accompany a deputation of the delegates to wait on the Messrs Ferguson to see if an arrangement cannot be come to in the dispute, and that they were willing to submit the whole dispute to arbitration of a competent party'.[47]

If the role of trades councils in the west of Scotland was taken to be to exercise a moderating influence on the women textile workers, the influence of the Reverend Henry Williamson on the Dundee and district workers was more explicitly to restrain and contain their action. A six-week-long strike and lock-out of factory workers at Forfar in 1875 against a reduction was resolved by the Reverend Williamson persuading the workers to accept 3½ per cent reduction as opposed to the 5 per cent[48] demanded, and he also succeeded in persuading millworkers in Kirkcaldy, who were on strike for an increase, to go back

[46] *Sentinel*, 5 Feb. 1875.   [47] Ibid., 16 Feb. 1889.
[48] *Glasgow Weekly Herald*, 29 Aug. 1885.

to work, form a union, and get their advance 'without having to resort to the desperate effort of a strike'.[49] There were innumerable examples of Reverend Williamson counselling workers to return to work and agitate by means other than strike for their demands, but he was not always successful. Blairgowrie millworkers, on strike for a 5 per cent increase, were strongly advised by Williamson to return to work because of their 'want of organisation', that is, they did not belong to a union. They chose to ignore his advice, sent another deputation to the employers, and received replies from two that they were willing to grant the full increase.[50]

Although no separate list of prices for spinning and weaving had been established in Scotland, the Scottish workers did use the existing lists in England as guides to their prices and deployed a number of other measures to ensure that their wages were protected. There are a number of cases where claims for parity with other workers were made and this seems to have been a favourite device of the women workers in the Kilmarnock mills. In 1865 the women employed in the power-loom factory of T. & J. Ferguson refused to work until the employer had guaranteed they would be paid the same prices as the Glasgow weavers. The majority of the women refused to go to work until the deputation they had appointed to visit Glasgow had returned. On this occasion they were successful in obtaining the Glasgow scale of prices although an attempt to gain parity in 1870 failed.[51]

In 1885 the spinners at Todd and Higgenbotham's and Grant's Mills in the east end of Glasgow struck against a reduction of piece wages ranging from 5 per cent to 7½ per cent or 6 per cent overhead. As a consequence of a previous strike in cotton spinning, it had been agreed that wages in Glasgow should fluctuate according to changes in Lancashire and, as there had been a recent reduction there, Grant's and Todd and Higgenbotham's had attempted to impose a similar reduction. The women felt that the state of trade in Glasgow did not merit such reduction and would only agree to 3½ per cent rather than 7½ per cent, although the fly-frame workers

[49] *Glasgow Weekly Herald*, 16 Feb. 1889.   [50] Ibid., 21 Sept. 1889.
[51] *Sentinel*, 11 Nov. 1865.

had already accepted a reduction. After a week-long strike the women returned on a 5 per cent reduction.[52]

It is clear that textile workers were aware of the different methods which could be adopted to protect their living standards and had no hesitation in resorting to what they considered would be the most expedient methods. Piece-workers were particularly alive to changes in working conditions which could affect their earnings; therefore, disputes over inferior material, speed-ups, and general efficiency measures were frequent.

Four hundred mill girls in the employment of Messrs Ferguson, Kilmarnock, took strike action in 1867 because they were adamant that they should receive the same remuneration whether the pieces were of the usual length (54 yards) or a few yards shorter. After a short strike the girls resumed work on their terms, which involved the same money for less work.[53]

In 1889, 600 female weavers at the same factory struck over the quality of the yarn supplied for weaving, which they claimed was difficult to work. The firm promised to remedy the defect, which they maintained was purely accidental, but the girls still remained on strike.

Whether or not their action was successful, the women did not always strike with impunity and on occasions the might of the law was brought to bear on them. Often an individual worker was made an example of and prosecuted as in a dispute of female pickers in Kelso in 1866. In 1873 several hundred female power-loom weavers in Nithsdale struck because of a notice posted throughout the works by the employers stating that they would have to be 'extra exacting' with reference to damages in worsted webs. In spite of the employers' assurances that this was not an innovation, and merely involved the existing rules being more rigorously applied, the weavers took this to be an innovation and immediately went on strike, throwing four or five hundred others out of work in consequence. The following Monday eleven of the workers were summoned before the Sheriff for breach of contract under the Master and Servant Act and threatened with severe penalties

---

[52] *Glasgow Weekly Herald*, 7 Nov. 1885.   [53] *Sentinel*, 16 Mar. 1867.

unless they returned to work. Whatever the final resolution of the dispute, the threats of the Sheriff were futile, as only a few of the several hundred resumed work.[54] An attempt by McPherson's Mill in Calton to increase productivity by making the women weavers work 60–66 yards to the piece instead of the usual 56 yards was strenuously resisted. The women demanded that the cloth be measured and also that the books of the employer for the previous ten years be submitted to a neutral person in order to ascertain 'how the work had hitherto been done'. The dispute came to an end after two weeks, with the employer conceding practically all the workers' demands.[55]

Spinners as well as weavers were alert to changes which might affect their earnings or conditions. A strike of about fifty weft spinners at Grant's Mill in the Mile End illustrates the more indirect methods used by the workers to maintain and improve their conditions. For nine years the spinning machines had been fitted with a 19-inch rim but, in the three months before the dispute, the rim had been changed for one of a smaller size because of the softness of the cotton which was being spun. When the rims were changed back to the original size, the spinners refused to work and as a result 1,000 workers in the mill were made idle. The spinners only returned to work when 'an amicable arrangement' had been reached.[56]

The weavers in most branches of the textile industry, particularly Glasgow, were extremely successful in resisting the introduction of more looms per worker. Contemporaries often argued that the inefficiency and obstructiveness of the female weavers in the Glasgow cotton industry was responsible for the failure to compete successfully with the Lancashire industry. Although other more important factors were responsible for the decline, it cannot be denied that the weavers directed a great many of their energies at resisting the introduction of more looms. A straightforward comparison cannot be made with Lancashire, as the type of material woven, that is, coarse or fine, often determined the number of looms which could be worked. It was, however, common for weavers to operate

---

[54] *Sentinel*, 5 July 1873.   [55] *Glasgow Weekly Herald*, 16 Apr. 1887.
[56] Ibid., 22 Feb. 1890.

four or even six looms in Lancashire whilst in Glasgow two- and three-loom weaving was the norm.

In 1858, 400 women weavers at St Rollox Mill, Glasgow, left their looms when the employers proposed to change the system from two looms to four looms per weaver and thus dispense with the services of 200 of their employees. The women were supported by the Glasgow Trades Council, although they themselves mounted strenuous opposition to the proposals. The two tenters who were responsible for implementing the new arrangements were constantly harangued not only by the strikers, but also by other workers in the locality who gave their support to the women:

At the meal hours those 2 men, father and son, are escorted to their houses amidst the shouting and yelling not only of the hundreds of the 'turn-outs' but by many of their sympathisers belonging to the factories and other public works in the same locality and not withstanding the presence of Mr Galbraith [the employer] and a possee of police, they were on Wednesday cheered and yelled to and from their homes. How far the roused feelings of the young women of St Rollox may overcome their judgement in this case of dispute about the terms of the employment, is very uncertain, as bills have been posted in the neighbourhood expressing 'Down with the nobs'. Nevertheless we trust that the Provost and his female workers will soon come to an amicable understanding and peace be maintained at St Rollox.[57]

The amicable understanding reached was that the women returned to work on their own terms and successfully resisted the introduction of four-loom weaving. Employers' attempts to increase the number of looms per worker were not restricted to Glasgow and, at a meeting of the Dundee Mill and Factory Workers' Union in 1888, a resolution was passed deploring the level of spinners' wages and opposing weavers working more than one loom.[58]

The longest strike of women weavers reported in Glasgow involved a number of issues which related to their productivity and their refusal to work more looms. Napier's Mill in Bridgeton proposed a reduction in piece rates on all quality goods and the firm also operated a bonus system. The women

---

[57] *Sentinel*, 14 Aug. 1858.   [58] *Glasgow Weekly Herald*, 11 Aug. 1888.

maintained that under the new scale they would not only make lower wages but to a considerable extent would lose the premium. The employers claimed that the reduction was necessary because of the obstructiveness of the women in refusing to work more looms. One of the partners of the firm maintained that:

Competition is very keen in our trade and the struggle has been interrupted by the passing of the McKinley Act and the new French tariff. Besides the Lancashire mills have had this system which we propose to adopt, in operation for some time, and as a matter of fact it has been the cause of most of the work going out of Glasgow to Lancashire.

The girls are under an erroneous impression that the change would result in a diminution of their wages. In the process of making it, the change might result in a temporary decrease but the ultimate result would be an increase in wages.[59]

Given the nature of the material worked by the women, it would have been virtually impossible to operate more looms and this was acknowledged by the Trades Council and the WPPL, who pledged their support to the women. As both these organizations had been involved in earlier attempts to get the women to work more looms in other firms, the reduction was undoubtedly an attempt by the employers to cut costs in the most obvious way, in the face of fierce competition. The strike lasted twelve weeks and was given widespread support, not only by fellow workers in Bridgeton, but by a number of other trades and localities. The details of the settlement are uncertain but, according to the Trades Council, the dispute was satisfactorily terminated and concessions made on both sides.

Most disputes involving the textile workers throughout Scotland were either directly or indirectly related to wages, but there were a significant number which specifically involved conditions of work and others which were expressions of solidarity with workers who had been victimized or unfairly dismissed. One such dispute involved the millworkers of the east end of Glasgow, who had taken action in sympathy with a young apprentice who had been imprisoned for thirty days

[59] *Evening Times*, 10 Mar. 1892.

with hard labour for refusing to tend more than ninety-six looms.[60] In Montrose in 1876, female workers at Messrs Richard and Company struck over the dismissal of four overseers who had been employed by the company for between thirty and fifty years. They also used the incident to demand an increase in pay. Despite being told by the employers that they would have to give a week's notice if they intended to strike, the women took to the streets after work and gave vent to their feelings in no uncertain terms:

> The girls returned to work and remained quiet till the work closed in the evening, when a large mob assembled in front of Mr Holland [the resident partner]'s house and began to make a disturbance. Mr Holland appeared and threatened to send for the police. This led to stones being thrown and nearly all the glass in the windows fronting the streets were smashed. The stone throwing being contained, Mr Holland took refuge in the house of a friend, but he was followed by a portion of the mob who hissed and hooted but did not resort to violence. After the disturbance had lasted an hour, the police appeared in force and the mob dispersed.[61]

The disputes, although concentrating on the wages question, encompassed the whole gamut of industrial relations issues and, in this respect, the women textile workers did not differ from the other groups. There were instances where the women struck for equal pay or an equal increase with the men, who were often awarded their advance without having to take action. Although the men were either obstructive or outright hostile on a small number of occasions, in the majority of cases there is no real evidence to indicate that they did not support women in their action, although this did not go so far as to strike in sympathy. Women on occasions were more militant than men and displayed a greater reluctance to submit to arbitration or defeat. A strike of millworkers in Kirkcaldy, in 1883, came to a partial close when all except fifty of the women resumed work on the old terms.[62]

The form of women's resistance was most frequently expressed by their refusal to work for certain wages. However, they also resorted to informal methods of resistance, which

[60] *Sentinel*, 16 Feb. 1866.   [61] Ibid., 22 Jan. 1876.
[62] *Glasgow Weekly Herald*, 3 Feb. 1883.

might be termed industrial sabotage. One such case resulted in a court case when the worker involved tried to sue her employer for unfair dismissal:

Sarah Seally, a weaver, sued the Constonholm Weaving Company, Pollokshaws, for her wages and for a fortnight's wages in lieu of working; but as it had been clearly proved that the weaver had been working her cloth thin by having changed the pinion of her loom (this being a contravention of the rules of the factory which were produced in court), the Sheriff assoilzied the defenders and taking into consideration the serious nature of the offence, and it having been established that she had been similarly guilty on more than one previous occasion, he considered that the manager had acted very properly in summarily dismissing her from the factory.[63]

This was obviously an attempt by the weaver, who was probably on piece-work, to ease the work process and push up her earnings. Although there is no written evidence of spinners resorting to this kind of resistance as they were not paid by the piece, it is likely that they devised methods of resistance, collective or individual, which were appropriate to their work situation. However, one can only speculate on the prevalence of these informal methods of resistance amongst women workers.

It has become commonplace to describe non-union labour as 'unorganized' and yet the vast majority of disputes which involved women were characterized by a high level of organization, although on most occasions they were not trade union members. The strikers usually held frequent meetings during a dispute, elected committees, sent delegates to employers, and on occasions distributed leaflets in the vicinity to advertise their case. Although most disputes were isolated, with only one firm involved, the Dundee workers often took joint action with a number of workers striking simultaneously, and in 1874 almost twenty mills were involved in action against a reduction in wages. In 1871, Kirkcaldy mill girls at McLaren's and Swan's attempted to generalize their struggle for an increase, and successfully involved most of the mills in the district.[64]

[63] *Sentinel*, 22 Jan. 1876.   [64] Ibid., 15 Apr. 1871.

In 1880 female operatives in the Glasgow cotton industry initiated action to obtain an increase for workers in Airdrie cotton works. Their motives were not entirely without self-interest as they had found trade dull in Glasgow and blamed unequal competition from their sister operatives in Airdrie, who were paid less. A deputation from Glasgow addressed a well-attended meeting but, as male workers had entered the meeting as spies, little progress was made as much time and energy was devoted to expelling the intruders.[65]

Two hundred female workers, pickers and menders at Teviotdale and Howland Mills at Hawick, who were on strike over an alteration in their wages terms, ensured that there would be no blacklegging by posting bills throughout the town warning workers against seeking employment in the mills whilst the dispute lasted.[66]

The Glasgow weavers' dispute in 1892 was a model of organization as deputations from the workers were sent to collieries, engineering works, etc. to plead their case and seek financial assistance. Although they were aided by the Trades Council and WPPL, they succeeded in collecting enough funds from collections at football parks, racecourses, and other works to sustain a twelve-week-long strike.

Obviously self-organization and self-activity were not the monopoly of the unionized workforce, but in addition the strike activities of women workers usually involved the participation of all levels of workers, with delegations having a changing composition and a variety of spokeswomen emerging in the course of a dispute. The concern of trade-unionists' leaders to endow their action with respectability and dignity often meant that official strikes had none of the excitement and vitality which characterized the activities of women strikers. As negotiations with employers were often conducted by a few leaders the rest of the membership were often not called upon to take any action except when summoned to meetings, although they did sometimes initiate independent action to publicize their grievance.

Women's disputes were almost without exception lively affairs and there are numerous references to 'gangs of women'

[65] *Sentinel*, 11 Sept. 1880.   [66] *Glasgow Weekly Herald*, 16 Feb. 1884.

roaming the streets during some disputes. Ridicule, derision, and hooting were the favoured weapons and in this respect their action is more reminiscent of the street demonstrations and disturbances of the eighteenth century than the 'respectable' unionism of the late nineteenth century. There is even an instance of women being locked out because of hooting and ridiculing their employers. Women millworkers in Greenock, who had struck because their employer refused them an hour for each meal, caused considerable amusement on leaving the works as they 'were somewhat remonstrative'.[67]

A typical illustration of the kind of activities indulged in by striking textile workers was the antics of the Dundee workers during what amounted to a general strike in the town in 1874.

At an early hour in the morning the operatives on strike mustered outside their respective works and formed in procession and marched through the principal streets of the town carrying as flags handkerchiefs and pieces of cloth on the end of sticks and poles and shouting and singing as they went along. Shortly after breakfast the procession met on the High Street, which they crowded, and after some jubilant demonstrations there, they broke up again into procession and marched about the town. At 3 o'clock the operatives gathered in front of some of the works and hooted and shouted at everyone who attempted to go in, indeed in some cases stones and other missiles were thrown. The police endeavoured to keep order but their efforts were comparatively fruitless . . . The operatives who had come out on strike on Monday continued to parade the streets of Dundee on Tuesday forenoon and to manifest their enthusiasm by singing and shouting wherever they went.[68]

It would be facile to juxtapose the behaviour of trade-unionists and non-unionists for the purpose of contrasting one with the other. The consistency with which the trade union leadership advocated dignified and respectable action did not mean that the official line was transmitted and acted on by the rank and file. Indeed one of the concerns of trade union leaders was the undisciplined nature of the activities of striking unionists and they were at great pains to dissociate the movement from the incidents in 1866 which came to be known as the Sheffield outrages, being instrumental in calling for a government inquiry. There is, however, a case for arguing

[67] *Glasgow Weekly Herald*, 16 Jan. 1875.   [68] Ibid., 12 Dec. 1874.

that, because women were not integrated into the formal labour movement, they were not influenced to any degree by the dominant ideology of unionism and its concerns with respectability and responsible action. They were even less influenced by orthodox economic arguments about the state of trade and displayed a willingness to take action even when trades councils and trade unions counselled that it was imprudent.

Given the propensity of women in the textile industry to strike, it is obviously necessary to reappraise the view of women as an apathetic and tractable labour force, a view which derives from our wholesale acceptance of contemporary views of women and an acceptance of contemporary definitions of organization and legitimate struggle. Trade-unionists could not have been unaware that, throughout the latter half of the century, women workers were engaged in a constant struggle to defend their wages and conditions, a struggle which may not have merited the designation 'battle', but which could at least be termed guerrilla warfare. It is clear that the partial definitions of organization and struggle held by contemporary unionists have obscured the history of those whose actions were not encompassed by these definitions and who have consequently been excluded from the historical landscape.

Women, both young and old, mothers and daughters, living within conventional family structures, or heading households, were involved in industrial action. This indicates the need to dispense with notions of exceptionalism and specially constructed explanations to account for militant collective action by women. The fact that women entered commodity production on different terms from men derived from their association with the domestic sphere and their role in the family as reproducers and maintainers of labour power. However, clearly this role did not prevent women organizing. Once women were involved in waged work outside the home, they adopted the most expedient methods available to them to protect their wages and conditions, irrespective of whether they challenged or contradicted contemporary views of them as passive or docile. This is not to deny that women to some extent accepted their allotted role and the idea of a 'woman's sphere', but to argue that gender stereotypes and the mantle of passivity were discarded when they conflicted with the imperatives of social reality.

Women have generally been defined in terms of their domestic role and it has commonly been assumed that their consciousness and attitudes and responses to work were shaped primarily by their domestic concerns. However, the evidence of Scottish women's industrial action suggests the importance of workplace conditions and circumstances in explaining their collective action. The issues at the root of the disputes and the predominance of wage demands indicate that women's primary concerns in the workplace cannot be assumed to be derived from their association with the private sphere. Although it is necessary to analyse women's work pattern and labour market position in terms of their dominant ideological role, in many ways their concrete experience was structured by the same forces which structured the experience of male workers. Therefore, occupational characteristics must be accorded some salience in the analysis of women's workplace behaviour, just as family situations and gender roles influenced men. One could argue that women's position in the labour market was patterned and mediated by the wider social division of labour. However, labour market position alone is not sufficient to explain industrial behaviour, and has to be combined with an analysis of specific workplace conditions and circumstances.

The fact that the majority of women's strikes were usually outside the portals of trade union organization and that women's collective action was generally not translated into trade union membership suggests that trade union structures and strategies need to be scrutinized in order to explain why women remained tangential to the formal organizations of labour. The struggle for acceptance by the mid-Victorian trade union movement and the fact that it was comprised largely of male skilled workers involved commitment to a set of values and concerns with a number of issues which were often irrelevant to women workers or against their interest. Therefore, it would not be surprising if women found it difficult to believe that their interests could be served best by these organizations.

The form of action women chose, the short, explosive strike, for all its limitations, should not be dismissed as the product of irrational behaviour; detailed examination of the specific context may reveal it to have been the most meaningful and relevant form of struggle available to women workers. What is certain is that non-membership of trade unions was not an index of apathy and docility. The actions of women in the various branches of the Scottish textile industry in the second half of the nineteenth century confirms that women did not meekly acquiesce to the demands of their employers and that they struggled constantly, if not always successfully, against wage cuts, for increases, and to maintain and improve their working conditions. It was not that they were silent, but that their voices could not be heard above the authoritative boom of respectable trade-unionism.

4. The Mill, the Factory, and the Community in Dundee's Jute Industry, 1860-1914

THE incontrovertible fact that women workers in the nineteenth century frequently resorted to various forms of collective action to redress their grievances seriously undermines general models of women's workplace behaviour, which assume complete submission and subordination to managerial authority and controls, and suggest that the locality and the industry rather than the labour market are more profitable contexts for exploring women's work experience. We have seen that social relations outside the factory impinged on both managerial and trade union strategies. Therefore, if we accept that the social relations of the workplace are not sealed off from wider social relations, we need to examine the linkages between the two in order to understand the everyday experience and responses of women in the workplace.

A detailed study of Dundee women jute workers which takes account of the production cycle of the industry, its labour process, and sexual division of labour, and of the social structure and relations of the town and the interaction between these factors within the industry and the town, should enable us to say more about the ways in which women were controlled and the particular circumstances and ways in which they resisted this control.

The standard histories of Dundee's jute industry usually portray women's docility as having a retarding effect on union organization.[1] The position which has gained the widest currency, and, indeed, has been elevated to the status of an eternal truth, is that women in the jute industry were low-paid because they failed to organize and were consequently

---

[1] B. Lenman *et al.*, *Dundee and its Textile Industry 1850-1914* (Dundee: Abertay Historical Association, 1969); W. Walker, *Juteopolis: Dundee and its Textile Workers, 1885-1923* (Edinburgh: Scottish Academic Press, 1979).

subordinated to the will of capital. This lack of assertiveness is often explained by reference to woman's more passive nature, her lack of interest in matters unrelated to the domestic sphere, and thus her relative quiescence. Thus it could be asserted with certainty by one contemporary commentator 'that the true reason for the employment of women is an economic one. They lack the faculty of efficient organisation and therefore the power of systematically increasing their wages.'[2] But this obviously fails to take account of the objective constraints on any attempts to improve wages or conditions. The jute trade was precarious and plagued by Indian competition, which provoked employers to over-expand and over-produce; this must have determined the response of the workforce to some extent.

Although Dundee was synonymous with jute manufacture, the regional textile industry involved more than the production of jute, with Brechin and Forfar producing heavy linen, North Fife specializing in finer linens and bleached goods, and Arbroath concentrating on canvas.[3] The textile industry had originally been based on flax and hemp, but its substitution by jute, a cheaper fibre, seems to have begun about 1833,[4] until by 1863 imports of raw jute considerably exceeded those of flax and hemp with 28,900 tons of flax and hemp imported compared with 46,900 tons of jute.[5]

Despite the systematic substitution of jute some firms continued to deal in flax for some time and only cautiously shifted to the cheaper fibre. Baxter Brothers had begun experimenting with jute in 1845, but it was 1867 before it appeared on the firm's monthly production statements.[6]

The economic fortunes of the jute industry were somewhat erratic, with frequent downturns of the business cycle being punctuated by booms of almost spectacular dimensions, usually occasioned by a war, which stimulated the demand for manufactured jute in its various forms. Thus the Crimean War, the American Civil War, the Franco-Prussian, and the Boer War

[2] D. Lennox, 'Working Class Life in Dundee for 25 years 1878–1903', TS, n.d., c.1906, St Andrews University Library.
[3] Lenman *et al.*, *Dundee and its Textile Industry*, 29.   [4] LC 196A (29).
[5] A. J. Warden, *The Linen Trade Ancient and Modern* (London: Frank Cass & Co., 1864), 63.
[6] A. J. Cooke (ed.), *Baxters of Dundee* (Dundee University Press, 1980).

all triggered booms in the jute trade and ushered in periods, however brief, of high demand and healthy profits.

The development of a low-wage jute industry in India, established in 1855, although initially having a marginal impact, was to be a constant thorn in the flesh of the jute industry as it steadily encroached on the cheaper end of the market, which had once been monopolized by Dundee. The consequences of this competition were probably to lower prices generally for jute products and to make it difficult for Dundee to exploit any rise in demand for jute as it was not the sole source of supply.[7] The industry was placed in an even more vulnerable position by the introduction of tariffs abroad, the first of which was the Morrill Tariff, which in 1860 imposed a duty of between 15 and 20 per cent on jute goods entering America. Although this was soon lifted, others followed towards the end of the century.[8]

Lenman and Donaldson have argued that the competitive threat of the Calcutta mills was not so immediately irritating to Dundee manufacturers as the fiercely competitive nature of the home trade. Often those who had successfully engaged in speculation in India returned to Dundee to establish a mill or factory and attempted to undercut established rivals in order to gain a foothold in the trade.[9]

The vicissitudes of the business cycle were exacerbated by the effects of the general economic climate, to which of course it was not immune. The industry was particularly vulnerable in a situation where prices were in a downward spiral such as obtained between 1873 and 1896, the period usually referred to as the Great Depression. Although demand for jute goods fluctuated during this period, prices were so low as to virtually eliminate profit.[10]

The vagaries of the fortunes of the jute trade were only partially a product of these external circumstances, which were largely outside its control. Part of the explanation lies in the response of the industry to the variety of problems it had to

[7] B. Lenman and K. Donaldson, 'Partners, Incomes, Investment and Diversification in the Scottish Linen Area, 1850–1914', *Business History*, 13(1) (1971), 5.
[8] Lenman *et al.*, *Dundee and its Textile Industry*, 30.
[9] Lenman and Donaldson, 'Partners, Incomes, Investment and Diversification', 6.
[10] Lenman *et al.*, *Dundee and its Textile Industry*, 32.

confront. The ever present threat of Indian competition, the fluctuating demand for jute, and cut-throat competition at home evoked a Pavlovian response to produce more.[11] An article in the *People's Journal* in 1851 argued that 'the remunerative nature of jute manufacture leads to its extension. To produce a few more tons a week seems to be the only course when prices will scarcely meet costs.'[12]

Manufacture was such a small proportion of final cost that in years when jute was cheap the reaction of the manufacturers was to produce more in order to squeeze as much profit as possible from a material which yielded such slender profit margins. Lenman argued that the roots of depression in the jute industry lay in this cycle of over-expansion, over-production, and glutted markets with little regard for the long-term economic and social consequences.[13] This contention echoes the fears of A. J. Warden expressed as early as 1864 when he noted the tendency for profits realized in a boom period to be laid out in the erection of extensive new works and the additions to old ones, so that money was locked up in buildings and machinery which ought to have been conserved and retained in the trade. He claimed that 'if these extensions are kept within legitimate bounds they will be profitable to the builders and beneficial to the community, but if not they will do injury to all'.[14]

The picture of the regional jute industry was not uniformly bleak, and many of the larger firms which had reaped enormous profits in the boom periods of the 1850s, and which continued to maintain healthy balance sheets throughout the Great Depression, did not indulge in an orgy of building but contented themselves with a slower and steadier rate of expansion.[15] Vertical integration proved to be another successful strategy, for, by controlling every aspect of production, some firms managed to survive the buffetings of trade depressions and more effectively exploit the boom periods.[16]

[11] Lenman *et al.*, *Dundee and its Textile Industry*, 33.
[12] Quoted in Lenman and Donaldson, 'Partners, Incomes, Investment and Diversification', 32.
[13] Lenman *et al.*, *Dundee and its Textile Industry*, 32.
[14] Warden, *The Linen Trade Ancient and Modern*, 619.
[15] Lenman and Donaldson, 'Partners, Incomes, Investment and Diversification', 8.
[16] Lenman *et al.*, *Dundee and its Textile Industry*, 33.

The profitability of certain enterprises is attested to by the extent of overseas investment where Lenman claims: 'Dundee and its associated textile area played a wholly disproportionate role in the remarkable expansion of British capital exports in the late nineteenth and early twentieth centuries.'[17] It is difficult to estimate how far this exportation of capital directly contributed to the low wage levels which characterized the jute industry. It is clear, however, that the failure to invest at home outside the jute trade and the consequent lack of industrial diversification exacerbated a situation already characterized by terrible poverty and periods of high unemployment.

The dominance of jute in Dundee was reflected in its industrial structure, which was heavily skewed towards textiles and clothing. Throughout the period 1841–1911, over 50 per cent of the population were employed in jute and linen textiles and clothing, whilst the other three main areas of employment combined, engineering, tool-making, and metalwork, building, and food, drink, and tobacco occupied, at most, just over 20 per cent of the workforce.[18] By the beginning of the twentieth century the industrial base was further narrowed with the sale of two shipping fleets, the decline of the whaling industry, and the contraction in the number of shipbuilding firms.[19]

Unsurprisingly, jute dominated the employment pattern of both men and women in Dundee. In 1911, from a total working population of 84,000, jute employed 34,000.[20] It was the single largest occupation for males, employing over 9,000 men and boys (one-fifth of the male workforce) with the metal and engineering industries and transport each employing over 6,000.[21] However, the female labour market was comprehensively dominated by jute, which employed between three-quarters and two-thirds of Dundee's working women in the years 1871 till 1911.[22] Of the total jute

[17] Lenman and Donaldson, 'Partners, Incomes, Investment and Diversification', 5.
[18] Richard Rodger, 'Employment, Wages and Poverty in the Scottish Cities 1841–1914', in G. Gordon (ed.), *Perspectives of the Scottish City* (Aberdeen University Press, 1985), 55.   [19] Ibid. 40–1.
[20] Census of Scotland, 1911.
[21] J. Butt, 'The Changing Character of Urban Employment 1901–1981', in Gordon (ed.) *Perspectives of the Scottish City*, 213.
[22] Census of Scotland, 1871 and 1911.

142   *The Background to Dundee's Jute Industry*

workforce 75 per cent were women. The demand for cheap female labour was such that Dundee became a town of migrant labour, drawing much of the workforce from the neighbouring countryside, the Highlands, and Ireland. In 1861 61.5 per cent of Dundee's population was born within the county, 20 per cent came from other counties, and 15.6 per cent from Ireland.[23]

Dundee was therefore a woman's town: women outnumbered men in the town by 3 to 2; they formed over 43 per cent of the total labour force; and 54.3 per cent of women aged over 15 were employed.[24] Dundee also had the highest percentage of married women working of all the Scottish towns. The official figure was 23.4 per cent, but a survey by the Dundee Social Union carried out in 1904 found that approximately half the wives in their sample of 5,888 households were working or temporarily unemployed.[25]

Women's dominance of the town was reflected in the disproportionately large numbers of households in Dundee dependent solely on women's earnings and the large number of households rented and leased by women. In 1871 the census enumerator noted that 'many factory girls keep independent households for themselves'.[26] In 1901 the proportion of women householders was 12,000 from a total of 37,000, the highest of any Scottish town,[27] whilst the DSU's 1904 survey claimed that in the west district of the town over one-third of the 3,650 households visited were rented by women. Of these 3,650, 111 were wives living apart from husbands either temporarily or permanently, 804 were widows, and 370 were unmarried women. The east district displayed a similar pattern of tenancy and it was calculated that the proportion of female householders in the whole town was about one-third.[28]

The population of Dundee grew from 78,981 in 1851 to 165,000 in 1911, although the rate of increase slowed down

[23] Quoted in Lenman *et al.*, *Dundee and its Textile Industry*, 74.

[24] Census of Scotland, 1911; M. L. Walker, 'Work Among Women', in *Handbook on Dundee* (Dundee: British Association, 1912).

[25] DSU, *Report on Housing and Industrial Conditions and Medical Inspection of School Children* (Dundee: DSU, 1905), 24.

[26] LC 222 (12).

[27] Walker, 'Work among Women'.   [28] DSU, *Report on Housing*, 17.

after 1871.[29] A consequence of the mushrooming population was severe overcrowding and a chronic housing shortage. Of all the Scottish towns and cities, only Paisley, where 37 per cent of all families lived in one room, had worse overcrowding than Dundee.[30] Although the population had risen by 30,000 between 1841 and 1861, only 568 extra houses were built in that period,[31] the problem being the reluctance to build houses for workers whose wages were too low to allow for economic rents.

The extent of migration to Dundee and the chronic shortage of housing meant that accommodation for many women implied lodging with a family, which could involve three or four lodgers sharing a two-roomed house with a family.[32] There were few attempts by employers to provide houses for their workers with the exception of Baxter Brothers, who built a tenement block for about eighty families in 1866.[33] Although initially intended for their own workers, they later rented them to those who were likely to be good tenants.[34] The occupations of the heads of the households indicate that the tenants of these employer-built houses were drawn from the ranks of the skilled and supervisory workers, who were therefore likely to be better-paid. This is confirmed by the fact that approximately 80 per cent of wives in these houses did not work,[35] an unusually high percentage in Dundee. Employers clearly did not feel constrained to secure the loyalty and services of women workers whose skills were not at a premium and, most importantly, could not afford to pay an economic rent.

Dundee's appalling housing conditions were frequently the object of philanthropic concern and investigation. The DSU investigation into housing and social conditions in the city established that, using the officially recognized definition of overcrowding, almost 50 per cent of Dundee's population lived in overcrowded accommodation.[36] As many of the workers had to live near the mills and factories, the centre of the town

---

[29] Census of Scotland, 1851 and 1911.
[30] Lenman *et al.*, *Dundee and its Textile Industry*, 79.   [31] Ibid. 80.
[32] Census Enumerator's Schedules, 1891, Dundee Registration District, St Clement's District, West Register House.
[33] Cooke, *Baxter's of Dundee*.   [34] Ibid. 56.   [35] Ibid. 56–7.
[36] DSU, *Report on Housing*, 1.

was particularly congested and the combination of 'bad ventilation, insanitary closets and filthy ashpits' created an appalling stench, according to the sanitary inspectors.[37] Examples of overcrowding cited by the DSU report referred to seven people (two men, four women, and one child) sharing one room and a closet and ten people (husband, wife, and eight children) sharing two rooms with no sanitary facilities. In the latter case the accommodation was also shared with a number of dogs, which the family bred.[38] The usual weekly rent for one-roomed houses varied from 1s. 3d. to 2s. 6d., depending on size and locality, and for two-roomed houses the rent was between 2s. 6d. and 3s. 6d. per week.

Rent and food represented a particularly high proportion of income in Dundee, given the low level of wages and the high cost of living. Up until the First World War, Scottish wages fluctuated at between 87 and 96 per cent of the United Kingdom average,[39] and, because of the predominance of low-waged female employment, Dundee wages were particularly low. Low wages were compounded by high price levels, which in Dundee, including rents, were 4 per cent higher than central London, the most expensive English city.[40] Poverty levels were exacerbated by the number of households in which women were the sole or chief bread-winners. Of a sample of 3,039 families, 1,062 were dependent solely on the earnings of women, and, in 655 cases, the income was less than 15s. per week.[41]

In contrast to those beleaguered families struggling to provide for dependants with a wage which was meant to be supplementary, there were a number of households (almost 500 of the above sample of 3,039), which consisted of single women living either alone or with a friend, with no dependants. Despite relatively low earnings, these women, sometimes by pooling resources, could achieve a reasonable standard of living and even manage to dine out either at a cook-shop or at a neighbour's house, thereby saving themselves time and labour.

[37] DSU, *Report on Housing*, p. xi.   [38] Ibid. 14.
[39] Quoted in Rodger, 'Employment, Wages and Poverty in the Scottish Cities', 42.
[40] Rodger, 'Employment, Wages and Poverty in the Scottish Cities', 43.
[41] DSU, *Report on Housing*, 25–6.

The DSU report cited three such cases of 'a class of household typical of Dundee'.[42] The first household consisted of two weavers:

Miss X and her friend are weavers, earning 14s. a week . . . These two girls have a very neat and pretty room, for which they pay 2s. They take coffee before starting for work, come back at 9 o'clock to breakfast, which consists of coffee, rolls, eggs, and butter, and go to a dining-room at 2 pm. They have meat and potatoes, rice or stewed fruit every day, for which they pay 4d. or 4½d. each. At six they have tea with jam or cheese, and sometimes porridge and milk before going to bed.[43]

In another household 'Miss Z and her sister live together. They are spinners earning 10s. 6d. and 11s. 6d. respectively. . . . For 1s. a week each a neighbour provides their dinner which consists generally of broth, sometimes, potatoes and vegetables, or suet pudding.'[44] It was not only the single women who availed themselves of the cook-shop facility. Another case cited by the DSU report was that of a millworker and his wife, a preparer, who had four children. Their combined income was 25s. a week, 4s. of which was paid to a neighbour for watching the baby: 'The children bought ½d. worth of soup for their dinner at the cook-shop, and she and her husband had tea and bread and butter, and sometimes soup from the cook-shop. For supper her husband and she had tea, bread and butter, steak, ham or fish.'[45]

The official statistics on wages indicate that jute wages were particularly low in comparison with other textile trades, and that this was the reason for the extent of poverty in Dundee. However, the most frequently cited rates, those taken by the Board of Trade in 1886, were based on a year when wages were at an abnormally low point, and therefore give a particularly pessimistic picture of earnings.[46] By 1890 the rates of wages of weavers had risen by 20 per cent, and those of millworkers, reelers, and winders by 25 per cent since 1886. This placed female wages in the weaving sector of jute on a par with cotton,

[42] DSU, *Report on Housing*, 31.   [43] Ibid. 41.   [44] Ibid.
[45] Ibid. 35–6.
[46] *Return of Rates of Wages in the Minor Textile Trades of the United Kingdom*, C. 6161 (London: HMSO, 1890).

the highest-paying sector, and wages in the spinning branch about half-way up the earnings table for female textile workers.[47] Therefore, the major reason for poverty in Dundee was not abnormally low wages in comparison with other textile centres, but the more fundamental fact that women were paid a wage which was assumed to be supplementary, when the reality in Dundee was that substantial numbers of households depended solely on women's earnings.

The jute industry dominated both Dundee and the lives of its workforce. A twelve-hour day was the norm, with two breaks, three-quarters of an hour for breakfast and one hour for dinner. In the 1870s working hours were shortened and the normal practice was to cease work on a Saturday at 9.30 a.m., rather than 1 p.m. For both mills and factories, work began at 6 a.m., although in winter some of the works would have a later start and compensate by having shorter breaks for breakfast and dinner.[48] Mill bells and factory whistles sounded half an hour before the starting time and as an added precaution some workers paid 'knocking-up boys', who would tap on doors and windows to waken them. Lateness was penalized by loss of earnings. The doors of the workplace were closed exactly on the hour of starting and workers would have a portion of their wages deducted even if only minutes late. Exit doors were padlocked once the workers were inside, and only the foremen had the key.[49] Although most workers lived near enough their place of work to enable them to go home during the dinner hour, others had some distance to travel and had to take their meals in some corner of the mill or factory, whilst others preferred to go to coffee-shops or cook-shops.[50]

The manufacture of jute involved an array of processes which were split between the spinning mills and the weaving factories.

[47] *Return of Rates of Wages in the Minor Textile Trades of the United Kingdom*, C. 6161 (London: HMSO, 1890).

[48] Royal Commission on Labour, *Fifth Report on Changes in the Rate of Wages and Hours of Labour in the United Kingdom 1898*, C. 8795 (London: HMSO, 1898), 28; Report by the Inspector of Factories, *Half-Yearly Report, 30th April 1872*, in *Industrial Revolution*, Factories, xv (Shannon: Irish University Press, 1970), 207–8; *Early Days in a Dundee Mill 1819–23: Extracts from the Diary of William Brown, an Early Dundee Spinner* (Dundee: Abertay Historical Society, 1980), 14.

[49] 'Sketches of Life in a Jute Mill', *People's Journal*, 14 May 1881.

[50] Ibid.

The coarse nature of raw jute meant that there were more preparatory stages involved in the process than in other textile industries before the material was ready to be spun. The first stage of the process was carried out in the mills, starting with the batching house where the jute was softened, combed, and teased; from there the softened and 'scutched' jute went to the low mill where it was converted by the processes of 'carding', 'drawing', 'doubling', and 'roving' into a soft, ropelike material and wound round big bobbins, which were taken to the spinning flats.[51] From the spinning flats the material went to the reelers, winders, and warpers before being transferred to the weaving sheds where the final stages of the process were carried out.

In both the mills and the weaving factories there was a fairly rigid sexual division of labour. However, in the weaving branch, which employed about 40 per cent of the jute workforce, the division of labour was most rigid, with weaving being an almost exclusively female occupation and men's employment confined to a small number of skilled workers such as beamers and dressers, supervisory and maintenance workers such as overseers, tenters, and mechanics, and the unskilled labourers. A few men were employed as weavers, many of whom had previously been hand-loom weavers; however, they generally hoped to move on to become tenters.[52]

Overseers and assistant overseers were at the apex of the hierarchy of authority in the weaving sheds. They were usually promoted from the ranks of the tenters and had responsibility for recruiting the workforce, although not on a subcontracting basis.

The tenters were the male workers who most frequently came into contact with the female weavers. One tenter would commonly oversee about twenty looms. Although their task was to set up the looms, tune them, and tend them when they broke down, tenters were effectively sub-foremen who exercised a degree of authority over the weavers and controlled the pace at which they operated. In his evidence to the Royal Commission on Labour, James Reid, a loom tenter, claimed that as 'a

[51] 'Sketches of Life in a Jute Mill', *People's Journal*, 14 May 1881.
[52] Ibid.

result of the bounty system', which involved the payment of a bonus on production over and above a certain fixed quantity, tenters had a vested interest in intensifying the labour of the weavers as they too were paid the premiums on production.[53] Consequently, the relationship between tenters and weavers was often an uneasy and antagonistic one. Weavers frequently complained about tenters. As one weaver commented: 'That was the only thing I had against the weavin'—the tenters. You get one or two good ones, but most of them were a lot o' rotten buggers, they really were.'[54] Another weaver complained that the tenters were 'a lot o' crabbit so-'n'-so's'.[55] Clearly the supervisory functions of the tenters and their skilled status differentiated them from the women weavers, but the fact that they could increase their earnings by increasing the pace of work of the women weavers introduced an additional dimension of sexual antagonism to these divisions.

There were a limited number of opportunities for occupational mobility for male workers in the weaving sector. There were apprenticeships available, including mechanic, tenter, and hacklemaker, and it was possible to move from one of the unskilled occupations into an apprenticed one. For a small handful of men there was always the possibility of becoming a foreman or sub-foreman. For the women, however, there was no opportunity for vertical mobility. Although weaving was not officially recognized as skilled work, there was an informal apprenticeship which involved the young girl entering the weaving sheds to serve her time as an 'ingiver'. During this period, which ranged from a minimum of six weeks to one year, depending on the availability of a loom, she would work alongside a fully fledged weaver, observing, servicing, and learning the requisite skills. Once she was given a loom of her own, the weaver could progress no further.

These distinctions between male and female workers in the weaving factories were replicated in their earnings. Apart from the apprentices, the men, including unskilled labourers, earned

[53] Quoted in *Dundee Year Book*, 1893.

[54] Interview with Winnie Porter (weaver) carried out by Billy Kay for the BBC 'Odyssey' programme, 1979. I am grateful to Mr Kay for making his transcripts available to me.

[55] 'Odyssey' interviews, Annie Reid (weaver).

TABLE 4.1. *Number of workers employed in the Bowbridge Works jute mill, Dundee, by age, 1907–1914*

	Men		Women		Total
	under 18	over 18	under 18	over 18	
April 1907	183	267	153	621	1,224
October 1907	181	266	160	622	1,229
July 1908	179	266	149	616	1,209
October 1908	169	270	146	537	1,122
April 1909	170	278	163	580	1,191
October 1909	171	284	142	598	1,195
April 1910	191	173	162	568	1,194
October 1910	187	279	133	599	1,198
April 1911	163	285	104	560	1,112
October 1911	159	298	119	611	1,187
April 1912	162	295	123	628	1,208
October 1912	157	300	127	590	1,174
April 1913	156	298	123	587	1,164
October 1913	155	284	112	571	1,120
April 1914	154	288	121	592	1,155
October 1914	131	229	120	569	1,040

Source: SIC, J. & A. D. Grimmond Ltd., JS 66/11/8/27.

more than the women weavers. In 1905, overseers earned an average of 31s. per week, tenters an average of 30s. 5d., mechanics 30s. 6d., beamers and dressers 18s. 9½d., and labourers 19s. 8d.[56] The women weavers earned an average of 13s. 7d.; however, as they were on piece-rates they had greater variation in their earnings, with some weavers earning very little in particular weeks and others capable of earning 24s.[57]

In the jute mills the ratio of females to males was 2 : 1. However, the prevalence of the half-time system in the mills, whereby children over 10 who had not attained school-leaving age were able to work alternate days in the mills and the school, and the youth of the shifters in particular resulted in a workforce with a relatively young average age. The ratio of adult women to adult men was about 2 : 1 (see Table 4.1).[58] Although about one-third of the workforce in the mills was

[56] DSU, *Report on Housing*, 55, drawn from a table of earnings of male jute workers.   [57] Ibid., table of earnings of female workers.
[58] DUA MS 15/46, wage records of an unidentified jute mill, 1860–2.

under 18 years of age, the largest single category of workers was women between 25 and 45 years of age.[59]

The mills were not so sharply differentiated occupationally as the weaving factories and there was not quite such a rigid sexual division of labour, as there were a few processes which engaged both men and women. However, this was confined to the batching house and the task of shifting, which was usually carried out by young boys and girls. Males and females were generally paid at the same rate in the few tasks they shared. However, in batching the workers were paid by the bale and the superior strength of most men usually enabled them to earn more than the women.

In the low mill or preparing department, women predominated, carrying out the task on the carding, drawing, and roving machines, which converted the yarn into a fine, regular material suitable for spinning. The ratio of females to males in the low mill was approximately 2 : 1 but many of the males were young boys who carried out the subsidiary tasks, and the ratio of adult women to adult men in preparing was approximately 3 : 1.[60]

Work in the low mill was generally said to be unskilled and therefore attracted casual female labour, often 'married women in necessitous circumstance'.[61] However, an account given by a former shifter in the preparing department who subsequently became a manager suggests that it was none the less an important part of the manufacturing process:

The women employed in the low mill have very important matters to look after. The first supply of jute to the breaker card is under their control and the whole subsequent texture of the yarn is dependent on the regularity of their feed. To aid them in this, the jute is weighed in bunches before leaving the batching house and the speed of the card is indicated by a rough kind of clock attached to it, so many bunches being spread out on the feed cloth during one round of the clock. The feed of the roving frame is also under female control, and everything depends on that supply being regular and unbroken. The intermediate processes—not requiring such exact treatment—are generally in the hands of the boys.[62]

[59] Census of Scotland, 1851-1911.   [60] DUA MS 15/46.
[61] Extract from the Royal Commission on Labour, *The Employment of Women*, C. 6894 (London: HMSO, 1893), published in the *Dundee Year Book*, 1893.
[62] 'Sketches of Life in a Jute Mill'.

In the spinning flats the ratio of women to men was approximately 10 : 1 with adult males confined to supervision and maintenance work. In one mill, the spinning department had 81 employees, 72 of whom were female. The females were either spinners, shifters, or piecers, whereas the men included the overseer, an oiler, and the boy shifters.[63] Of the hierarchy of spinner, piecer, and shifter, the spinners were at the top although they had no supervisory powers over the piecers and shifters. As well as working one frame or a pair of frames, the women were expected to keep their own frames in good order, a regular time being set apart for cleaning them. The piecers, who were young women, went from one frame to another fixing up, or piecing up, any ends which were dropped by the spinners. The shifters, many of whom would be half-timers, removed the filled bobbins from the frame and replaced them with empty ones.[64] The shifting and piecing tasks functioned as an informal apprenticeship to spinning, as most spinners had been shifters and piecers before acquiring a frame of their own.[65]

The spinners and piecers were supervised by an overseer and the shifters managed by a shifting mistress, who carried a light strap or tawse, which she used to keep her young charges in tow, and a whistle, which she blew as the signal to start shifting the filled and the empty bobbins.[66] The final stages in the mill were reeling, winding, and warping, which were exclusively female tasks, the only males in these departments being the overseers.

Apart from the half-timers and the boy shifters and rove- and bobbin-carriers, most of the men in the mill earned more than the women. Overseers could earn between 22s. and 27s. per week whilst the highest-paid women were the shifting mistresses, who earned 14s. per week. They were the only women in the mills who earned a higher rate than some men. The female piece-workers such as winders and batchers could put their earnings up in good weeks, but only to the level of the lowest-paid men.[67] The piece-workers such as the winders,

[63] DUA, MS 15/46.
[64] Interview with Mrs McD. (former spinner), b. 1890.   [65] Ibid.
[66] 'Sketches of Life in a Jute Mill'.
[67] *Return of Rates of Wages in the Minor Textile Trades of the United Kingdom*, C. 6161 (London: HMSO, 1890), 5–8.

warpers, reelers, and batchers were the highest paid of the other women, earning an average of 12s. per week, whilst the spinners and preparers, who were on time wages, earned about 10s.[68]

Effectively the jute workforce was differentiated along gender lines with men occupying the few positions of authority and the higher-paid jobs. The division of labour and authority in Dundee's jute industry was not so hierarchically organized as the Lancashire cotton industry where authority and discipline were devolved to the male senior minders, who supervised three or four workers. In the Dundee jute industry supervisory functions resided with a small number of male workers; in the spinning departments of mills one male overseer to fifty or seventy female spinners, shifters, and piecers was not uncommon, and, unlike in Lancashire, spinners had no authority over other workers in the squad and occupied the same subordinate status in the hierarchy of labour as piecers and shifters.[69]

Labour turnover in the industry was particularly high, especially amongst the 'unskilled' operatives. The records of the Victoria Spinning Company indicate that, in the five-year period between March 1894 and March 1899, the annual labour turnover varied between 80 per cent and 85 per cent, whilst over this five-year period, the attrition rate rose to 90 per cent.[70] The supervisory and skilled workers provided a more stable workforce. Although there was still a significant turnover in the mechanic's section, only the overseer remaining unchanged throughout this five-year period.

The high turnover was partly a reflection of the erratic trade cycle of the jute trade, which was punctuated by frequent bouts of boom and slump, and partly related to the absence of uniform wage rates throughout the industry. Both of these factors encouraged frequent job changes, particularly in periods of labour shortage. A former spinner recalled that, on hearing that another mill was paying higher wages, she wasted no time

[68] DSU, *Report on Housing*, 55, table of earnings of jute workers.
[69] DUA MS 15/46.
[70] Wages Records of the Victoria Spinning Co. 1894–8, MS GD/Mns 105/1/3. City Archive and Record Centre, Dundee.

in leaving: 'if I got extra money I'd say "that's it, I'm away on Saturday". My father would say "You're leaving that place for another sixpence and you're wearing mair shoe leather". But at that time you could get a job anytime.'[71]

Unlike in Lancashire there is little evidence of a family economy or patrimonialism in the Scottish jute industry. This was probably due to the absence of a subcontracting system and the fact that hiring and firing was the prerogative of the overseer of a department. Members of one family might work in the same factory or mill, but it was unusual for husbands or fathers to be in a position of authority over family members in the workplace.

There were a small number of firms whose policy was to give preference to those whose family already worked in the firm. Both Halley's and Baxter's followed this recruitment practice. According to former employees, 'you had to be asked' into these firms. However, one weaver remarked that although both her father and mother worked in Halley's it was her mother's neighbour who 'spoke for her'.[72] Although there was no established tradition of shop-floor recruitment, family and neighbourhood connections probably had a limited role to play in the recruitment process.

The supervisory and skilled jobs were the exception to this general pattern, particularly in the mechanics shop, which contained most of the skilled workers. This department not only had a stable labour force, but clearly operated a system of patrimonialism with apprenticeships going to the sons or other relatives of those who worked in the department.[73]

Although Dundee generally had a high percentage of married women working, the skilled men and the supervisors in jute tended to have non-working wives. In a survey of 2,196 households in the east of the town, it was found that 36 out of 57 married men who worked in skilled trades in the weaving factories had non-working wives, 20 out of 25 mechanics and 9 out of 12 overseers also had wives who did not work.[74]

[71] Group interview with former weavers in Halley's mills, b. 1899–1908.
[72] Interview with Halley's weavers.
[73] Wages Records of the Victoria Spinning Co.
[74] DSU, *Report on Housing*, 55, table of occupations of able-bodied man and wife.

When their wives did work it was frequently in the factories as weavers or in the mills as winders, although a small number worked as preparers and spinners.[75] By contrast the majority of unskilled men in the jute mills had working wives. Of 380 millworkers, including batchers, preparers, rove-carriers, and mill labourers, 75 per cent had working wives. The vast majority of their wives worked in the jute industry, usually as spinners and preparers; 102 wives were spinners, 72 preparers, and only 23 were weavers and winders.[76]

In the jute industry about one-third of the female labour force over 20 was married.[77] It is more difficult to establish where the married women were located in the industry. Margaret Irwin's report for the Royal Commission on Labour estimated that in one large mill 97 per cent of the preparers, 19 per cent of the spinners, 32 per cent of the warpers and reelers, 14 per cent of the winders, and 34 per cent of the weavers were married women. However, this conflicts with both oral evidence and the findings of the survey by the Dundee Social Union, which indicate that spinning had a higher percentage of married women than weaving. It is possible that the percentage given for spinning in Margaret Irwin's report includes young shifters and piecers who worked with the spinners and therefore underestimates the percentage of spinners who were married. Therefore, to the division of authority and earning between small groups of skilled and supervisory male workers and the female workers was added a further divider which related to one of the pivotal components of respectability, the ability to maintain a non-working wife. This differentiation was most acute in the mills, where it would be unlikely that spinners or preparers were related to any of the supervisory workers, whereas in the weaving department it would be more common for the women to be either the wives or daughters of overseers and tenters.

Despite the pace of work, which in spinning was dictated by the machine and the overseer, and in weaving by the fact that it was piece-work, mill and factory shop-floor life could

---

[75] DSU, *Report on Housing*, 55, table of occupations of able-bodied man and wife.   [76] Ibid.
[77] Census of Scotland, 1911.

have a rich and robust character, which was barely stifled by the level of supervision which prevailed. Margaret Irwin complained in her report that:

one existing evil in mills is the slack time the workers have; then they gather together and talk over the experience of the previous evening's so-called pleasure or amusement, which is often not of an elevating nature . . . A division of the workers, and the oversight of a motherly matron, might obviate the difficulty.[78]

This informal factory culture could also be of a ribald nature as, according to the reminiscences of a former factory boy, the women used to sing obscene songs, which would be taught to the younger workers.[79] Although designed to illustrate the moral degradation of spinners and therefore undoubtedly exaggerated, he gives an account of the process of transmission of mill girl culture:

I have known a woman of bad character pollute the whole juvenile workers of the flat in which she was employed. She could fill their young minds with wanton and lascivious ideas, teach them to sing obscene songs; gradually introduce them to low dancing; lead them to houses of bad fame and finally accomplish their ruin.[80]

However, the shop-floor culture of the mill could also be a powerful force for generating networks of solidarity and mutual assistance. The same writer recounts the efforts made to help the family of a male worker who had fallen into ill health: 'a benefit concert is organised, and almost everyone appears at it. A great enthusiasm is displayed about it and frank help is afforded in disposing of the tickets, or even in platform service in order that this venture may prove a success.'[81]

Despite the individualized nature of the work in weaving, informal networks of solidarity still thrived. One weaver described how, if someone had a 'smash' when the material broke and the weaver had to put off the machine to fix it, 'your neighbour would holler and everybody came running to help you',[82] despite the fact that the stoppage would affect their

---

[78] Royal Commission on Labour, *The Employment of Women.*
[79] J. Myles, *Chapters in the Life of a Dundee Factory Boy, 1851–57* (William Kidd: Dundee, 1887).   [80] Ibid.
[81] Ibid.   [82] Interview with Halley's weavers.

earnings as they were all on piece-work. Weavers talked of the friendly atmosphere in the factory and how books and magazines would be passed round. The noise level was such in the weaving sheds that weavers developed lip-reading skills and a repertoire of sign language in order to communicate. In this way information about the events of the previous evening or the impending marriage of one of the girls would be passed from one end of the factory to another.[83]

Although the pivotal distinctions of earnings and authority clove the jute workforce into a small group of relatively well-paid men and the mass of mainly female workers, there were subsidiary distinctions and divisions amongst the workers, the most significant being between the weavers and the women who worked in the mills. In popular consciousness the division was between spinners and weavers, although in practice it was the women of the low mill and the spinning flats who comprised the category labelled 'mill girls'.

Weavers were often accused of regarding themselves as a 'cut above' the spinners. Comments of former spinners observed that 'weavers thought themselves somethin', aye and the winders tae'.[84] The weavers 'were different from us altogether—they never looked at us . . . They thought they were something special . . . They used to walk past you as if you were something low and they were "it".'[85] There does seem to have been some basis for these comments, as weavers themselves confirmed that they considered themselves a 'breed apart': 'They were a rough lot the spinners . . . [but] some nice girls worked in the mill, in the winding.'[86] 'You were a cut above the mill—you really were a cut above them.'[87]

Undoubtedly these divisions were buttressed by the physical separation of the mill and the factory, which clearly demarcated the territories of the two workforces. One weaver noted:

[83] Interview with Halley's weavers.
[84] Interview with Mrs G. (former spinner), b. 1893.
[85] 'Odyssey' interviews.
[86] Interview with Halley's weavers.
[87] 'Odyssey' interviews.

I was never in a mill in my life, I'd never even seen the
inside o' the mill. When you went into your work the factory
was on one side, the mill was on another side and you'd no
occasion—maybe you were allowed, maybe you weren't, I don't
know, but I was never in the mill in my life. Just my own factory
bit.[88]

There were obviously a number of concrete differences
between spinners and weavers which could have formed the
basis for the divisions between mill girls and weavers. The
earnings of the weavers were generally higher than the
millworkers. More importantly the weavers were piece-workers
and, although this made their earnings dependent on their own
exertions and therefore more variable, it connoted a degree
of job control denied to the spinners, who were paid a set wage
irrespective of individual effort. This perhaps explains why
those women in the mills who were piece-workers, such as
the reelers and winders, were more often bracketed with the
weaving community. As one spinner commented: 'In the
spinning flats you had to keep goin' whether you liked it or
not. In the weavin' you could take your time—but then you
got less pay.'[89]

The weavers themselves acknowledged that 'they made
their own wages'.[90] Neither spinners nor weavers gave much
credence to the argument that weavers were more skilled,
although one spinner commented that the weavers' work
was 'more particular'. Although neither trade was officially
recognized as skilled or paid accordingly, both had informal
apprenticeship systems. In the mills the only form of upward
mobility for women was through the stages of shifting, piecing,
and finally spinning. Indeed this was a necessary progression
in order to learn how to operate the frames. Spinning was one
of the most skilled of all the female occupations in the industry,
although there was no official or indeed financial recognition
of this. A former mill manager remarked that whilst many of
the processes about both mill and factory were very easily
learned:

[88] 'Odyssey' interviews.
[89] Interview with Mrs Cummings (former spinner), b. 1900.
[90] Interview with Halley's weavers.

in other cases there must necessarily be a long course of training. Where much depends upon personal attention in equalising the feed of jute or in securing the exact twist of the yarn—both processes being controlled by the workers alone—it takes a long time to acquire the requisite skill; and a good feeder or a good spinner is therefore highly appreciated.[91]

Although there was also a period of apprenticeship in weaving, referred to as 'in-giving', most commentators acknowledged that spinning was more skilled. The DSU investigators confirmed this assessment when they claimed that 'spinning is highly skilled work and requires a long apprenticeship, but is less well paid than weaving, which can be learned in a shorter time'.[92] The same investigators attributed the higher wages in weaving to the fact that when machinery was introduced the male hand-loom weavers refused to adopt power-looms and, 'a class of women superior to those already engaged in spinning were tempted to become weavers'.[93]

It has been suggested that millworkers were drawn from the poorer sections of the working class as it was the mills which employed half-time labour and a likely indication of poverty in a family was having to send its children out to work.[94] Financial circumstances may indeed provide part of the explanation for the different status of the two groups. Apprenticeships in weaving could only begin after leaving school, and would have required a period on a set rate of about 6s. per week whilst being an 'in-gi'er'. At this age a young girl in the spinning flats might already have progressed through the stages of shifting and piecing, and acquired her own frame. Even if she was still piecing, there was the possibility of undertaking some shifting in order to boost her earnings. A former spinner observed that her sister only earned 6s. 3d. whilst learning weaving, whilst at a similar age she had been earning 10s. 9d. as a spinner.[95]

[91] 'Sketches of Life in a Jute Mill'.
[92] DSU, *Report on Housing*, 49.
[93] Ibid.
[94] W. M. Walker, 'Dundee's Jute and Flax Workers, 1885–1923', Ph.D. thesis, University of Dundee, 1976, 45.
[95] Interview with Mrs McD.

Financial considerations were probably the major factor precluding horizontal mobility from spinning to better-paid weaving as spinners would have to take a cut in earnings whilst learning weaving. For this reason it was likely that, having entered the mill as a half-timer, there was little prospect of a sideways move into the weaving factories. Although this sealed the divisions between the two groups, there is also evidence that there were spinners, preparers, and weavers from the same family and that the fathers of some millworkers were tradesmen. The precarious nature of employment for men and the extent of seasonal labour makes it likely that the two groups did not represent completely distinct strata in the hierarchy of the working-class community and that the family of tradesmen may have entered the mills in periods of financial hardship. The reputation that the mill gained for attracting the poorer class of worker was bolstered by the composition of the preparing departments, which were located in the low mill (a term which connoted the geography of the department rather than the class). It was universally acknowledged that the preparing departments offered the least-skilled work in the industry and the only kind of work which women with no previous experience could enter directly. Therefore, the many widowed and deserted women who migrated to Dundee, driven by poverty, were more likely to enter the mill and augment the numbers in the mill drawn from the poorest section of the community.

The higher earnings of the weavers and the likelihood that they were drawn from the less financially beleaguered families may have been an important factor in the formation of this caste system. However, both weavers and spinners perceived the differences in terms of the cleanliness of the work in weaving: 'spinners' work was a lot dirtier than factory workers'. Ours wasna such a *dirty* job, no much dirt in it . . . It was a bit o' this uppity business, you know.'[96]

One weaver remembered that the spinners used to be given the nickname of 'snuffy spinner':

[96] 'Odyssey' interviews.

because long ago they did snuff, you know in the mills, they really had to do it. Because at that time the dust was flying across the place. No now, its a' modernised now, but at that time there was nae ducts or anything to tak it awa'. Wi' the results it choked them and that's the reason they took snuff and it always got that name—the snuffy spinners.[97]

And in explaining why she as a weaver felt 'a cut above the spinners', she pointed out that 'I mean we were never what you would say really dirty, the way they got dirty, because they were covered in mill dust when they came out their works.'[98]

The weavers underlined this difference by dressing up to go to work: 'You wouldn't have dreamed of going to the factory without a hat, you would have been a scruff.'[99] Similarly, a former spinner claimed that the weavers thought they were 'somethin' special because they did the finishin' of the jute', by which she meant they had the clean work. She remembers their emblem of status as their hat and gloves: 'an they wore gloves . . . see we were low mill hands and we used tae just come wi' wir jackets on—nae hats, nae gloves.'[100]

The importance placed on clean work and the accoutrements of hat and gloves is not surprising when the meaning of respectability for women was so tied up with the notion of femininity and gentility, the outward manifestation being pride in one's appearance. The weavers also seemed to have aspirations of marrying men with a trade and becoming non-working wives, that other symbol of working-class respectability. A former spinner remarked that:

An awful lot of the weavers married a wee bitty better men—men that had good jobs. On the mill you might marry a man that had worked in the mill, but a weaver looked out for somebody who had served his time—an engineer or something. And they got on a wee bit better—that's how they classed themselves as better.[101]

The consensus amongst ex-weavers was that 'If anybody got married . . . it was an awful slur if they had to go back to work . . . It was only the millworkers [that went back].

[97] 'Odyssey' interviews.   [98] Ibid.   [99] Ibid.   [100] Ibid.
[101] Interview with Mrs Cummings.

Outside the mills very few women when they got married worked.'[102]

There was also some recognition that a different code of conduct applied to the millworkers, presumably because different and lower standards were expected from this 'rougher' element of jute workers. Again the weavers claimed that 'Long ago it was the done thing for a woman who had worked in the mill just to go back to work . . . and often they had children—they may have left one day and had a child the next and they were back within a week—because you see, it was the done thing.'[103]

The marriage patterns of weavers and millworkers confirm the contention that weavers tended to marry 'better men'. The majority of unskilled male millworkers married women in the mills, many of whom carried on working after marriage, whilst in the weaving factories the skilled and supervisory workers were more likely to have wives who worked as weavers if their wives worked at all.[104] The married women in weaving may not have been such a permanent part of the labour force as the married women in the mill if it was the case that their partners had better jobs. Only when financial circumstances dictated did the wives of tradesmen take up employment. A spinner whose mother was a weaver and father a tailor confirmed that the occasion for her mother seeking work was during a financial crisis: 'My mother went out for maybe a month or so in the winter, but that was it finished. My father wouldn't allow her.'[105]

Social relations between the weavers and millworkers were characterized by social distance and cultural exclusiveness, although tempered on the part of the weavers by an affectionate tolerance for the roguish antics of the millworkers, whom they regarded as a 'happy crowd who liked their work'. For the weavers the memories evoked by the spinners concerned singing and alcohol. One incident in the inter-war years was recalled when a mill had to be closed down 'because they were all tipsy' and their example of the songs sung by spinners was the Will

---

[102] Interview with Halley's weavers.   [103] Ibid.
[104] DSU, *Report on Housing*, 55, table of occupations of able-bodied man and wife.   [105] Interview with Mrs McD.

Fyfe tune 'How can you be happy when happiness costs such a lot?'[106] (This refers to the price of 12s. 6d. for a bottle of whisky.) Another memory related to a spinner who one day appeared with two black eyes because 'her man had hit her for being drunk'. No doubt these memories had some factual basis but spinners also talked of the stigma attached to women going into pubs and how drunkenness was confined to the Overgate, the haunt of down-and-outs, prostitutes, and the 'rough' element. One spinner remembered that spectating at the Overgate was a cheap form of entertainment: 'If you had no money you used to say to your chum—"Come on, we'll go down the Overgate and see how many fights there are tonight".'[107]

Although there were 63 cases of disorderly conduct among female millworkers and a handful involving weavers in 1854 the number of prostitutes apprehended for this offence was 439,[108] indicating that, in the hierarchy of female respectability, spinners were probably far from the bottom rung.

It is more likely that for the weavers these activities symbolized the cultural gap between themselves and the spinners and therefore were projected as the norm rather than the exception in order to highlight these differences. According to the accounts of weavers and spinners, leisure patterns for both groups were remarkably similar and consisted of promenading, dances, concerts, and picnics. Weavers talked about the number of dance-halls there were in Dundee and how 'You would walk up the Perth Road—you would meet somebody and you would speak to them and then you would carry on and meet some other budy.'[109]

The object of the exercise seemed to be 'Lettin' everybudy see you while you're seein' everybudy else'.[110] This was similar to the recreation of the spinners who remembered that 'In the evenings you would walk down the town, see somebody you would talk to—have a walk around and a talk.'[111]

[106] Interview with Halley's weavers.
[107] Interview with Mrs Cummings.
[108] From the *Return of Crimes and Offences in Dundee, 1860*, quoted in Walker, 'Dundee's Jute and Flax Workers', 41.
[109] Interview with Halley's weavers.   [110] Ibid.
[111] Interview with Mrs Cummings.

Dances and concerts were alternative diversions but the ritualistic promenading, meeting with friends and 'ha'in' a gossip', seemed to be the favoured pastime. According to one spinner, 'the streets were packed at night'—possibly this was a form of recreation which was available to the married women with their families, albeit less frequently. Although leisure patterns were similar for weavers and millworkers, the social relations of the community replicated those of the workplace and therefore leisure was pursued in mutually exclusive groups. According to the weavers: 'we were friendly enough but we didn't go out together . . . you seemed to chum up with somebody beside you.'[112]

Another weaver claimed that she 'had no friends among the spinners, they all seemed to clan together you know with each other—we had nothing to do with the spinners'.[113]

This exclusivity was confirmed by a spinner who detailed its operation:

The weavers seemed to keep themselves by themselves. If I was a weaver and you were a weaver you could be my chum—we would go out together. If you were in the mill, you would go out with your chum maybe to picnics on a Saturday. There was evening drives during the summer—the mill folk would have their drive and the weavers would have theirs—a bottle of lemonade and a pie at the end and we all sang on the way back.[114]

The nature of the jute workers' leisure activities prompted a discussion at a conference of Dundee's Committee on Public Morals in 1913, which felt constrained to try to minimize the practice of promenading, which was considered an unsuitable and unseemly activity. The Chief Constable whilst regretting its extent felt there was little which could be done as the law was not being infringed and blamed the industrial and social conditions of the city: 'They had so many young workers of both sexes who lived in lodgings, entirely removed from parental control whatever.'[115]

Whatever distinctions existed between millworkers and weavers, the latter were an important element in constituting

---

[112] Interviews with Halley's weavers.   [113] 'Odyssey' interviews.
[114] Interview with Mrs McD.
[115] Reported in *Glasgow Forward*, 22 Mar. 1913.

Dundee's reputation as a women's town, a reputation which stemmed from the dominance of the jute industry and its association with women's work. Such was the extent of women's work that men in Dundee earned the nickname 'kettle boilers', a reference to the fact that many men remained at home while the women of the family went out to work. Poverty and the dearth of employment for men may well have been the factors driving women out to work but there is evidence that they took pride in the fact that they worked hard for their money. The weavers' allusions to the intemperate behaviour of the spinners always contained the caveat that they were hard workers. A former weaver remembered that, when her husband's mother was informed that they were going to Glasgow, she said: 'That's where all the big, fat, lazy women are.'[116]

The extent of women's employment in Dundee and concern over its effects on the moral welfare of working-class families deprived of a non-working mother was a constant theme in the discussion of middle-class benevolent associations. A report in the *Dundee Yearbook* questioned 'if anywhere there is more done for the elevating and ameliorating of the lot of the working girl than in our city',[117] and went on to document the extent of philanthropic endeavour in Dundee. Most schemes involved instruction in dressmaking, millinery, cookery, laundry, and other home management tasks, for notwithstanding the permanency of women's work in Dundee, its reputation as a women's town, and the appellation of 'kettle boilers' given to Dundee men who remained at home, the association of women with the domestic sphere and men with the world of work was not undermined. It was not only public conceptions of gender roles which were unrevised, for it can be detected from the testimony that traditional domestic roles persisted despite women's primacy in the jute labour market. This was succinctly expressed by a spinner who claimed that 'In those days women served the men—the men didn't do the work at all . . . You never saw a father taking his bairns out on a Sunday.'[118] This evidence is corroborated by the DSU investigation, which cited

---

[116] Interview with Mrs Cummings.
[117] 'Work Amongst Working Girls in Dundee', in *Dundee Year Book*, 1911.
[118] Interview with Mrs McD.

a number of instances where husbands were unemployed, wives were working, and yet the children were looked after by a neighbour.[119]

Moralizing agents directed their attention primarily to married working women. However, other groups of women did not escape the attempts to educate and inculcate the skills of domestic economy. One commentator quoted the case of 'an intelligent wife and mother' who had successfully managed her household budget when her husband was out of work. On being asked how she had managed, the woman responded: 'You see . . . I have been at the St . . . Mission cooking classes for two past winters and I can mak a tasty dinner noo oot o' scraps and have learned to be real economic in ither ways.'[120] The writer concluded that the woman intended to go to a laundry-work class in order that 'She may learn how to do her husband's and boy's fronts and collars, so that she may send them out decently clad to church on Sundays.'[121]

The single women were also encouraged to take instruction in sewing, cooking, etc., and, in a boarding-house run by the Ladies' Union, girls were afforded every facility for doing their own washing, 'an occupation which seems to afford them a certain amount of pleasure, and appeals to their housewifely instincts'.[122] Philanthropic organizations, with the aid of funds from employers, constructed model lodging houses calculated 'to exercise a beneficial effect upon young females',[123] which probably referred to the desire to protect the morality of working girls. However, this kind of philanthropic provision was resisted by the women, very few taking advantage of it because of the strict discipline and close supervision of their time and actions in these establishments.[124]

The young children of working mothers were the uppermost concern of the panoply of philanthropic and middle-class voluntary organizations. In 1904 Dundee headed the infant mortality list of the fifteen principal towns in Scotland, with a rate of 174 per 1,000 births, compared with 151 per 1,000 for Aberdeen, the next highest.[125] Middle-class observers had

[119] DSU, *Report on Housing, passim.*
[120] 'Girls in Dundee', *Dundee Year Book*, 1903.   [121] Ibid.
[122] 'Work Amongst Working Girls in Dundee'.   [123] LC 196A (29).
[124] Ibid.   [125] DSU, *Report on Housing*, 68.

no hesitation in attributing this high rate to the prevalence of married women's work in Dundee. The statistics certainly provided the ammunition for inferring this correspondence between the two. St Mary's, the district in Dundee with the highest number of married women working, also had the highest infant mortality rate. However, Lochee, which had the second highest percentage of married working women, had the lowest infant mortality rate.[126] Of 616 occupied married women in Lochee, 69 per cent had children, and 42 per cent had children under 5.[127] These contradictory statistics suggest that there was no easy one-to-one correlation between rates of married women's work and infant mortality.

Although Dundee employers were not noted for their paternalism or philanthropy, their need to reconcile their employment of large numbers of women with the prevailing ideology of domesticity, and the discomfiture caused by these damning statistics, prompted some of them to contribute money towards the provision of crèches in the city and to organize evening classes in household skills. By 1905 there were three crèches in Dundee and one in Lochee, in the west district of the city. The crèches consisted of three rooms, two of which were used as nurseries and the third reserved for meals. There were usually three attendants, who did the cooking and housework in addition to looking after the children. Although the charge for the crèches was 1s. 6d. for children over a year and 2s. for babies under a year, compared with the usual 3s. charged by child-minders, they were not used to full advantage by working mothers. The daily attendance seldom reached the full quota and the combined average daily attendance for the four crèches was 76 in 1904 whereas the full complement was about 120.[128]

The migrant status of much of Dundee's labour force made it unlikely that there was an abundance of kinship networks on which women could rely for these kinds of service. As husbands might look after older children, but less frequently young babies, one can only speculate that women's preference

[126] Royal Commission on Labour, *Fifth Report on Changes in the Rate of Wages and Hours of Labour*, C. 8795, 37. [127] Ibid.
[128] DSU, *Report on Housing*, 4.

for the child-minding services of neighbours signified their resistance to the kinds of philanthropic provision which smacked of regulation and social control. The centrality to Dundee's labour market of women's employment, particularly married women's work, violated all the precepts of middle-class Victorian domestic ideology, which was defined by the interrelationship between respectability, the domestic ideal, and the ideology of separate sexual spheres. However, the prevalence of women's work and the high percentage of households which were dependent, either solely or partially, on the earnings of women did not undermine the dominant ideology of gender divisions, but led to its reformulation to fit the specific employment structure in Dundee. In the wider community concerted efforts were made to ensure that existing gender divisions of patriarchal authority were not decomposed by women's involvement in waged labour outside the home by providing training in domestic and household skills for female operatives. Similarly, the efforts of various organizations to 'elevate' and 'ameliorate' Dundee's working women were designed to control their behaviour so that it conformed to their culturally prescribed role. And of course the authority structures of the workplace replicated those of the patriarchal household.

Women were still defined as the dependants of husbands or fathers and associated with the domestic sphere; indeed it was the assumption of dependency which determined their status as cheap labour. However, the notion of dependency had wider implications than financial dependence, as the relation between men and women was constituted on the basis of general male dominance in society. Therefore, although substantial numbers of women in Dundee were independent of men, in the sense that there were no men in many households and women were frequently bread-winners, they were still defined by the dominant gender role of wife and mother and deemed to be subject to the authority of men. Although patriarchal authority relations had wider significance than authority relations in the family, it was universally accepted that women and girls should be subject to the control of their husbands or fathers. Thus the Reverend Henry Williamson, President of the Dundee and District Mill and Factory Operatives' Union, could chastise a crowd of strikers by inquiring what their fathers thought of their behaviour, in spite of the fact that the majority of them were adult women, many of whom would be married. The potency of the ideology of separate sexual spheres is further attested to by the assertion of a leading Dundee employer that 'A woman is better employed exercising the baby than exercising the franchise.'[129]

Although in important respects it is necessary to analyse women's experience in relation to the gender ideologies, it should be remembered that Victorian domestic ideology was essentially a middle-class notion, and may not have been so enthusiastically embraced or shared by working women. Dundee women's participation in the formal economy conferred on them a degree of economic independence, freedom from direct patriarchal control, and a public role which arguably undermined the material basis of this ideology of gender divisions. The middle classes and perhaps working-class men may have perceived and defined women workers in terms of their domestic roles and their association with the private realm, but there is little evidence that this is how women jute workers perceived themselves. It has already been indicated that, far from feeling ashamed or apologetic about having to work, they took pride in their skill and their labour. The Dundee Social Union report commented that 'the statement is often made that married women find the home dull in comparison with the factory and go out to work for preference'.[130] It would be foolhardy to accept this statement at face value, but it does suggest that Dundee's women jute workers evaluated their work more positively than others did, even if they did not consciously challenge or resist the ideology of domesticity.

Whilst women's experience of work was shaped by their subordinate status in society generally, and their low wages, and their position in the division of labour and authority in the workplace reflected and reinforced this subordination, this did not preclude resistance and struggle to either patriarchal authority or exploitation at the point of production.

---

[129] *Telegraph and Post*, 5 Mar. 1906.
[130] DSU, *Report on Housing*, 72.

5. Disputes in Dundee's Jute Industry

THE equation of absence of institutional organization with absence of effective opposition has led to a neglect of the variety of forms which resistance takes, at the level of both the workplace and the community. Once we are alert to this we can gain more profitable insights into the specific historical experiences of different sections of the working class; insights which should enable us to acquire a more vivid and detailed picture of working-class life, and the diverse patterns of opposition and resistance which particular material conditions and ideological forces evoke. By confusing an absence of formal organization with silence and deference, we are compelled to view these groups as totally subordinated to the dominant social order. We therefore fail to appreciate the contradictions and conflict which are inherent in social relations and fail to see class struggle as a permanent feature of these relations.

A study of the women textile workers of Dundee, their 'unorganized' action over wages and conditions, and their response to trade-unionism should serve to illustrate that, whilst the structural constraints on the organization of women workers were substantial, organization did exist and was imaginative and oppositional, and that the history of Dundee's textile industry was not one of the unfettered control of employers over a passive labour force.

There was little in the way of formal trade union organization amongst the various sections of the jute workforce before 1885, although reference is made to a branch of the Scottish Powerloom Tenters' Association being in its infancy in 1874. An East of Scotland Mill and Factory Workers' Protective Association had a relatively short-lived existence and was dissolved in March 1881.[1] The transitory nature of trade

---

[1] LC 196E (3).

union organization amongst textile workers must be placed in the context of the relative impotence of unionism generally in Dundee. Echoing the national pattern in Scotland, the ebb and flow of trade union membership usually reflected the vagaries of the economic climate. In 1875 the Dundee Trades Council claimed to represent 4,000 unionists.[2] Such were the fluctuations of membership that the Trades Council's existence was short-lived, although it was revived in 1885 when unionism throughout Britain embarked on a period of sustained and unprecedented growth.

The absence of institutional continuity in the organization of the higher-paid male workforce should not necessarily be construed as evidence of weakness. From the 1850s until 1874 the Dundee textile industry was characterized by prosperity and booms, with the occasional hiccup, which usually resulted in some short-time working. However, the labour shortage in Dundee was so acute during this period that depressions in the trade did not seriously affect the workforce and unemployment was not a serious problem. This period of almost uninterrupted prosperity resulted in a steady rise in money wages for all sections of the workforce,[3] but the relatively privileged position of the male supervisory and maintenance workers was further consolidated and enhanced, without the need to resort to the strike weapon or even trade union organization. It was this advantaged position in relation to the majority of the female labour force which provided the bedrock of their respectability and shaped their attitudes to society and how they might improve their position within it.

The agitation over Mundella's fifty-four-hour Bill in 1872 illustrates the extent to which these demands were couched in terms of moral and intellectual improvement and as aiding the struggle for respectability. At a meeting of mill and factory workers in 1872 to support Mundella's Bill, the debate centred on the incentive to self-improvement which shorter hours would provide. This view is encapsulated in the Reverend George Gilfillan's contribution:

[2] LC 196E (69).
[3] LC 196D (1).

I am no political economist. I have never read Adam Smith through, and I have never even attempted to read Ricardo or MacCulloch. I cannot argue shorter hours upon principles I do not comprehend. But sir, I can argue them upon principles that I do understand. I can argue their advantage as a friend, to the intellectual and moral advancement of the people. (*Applause.*) I can support them on the very same principles on which I have all along advocated Free Libraries. Short hours and opportunities of mental culture go hand in hand. (*Applause.*)[4]

The values of respectability and moral advancement did not preclude militant action nor produce a section of workers who accepted wholesale economic orthodoxies. Indeed the above quotation illustrates how these values could usefully provide a lever for improved wages and conditions which involved challenging the economic tenet of supply and demand. None the less, the pursuit of these values was a strategy which was attractive, and indeed possible, only for those sections of workers whose privileged position gave them a stake in the existing organization of society and who had opportunities to ameliorate this position within its framework. The small number of male skilled and supervisory workers in the jute industry were not necessarily amongst the highest-paid workers in the country or indeed the most strategically central to the economy. However, their position in relation to the mass of unskilled labour in the industry was such that they represented an élite of labour whose ideology derived in part from their relatively advantaged economic position but which incorporated attitudes that encompassed much more than the economic dimension.

A meeting of Dundee Working Men's Clubs in 1875 which was called specifically to discuss the establishment of infant nurseries and the 'better education of female operatives in domestic economy' highlights some of the notions embodied in their concept of respectability and which were adapted to the specific employment structure of Dundee's textile industry. A mill overseer noted that 'There were plenty of tradesmen whose wives went to work that had no need to go, and they should stay at home and keep their children. (*Applause.*)'[5]

It was recognized that the low wages of some men were not sufficient to support a family and therefore economic necessity would drive some women to work. The deleterious effects of this could be offset by training the women in the habits of domestic economy. Another contributor felt that, if nurseries were established, there should be connected with them 'classes for the instruction of mill girls in domestic cookery, washing, ironing etc.'.[6]

The conception of the family as an arena for the formulation and reproduction of the values of respectability was to a large extent posed in terms of woman as homemaker and this primary identification with the domestic sphere served to shape men's perceptions of her and attitudes to her, even when she worked in full-time paid employment. Although the higher wages of the small stratum of male workers in the jute industry contributed to the segmentation of the workforce, this differentiation was further strengthened by the articulation of an ideology which identified the industrial sphere as the domain of men and imbued workplace relations with a patriarchal character.

At the workplace the objectives and demands of this section of male workers, and more significantly their mode of organization and what they considered as legitimate activity, reflected their status within the industry. The subordinate position of women workers in the labour process and in the hierarchy of labour produced quite a different experience and this was to have important implications for how they organized and the issues on which they mobilized. The agitation over the extension of mealtimes in the jute industry in 1871 highlights not only the conflicts of interest engendered but also how the strategic position of one group of workers enabled them to get their definition of a situation accepted and their strategy and tactics defined as the most legitimate.

The movement for the extension of mealtime began in September 1871 and it appears that the issue was instigated by the men in the industry and the campaign conducted by a committee of delegates composed almost entirely of male supervisory and maintenance workers. A report of a meeting

6 LC 219 (4).

0.0787681

of the delegates stated that there were seventy-five members of the committee (all male) and the contributions from the body of the hall from tenters, overseers, who represented various branches of the industry, and a mill foreman,[7] are indicative of the prominent role of the higher-paid stratum of workers in the direction and leadership of the agitation. The committee were certainly regarded as the élite of the industry by those middle-class philanthropists who supported the movement. Sir John Ogilvie addressed a meeting of the delegates and expressed his delight 'in being present, and seeing such a meeting as this—such an intelligent gathering of representative men, being the élite of the factory workers of Dundee'.[8]

The initial demand of the workers was for an extension of all mealtimes to one hour, thereby reducing the working week from sixty hours to fifty-seven hours. From the outset the committee emphasized that its priority, indeed its sole concern, was to achieve the extension of the meal hour and that this was to be achieved by conducting negotiations with the employers and without resort to strikes. However, almost immediately operatives in a number of mills and factories struck for an increase in wages. This was interpreted by those who supported the movement, and by the committee themselves, as jeopardizing the negotiations with the employers and side-tracking and diverting the issue. An article in a Dundee newspaper complained that:

It is much to be regretted that a considerable number of the females and lads at several mills in Dundee, doubtless led by the foolish and unthinking, yesterday helped to embarrass the negotiations now going on between the employers and employed by striking work. This taking of the question out of the hands of their delegates is very rash and ill advised. They might surely wait a few days to see what is the result of the negotiations. The men they have appointed to represent them know best how to put forward their case if it is for the meal hour they are striking, but if it is for wages then they are really opposing what the delegates are doing, by demonstrating to the employers that they have, contrary to the Committee's circular, to deal with both demands.[9]

[7] LC 196D (47–51). [8] LC 196C (85). [9] LC 196C (25).

It was argued by some that the women, by striking for a wage rise, were being irrational and short-sighted and that they did not appreciate the value of extended time. It was claimed that an increase in wages was an easier demand to achieve as it represented no challenge to the employers, would be quickly eroded, and most importantly would result in the meal hour question being eclipsed. However, it is clear that the women did not regard the two demands as alternatives but took the opportunity to capitalize on existing discontent to rally support for another issue which they considered equally important. At one works, where there were stoppages affecting 900 workers, the strikers were approached by one of the partners of the firm and offered a rise in wages. They were also promised an hour for each mealtime, provided it was given at the other works in the town. However, the strikers were still dissatisfied, and could not be induced to return to work unless both demands were guaranteed.[10] The inclemency of the weather did not seem to deter them from parading the streets to manifest their discontent.

After a five-week struggle the dispute reached a successful conclusion, with the employers granting a rise of 5 per cent and a reduction in hours, although some employers would only grant two hours instead of the requested three. The credit for the successful resolution of the dispute was given to the committee of delegates and was seen by some as a vindication of the policy of moderation and conciliation which they had pursued and a triumph which had been achieved despite the irresponsible action of the women confounding the issue.[11]

It is clear that the wage increase would not have been granted without resort to strikes and that the women also had a commitment, if less firm, to the demand for an extension of the meal hours. Their stance can be explained by reference to their position in the hierarchy of labour and the economics of working-class differentiation. The leadership of the movement was firmly in the grip of the minority of workers whose earnings were substantially higher than the majority of the workforce. The favourable climate of the jute industry in the previous two decades had enabled them to secure a number

---

[10] LC 196c (23).   [11] LC 196c (39).

of increases which guaranteed them a fairly high and stable income, and the operation of the 'bounty system', at a time of expansion and increased output, further enhanced their position. The unskilled mill- and factory workers had also enjoyed a period of virtually uninterrupted advances in earnings but their wages were already very low and their position in the structure of authority relations prevented them from eroding the widening differential between them and the supervisory and skilled workers in the trade.[12] At an early stage in the dispute the committee issued a circular stating that they did not wish to raise the question of wages at all and that they would be willing to accept a reduction in wages to allow the concession.[13] This obviously reflected the interests of the élite in the industry, whose economic position afforded them the luxury of ameliorating conditions at the expense of earnings. In these circumstances the women who struck appeared to be responding rationally to a situation where they feared that their interests would not be adequately served by a committee exclusively composed of higher-paid men who had quite distinct and different priorities.

The desire of the higher-paid male workers to reduce their working hours even at the expense of a fall in earnings seems a clear-cut illustration of a sectional policy which ignored the interests of lower-paid workers, who might also have to intensify their labour in order to recoup some of their lost earnings. The fact that the vast majority of low-paid workers were women introduced gender divisions into this sectionalism, given that women's earnings were related to the sexual division of labour in the home and the family.

There were occasions when conflicts of interest between men and women workers arose directly from their distinct gender roles. Some workforces managed to reach voluntary agreements with the employers in the pursuit of a fifty-four-hour week; however, there was a great deal of contention amongst workers about how best to implement these agreements. The variety of schemes adopted was noted by the Factory Inspector for Dundee district, who doubted the popularity of the arrangement whereby work ceased at 9.30 a.m. on Saturdays: 'It is neither

[12] LC 196D (75).   [13] LC 196C (51–3).

a day of work nor a holiday. The time until the dinner hour is of little use to the men, who have no occupation for that period of the day.'[14] This seems to refer to the fact that the leisure pursuits of men were usually carried out on Saturday afternoons or evenings and therefore free time on Saturday mornings might only extend their domestic and family responsibilities. This interpretation is supported by the Factory Inspector's reference to the opinion of an engineer on the subject: 'What's the use, Jock, o' gangin' hame to haud the weans?'[15] The sexual division of labour in the home and the family powerfully influenced women's experience at work. Clearly it could also generate conflicts of interest which may have been manifested at the point of production but which stemmed from wider cultural roles, thus illustrating the potency of gender divisions in fragmenting the working class.

There was further tension between those who had assumed the leadership of the short-time movement and the women over the conduct of the dispute. The committee stressed the need for a conciliatory approach and insisted on moderation in respect of both the claim and the method by which it was pursued. At a meeting between the representatives of the employers and the employed their propriety was given fulsome praise by the *Dundee Advertiser*, who advised the workforce that:

Their case could not have been more ably pleaded than it was by the delegates. The representatives of the employers first of all spoke in the most conciliatory, candid, temperate, and even serious manner . . . On the other hand the delegates put their view of the question with remarkable skill and tact not giving way on the ground they had taken, remaining firm in their quest for a decided answer . . . One of the employers went so far as to say that failing the Act he would then give the hour, and this was reciprocated by one of the delegates saying that failing other towns following the example of Dundee, they would give it up.[16]

The extent to which the delegates were prepared to mollify the employers and perhaps the extent to which they shared their frame of reference is demonstrated by the nature of the

[14] *Fortieth Report by the Inspectors of Factories 1872–73*, in *Industrial Revolution*, Factories, 15 (Shannon: Irish University Press, 1970), see ch. 4 n. 48.
[15] Ibid., 10.   [16] LC 196c (23).

arguments they used to justify their case. At one meeting between the two parties, one of the employees' representatives claimed that the adoption of one-hour breaks would resolve the problem of unpunctuality in the trade.[17] Similarly, after the successful conclusion of the dispute, a meeting of the meal hour committee voted 'three hearty cheers to those employers who have seen it to be their duty to come forward and grant our request in full'.[18]

The oft-repeated request of the committee to confine the struggle within the walls of the negotiating hall went unheeded by the women and was a constant source of conflict and recrimination. The committee vainly appealed to the women to return to work and frequently expressed their disapproval of the strikes, and on one occasion called upon all delegates and overseers to use their influence to prevent the 'demonstrations' whilst the dispute was pending.[19]

The Secretary of the committee complained to the employers that the 'agitation' and 'uneasiness' was principally amongst the female workers and that there was little need for agitation amongst them as it was like 'putting a light to a powder magazine'.[20] Certainly the strikes seemed to be conducted in the time-honoured Dundee fashion of parading the streets, dancing, and singing, with the inevitable foray into the Cowgate, the territory of the masters. Shouts, insults, and good-natured banter were invariably hurled at employers, who seemed to accept it as part of the required ritual of strike activity. One newspaper report of the strikes conveys the flavour of the demonstrations:

Those on strike paraded the streets yesterday in grotesque processions bearing emblems of their trade, suspended from poles, such as mats, jute etc. They also indulged in shouting and singing, the latter being a peculiar sort of march, the words of which were principally intended to convey the information that they were sombody or other's 'band'. Besides this, they held threatening demonstrations in front of the works where nobody had turned out. Between 2 and 3 o'clock large droves of them marched to the Cowgate, and here they held an indignation meeting, in the midst of the merchants who were assembled there in large numbers, it being market day.[21]

---

[17] LC 196c (29–33).   [18] LC 196c (51).   [19] LC 196c (27).
[20] LC 196c (29–33).   [21] LC 196c (27).

Whatever criticisms were levelled at the women, ranging from 'foolish and unthinking' to 'less intelligent' and 'unreasoning', the efficacy of their action seemed to have been recognized by the delegates. At a meeting of the meal hour committee to discuss whether it should be dissolved or maintained, it was argued that it would be foolish to continue as people at the workplace had more powers than the committee. The example was given of an employer who was requested by the committee to grant the full hour and refused, but who yielded to the women who went in a body to demand the hour. The speaker concluded that 'the better plan would be to get the fair sex on your side and go to the employers and you will get the hour from them'.[22]

The healthy state of the Dundee textile industry before 1874, which was in large measure due to the various wars, which stimulated demand for manufactured jute, also created a demand for labour. The relative scarcity of labour not only ensured security of employment even when there was a temporary decline, but affirmed spontaneous strike action as the most apposite form of resistance to a workforce denied the status of skilled workers and the appropriate methods of organization, and whose subordinate position in the production process provided them with no other lever to secure their interests. The series of wage increases gained by the operatives in the 1860s and early 1870s were occasionally unsolicited increases granted by the masters, but more often they were won by recourse to strike action which was characterized by spontaneity. A strike of power-loom weavers in 1872 over a demand for a day's holiday pay illustrates both the efficacy of immediate action and the extent of the labour shortage. The head of the firm complained that the workers were getting the beef and he the bones, which elicited the response from one of the women: 'Very well, I'll gie him my beef if he gies me his banes.'[23] The women struck and refused to recommence work whilst management made their decision. After only one day's stoppage, the employers conceded the day's holiday pay and the women resumed work with the exception of those who had obtained work elsewhere.

---

[22] LC 196c (71–9).   [23] LC 196c (83).

However, by 1874 the tide was turning and short time, falling profits, and eventually unemployment were to become the traits of the jute industry. That year there was a general strike in the trade, involving between 20,000 and 30,000 against an attempt by the employers to impose a reduction of 10 per cent. The reduction seems to have been restricted to the unskilled majority of workers and excluded the male supervisory workers and the skilled and semi-skilled men. The male operatives who were locked out as a consequence of the strike held meetings to discuss the issue and debated whether or not they should give the women their support. They eventually agreed to back them but it was felt that every endeavour should be made to persuade them to accept a 5 per cent reduction.[24]

In this dispute, as with many others, the hoary issue of the conduct of the strikers was another source of irritation to the men, who advised the women to conduct themselves in a quiet and orderly manner and attempted to exercise a restraining influence on their exuberance. A particular incident which aroused the displeasure of the men involved women following two of the masters and hooting and yelling at them. One operative complained that 'If there was another scene like that the men and women of Dundee would be disgraced. (*Hear, Hear.*)—They should treat with the masters calmly, fairly and argumentatively and not by yelling and hooting.'[25]

This particular strike concluded in the women's favour but the next thirty years witnessed varying fortunes in the trade, characterized by intense cyclical fluctuations, which obviously constrained the ability of the jute workers to make gains. The employers managed to impose some reductions but others were successfully resisted and when trade was buoyant gains were made. Whatever varying degrees of success and failure the workers experienced in those years, there was a constant flurry of activity with strikes against reductions and for increases assuming a virtual permanence of the landscape. The Reverend Mr Henry Williamson, who was instrumental in forming the first trade union in Dundee aimed specifically at the female mill and factory workers, wrote that:

[24] LC 196D (67–9).   [25] LC 196D (77–9).

When walking down Lochee Road in those days, it seemed to me that never a week passed without presenting at some part of the route the same sad familiar scene—a band of tousled, loud voiced lassies with the light of battle in their defiant eyes gathered together in the street and discussing with animation and candour the grievances that had constrained them to leave their work.[26]

The pattern of labour organization which emerged between 1875 and the First World War crystallized the tendencies which had been manifested in the struggle over the extension of mealtimes; namely, the conflict of interests between the male skilled and supervisory grades in the industry and the female workers, and the women's proclivity for independent and spontaneous action. While the skilled and supervisory grades of male workers in the industry organized themselves into a number of trade unions and societies which remained obdurately opposed to the women operatives, another union was formed for the female workers in the industry which was independent of the established union movement in Dundee, and the women persisted with their pattern of spontaneous strikes.

The established trade union movement in Dundee was taken to task by James Morton, chief organizer of the Scottish Federal Union and member of the ILP. At a mass meeting during an industry-wide strike in 1893, Morton spoke of the great need for organizing female labour in Dundee and chastised the Trades Council for not undertaking the task of educating workers. He observed that there were those who maintained that women were difficult to organize, at which one female worker shouted: 'Gae awa' man, and dinna haver.'[27] But he claimed that had not been his experience. He also condemned the practice of those organized men in the industry such as those belonging to the Amalgamated Society of Engineers, for staying at their employment whilst the women struck. Claiming that this contravened the principles of trade-unionism, he maintained that 'It was one of the things . . . which disgraced unionism in Dundee. (*Applause.*) Trade

[26] *People's Journal*, 14 Oct. 1922, from a series of articles written by Williamson entitled 'Fifty Years in Dundee's Stir and Strife'.
[27] *Dundee Advertiser*, 1 May 1893.

Unionists looked down upon women as their inferiors, but in a great many cases women set an example to the best of them.'[28]

The failure of the labour movement in Dundee to support the spontaneous strikes of the women textile workers did not breach the principles of trade-unionism as claimed by James Morton, but rather was concordant with these principles. They favoured negotiation and moderation and prided themselves on their ability to meet with the employers on their terms and by dint of logic and reasoned argument to persuade them of the merits of their case. The democratic principles of trade-unionism were not defined by mass action but by delegation and representation. Thus the Trades Council in Dundee advised striking women in 1899 to return to work whilst promising that their cause would be vigorously pursued by negotiation.[29] At a meeting of the Trades Council which discussed the strike of textile workers for an increase of 5 per cent, James Reid, a power-loom tenter and President of the Dundee Textile Union, condemned the action of the strikers as 'most ill-advised and ill-timed . . . if they had waited three or four weeks the advance would have been granted without striking'.[30] He urged the strikers to return to work and observed that the lesson of this struggle was that priority should be given to organizing the jute workers into a union. He hoped that the employers noted that it was the union members who refrained from striking and that in future they would not discourage their employees from joining unions. A former spinner who talked of a dispute in which she was involved in the early 1900s remembered that her father, a tailor, a union man and a member of the ILP, was displeased at her coming out on strike and told her: 'If you come out with them, I'll kill you.' Her explanation was: 'You see, he was mad at us going with a crowd of lassies. You see, he said it was too gallus, that wasn't the right way to go about it. There was a right way and a wrong way.'[31] He even forbade her to sing the strike song in the house. Her father's objection to the strike, that they were not in a union and therefore 'it wasn't done properly', indicated

[28] *Dundee Advertiser*, 3 May 1893.   [29] Ibid. 8 Sept. 1899.
[30] Ibid.   [31] Interview with Mrs McD.

the disapproval of women taking independent action which was not sanctioned by men. For not only was the trade union movement comprised mainly of men, but its principles, policies, and strategies were fashioned by men. Similarly, the use of the term 'gallus' implies disapproval of autonomous action by women which ignored male controls and which therefore had to be condemned or dismissed. His claim that if you were in a union you had something to fall back on indicates that he saw the contribution of trade unions as making the strike more effective, but his attitude was more than simply instrumental. He associated unions with a trade and hence with security and respectability, illustrating the fusion of economics and ideology and the extent to which they were mutually reinforcing. If unions contributed to the successful resolution of a strike by providing financial support, they also endowed industrial action with legitimacy, dignity, and discipline, which were essential components of independent working-class action and organization.

The Dundee Trades Council and the unions of skilled men in the jute industry constantly counselled striking women to return to work. Women's action was usually described as 'rash', 'hasty', or even 'downright folly', but the women obdurately refused to abandon the spontaneous strike as their favoured weapon.

It was the prevalence of women's strikes and the belief that the interests of women jute workers were not adequately represented by the male trade union movement which prompted the Reverend Mr Henry Williamson to form the Dundee and District Mill and Factory Operatives' Union (DMFOU) in 1885, the first trade union in Dundee aimed specifically at the female mill- and factory workers.

Williamson claimed that the workers, before his intervention, were absolutely without organization, that they were like a flock of sheep without a shepherd, and that the usual outcome of their strikes was a return to work 'without nearness to their grievances'.[32] This somewhat one-sided and pessimistic picture of the mill girls had little bearing on reality, although it should not be denied that wages were low and that the

---

[32] *People's Journal*, 14 Oct. 1922.

women had no particular leader. Williamson's intention was to underline his role in ameliorating the wages and conditions of the mill girls (the article was entitled 'Helping the Mill Girls in the Fight for their Rights'), and for this purpose it was expedient to portray them as the helpless creatures of the master prior to the establishment of his union.

The DMFOU was formed in September 1885, in the aftermath of an extensive strike against a reduction in wages. The women strikers were holding a meeting in the Barrack Park one afternoon and the Reverend Williamson, at the behest of several of the male workers, addressed the meeting, and succeeded in persuading them to return to work and form a union.[33] The concern of the men in fostering union organization amongst the women is perhaps some indication of the measure of success the women had attained by their informal pattern of mobilization, or at least the extent to which they had threatened the interests of the élite stratum of workers. Women's strikes impinged on men in that they incurred broken time[34] and the portion of their wages they received would be subject to negotiation. It has been argued that the organized male minders in the Lancashire cotton industry stifled union organization of the piecers in order to maintain their dominance,[35] but in Dundee it appears that it was in the interests of the better-paid men to encourage unionism in the hope that it would exercise a restraining influence on the women, curb their inclination for spontaneous action, and channel their dissatisfactions towards more orderly and contained negotiating procedures. According to the account of Williamson, the employers also welcomed the establishment of the union and favoured the policy of negotiation as a first step in any matter under dispute.[36]

Originally the union permitted only women as members, with an entrance fee of 3*d.* and weekly payments of 1*d.*, but, within a year of its inception, it opened its doors to male operatives. By Williamson's own admission membership was

---

[33] *People's Journal*, 14 Oct. 1922.   [34] SIC MS 66/11/9/3.
[35] W. Lazonick, 'The Division of Labour and Machinery: The Development of British and US Cotton Spinning', Discussion Papers Series, Harvard University, May 1978.
[36] *People's Journal*, 14 Oct. 1922.

not stable, with some joining and leaving within a few weeks. In 1889 the union claimed to have a membership of about 4,000[37] with membership reaching a peak in 1902 at 6,000 and remaining relatively stable at about 5,000 till 1906,[38] although the Forfar branch of the Scottish Mill and Factory Workers' Federal Union rejected the membership figure as grossly inflated. The ratio of women to men in the union was particularly high, but this was to be expected in a workforce where women vastly outnumbered men. Initially Williamson experienced difficulties in persuading the women to become committee members; however, by 1889 the Executive Committee consisted of twenty-two workers plus the President, Secretary, Treasurer, and Vice-President, and the vast majority were women. There are no figures which provide a breakdown of the membership in terms of the relative numbers of spinners, preparers, weavers, etc.; however, in 1906 Williamson rejected an accusation by weavers that the union did not represent their interests as its composition was predominantly millworkers by claiming that piece-workers constituted the majority of the membership.[39] Similarly, there are no reliable sources to indicate the proportion of married women in the union but, in Williamson's evidence to the Royal Commission on Labour, he stated that he thought there were few members of the union who were married.[40]

The policy of the DMFOU was resolutely conciliatory and had as a guiding principle the prevention of strikes at all costs. Indeed it was stated by Williamson in a lecture entitled 'A Defence of the Constitution, Principles, Methods and Aims of the Dundee District Mill and Factory Operatives' Union' that the union 'was started with the view of finding a remedy for the evils of strikes'.[41] The union subscribed to the major economic orthodoxies of the labour movement, principally to secure 'a fair day's work' and the need to take cognizance of the state of trade in wage bargaining, but Williamson's

[37] LC 197 (34).
[38] W. Walker, *Juteopolis: Dundee and its Textile Workers, 1885–1923* (Edinburgh: Scottish Academic Press, 1979), 49.
[39] *Dundee Advertiser*, 2 Mar. 1906.
[40] *Dundee Year Book*, 1891, extract from the *Royal Commission on Labour*.
[41] DMFOH 9 (May 1889).

commitment to preventing strikes was founded on a sense of Christian justice which went beyond the essential pragmatism of the established union movement.

Williamson's belief was that strikes not only caused misery amongst the working class and were an ineffectual means of improving wages and conditions, but that they caused misery, unhappiness, and loss to the employers. This contrasts with the attitude of mainstream unionism of the period, which, although having a commitment to moderation, was capable of resorting to the most expedient method of redressing grievances, including strike action, regardless of the social philosophy which it espoused. However, for the Reverend Williamson, the economic order assumed not only a permanence and universality but had the properties of a law of nature which was outside human control. Thus in justifying the union's action in persuading strikers to return to work he argued that 'We, however, see no reason to regret the activities taken in advising the persons on strike to return to their employment and meanwhile submit to what could not be helped.'[42]

Throughout the period, Williamson's intervention was characterized by either counselling workers not to go on strike, advising them to return to work if they had already struck, or inducing them to accept a compromise which would end the strike. Although Williamson recognized the injustice of the Dundee jute workers' position, he did believe that often their grievances were trivial or fanciful and, even when legitimate, certainly provided no grounds for striking. In his article of reminiscences, he recounted an incident which was to serve to illustrate the state of anarchy and disorder which prevailed in the industry before unionization:

The girls were winders and it was their business to place the result of their labour in buckets, each of which had to be brought up to a certain weight. It came about in the course of the operations that many of these buckets were deprived of the handles by which they were moved about, but although the receptacles themselves were lightened to this degree, the rule was adhered to that when filled they must still come up to the specific standard in weight. It followed that the deficiency represented by the weight of the handles had to

[42] *DMFOH* 2 (May 1886).

be made up by the worker in materials, and that the employer was securing an advantage at the expense of the girls through the defective character of his own appliances . . . labouring under a sense of injustice the girls 'went out'. It is inconceivable that such a thing would occur today.[43]

The unorthodox nature of the DMFOU under the somewhat idiosyncratic leadership of Williamson did not endear it to the established union movement in Dundee. Their differences in approach and policies did not involve them in embarking on a collision course but there undoubtedly existed tension between the two, which took the form of verbal recriminations and the isolation of one from the other. Many years after the establishment of the union, Williamson complained that 'A measure of sympathy and support might have been expected from the Trade Unionists of the Town, but they stood aloof and offered no help.'[44]

The hostility of Dundee's trade union movement to the DMFOU derived more from the nature of its organization than any economic heresy it subscribed to which violated the principles of trade-unionism. The principal objection held by the Dundee Trades Council to the union was the degree to which it was in the control of Williamson, who, being a Unitarian minister, was not employed in the trade which the union represented. For this reason Williamson, who was the Honorary President of the union, was refused a seat on the Trades Council and the union prohibited from affiliating. There is further evidence of the nature of their objections to the union in the advice given by the Trades Council workers who were involved in a strike in 1895. They suggested that another union of millworkers should be formed which was democratic 'not autocratic'. Williamson's union was unpalatable to the labour movement in Dundee because it undermined working-class autonomy and the independence of working-class institutions from the control of middle-class philanthropists. The labour movement was not averse to the support and aid of such groups or individuals, particularly for women workers, but was inimical to attempts to control the working-class movement from outside. These criticisms did not preclude some measure

---

[43] *People's Journal*, 14 Oct. 1922.   [44] Ibid.

of co-operation between the two, particularly in relation to the thorny problem of strikes. When workers struck over the refusal of employers to maintain the rate of pay for a working week reduced by one hour, representatives of the Trades Council met with the Reverend 'with a view to devising some means whereby development of the strike might be avoided'.[45]

It was dissatisfaction with the DMFOU's methods which led to the establishment of an alternative textile workers' union, the Dundee Textile Union. This union was sanctioned by the Trades Council and drew the core of its membership from the skilled male workers in the industry. It claimed to have a membership of 2,000 but had a relatively short existence, its organization in tatters after a dispute over lock-out pay in 1899.

Williamson's union also encountered dissension and criticism from within its own ranks, over what was regarded as the undue sway exercised by Williamson over the Executive Committee. The Brechin branch of the union seceded when its proposals to alter the rules in favour of a federal structure were rejected,[46] and subsequently combined with other disaffected branches to form the Scottish Mill and Factory Workers' Federal Union.

It has been argued that the existence of Williamson's union as the leading labour organization amongst Dundee's textile workers was a measure of the apathy which existed among them.[47] It is, however, debatable to what extent the union influenced either its members or the bulk of the non-unionized workforce, or indeed had any significant impact on the workers' struggle to defend their living standard. Williamson's interventions were usually directed at dissuading the women from striking or counselling them to return to work and 'agitate by means other than strikes' for their demands. However, he was by no means always successful in his exhortations, for, despite his efforts to avert strike action, in 1893 there was a strike involving over 20,000 operatives against a reduction of 5 per cent.[48] Similarly, those involved in the general strike in 1895 for an increase in wages remained impervious to the

[45] *Dundee Advertiser*, 11 Jan. 1902. [46] *DMFOH 7* (Mar. 1889).
[47] Walker, *Juteopolis*, 150.
[48] *Dundee Advertiser*, 1 May 1893.

attempts by Williamson to persuade them to return to work, and women in Dudhope Works successfully resisted a reduction of 10 per cent in 1894 by resorting to strike action although they had been addressed by Williamson and advised against it.[49]

The labour force continued its tactics of spontaneous mobilization, while the presence of the union seemed to make little impression on this time-honoured pattern, and failed dismally to contain the eruption of disputes. This was admitted by Williamson in his address to the ladies' meeting of the TUC in 1889 when he stated that 'At the present time the members are hopeful that a further rise of wages will be obtained though it may not be till after some of the adventurous operatives have taken the matter into their own hands and resorted to the old method of a strike.'[50]

It is doubtful whether the DMFOU, which represented, by the most optimistic of estimates, 14 per cent of the workforce, was responsible in any degree for winning and securing wage demands, or was necessary for the successful prosecution of a strike. There already existed an informal network of contacts which was tapped and mobilized to give support, principally financial, whenever a section of the workforce was in the throes of a dispute. Collections were an indispensable component of strike activity and in this respect the workers exhibited a level of organization which at least equalled that of the formal labour movement.

If the union was so peripheral to the experience of the bulk of the labour force, why then did it still attract 5,000 of their number of its ranks when the officially sanctioned union had a transitory existence and only succeeded in recruiting 2,000 members? Part of the explanation lies in the nature of the union itself and the charismatic leadership of Williamson, but part of the explanation can be located in the composition and character of the established union movement in Dundee, which represented the interests and concerns of particular categories of male workers.

The appeal of Williamson's union lay not so much in the concrete benefits for the membership but in the language and

[49] *Dundee Advertiser*, 6 Mar. 1894.   [50] LC 197 (34).

manner in which Williamson pursued their claims. Williamson often deplored the fact that relations between masters and servants were increasingly governed solely by market considerations and that paternalism and mutual obligations were fast disappearing. He criticized the 'heartless officialism' of firms which dismissed women who were compelled to stay at home for a day or more as a result of illness. He chastised those who dispensed sanctimonious charity, arguing that 'There is no reason why the poor should be treated with disrespect even by the agents of benevolence.'[51] He implored that workers should be considered 'as human beings and not as so many working factors'. More importantly it was his aim that the union should be 'distinctly valuable and interesting to women'. Therefore, a major objective was to raise the wages of those considered the lowest paid in the industry, principally the spinners and preparers. In so doing, he affirmed their worth as human beings and workers, arguing that their work should be recognized as skilled:

Spinning is a trade; that is to say, a woman must be trained to it from childhood in order that she may become a really good worker. That means she is a spinner and nothing else. Her work is said to be very important, for although machinery can be made to do many wonderful things, it cannot get along without the human eye, hand, brain and skill.[52]

Williamson also spoke of women's role in a way which had a particular resonance for Dundee's working women, although he adopted a high moral tone. Recognizing that the dominant cultural imagery of women's role was inappropriate and inapplicable to many working women, Williamson urged that women should be aware of and develop their self-worth and not regard themselves as mere appendages to men:

The temptation to which our girls are most exposed is to live a surface life for a mere surface effect, to acquire those gifts and graces which please more the eye than the mind or heart of men, the cultivation of which will give them no inner resources of independent enjoyment, and will leave them to a joyless, aimless existence, should they fail in what has hitherto been considered the chief end of women—namely

---

[51] *DMFOH* 1 (Sept. 1888). [52] Ibid.

the marriage state. Under existing conditions of society not every woman can reach this commonly supposed most desirable status. A very large proportion have to make a status of their own, not to be mere drones in the hive of humanity, to have within themselves in their developed minds and tastes, that which will make life good and sweet to them should they never find a husband or should the husband when found prove not exactly the ideal man.[53]

The concern of the union to represent the interest of the female workers and the fact that they were accorded status, dignity, and respect must have had a strong appeal to the women whose position in Dundee's jute industry consigned them to the lowest rung in the hierarchy of labour. Therefore, any adherence to the Reverend Henry Williamson and his peculiar brand of unionism cannot be attributed simply to the absence of class consciousness in a backward labour force which clung to the essential individualism of religion and the pious expectation of salvation after death. Williamson himself complained how few of the operatives came to listen to him on a Sunday.

Undoubtedly the outstanding feature of the pattern of worker resistance in the Dundee jute industry continued to be the persistence of spontaneous strikes by women workers, the majority of whom remained outside the portals of formal trade union organization. The official statistics which were collected from 1889 indicate that between 1889 and 1914 there were 103 strikes involving women in Dundee's jute industry.[54] Evidence gleaned from newspaper accounts suggests that the majority of strikes were short-lived affairs, many lasting only a matter of hours. It is likely, therefore, that this official figure underestimates the frequency of strikes amongst women.

The vast majority of strikes were initiated by women and involved only women. A small number of these strikes included men: for example, in one instance male calender workers went on strike and women spinners came out in sympathy: in two cases weavers struck and tenters and mechanics supported

---

[53] *DMFOH* 1 (Sept. 1888).
[54] Annual Reports by the Chief Labour Correspondent on Strikes and Lockouts in the United Kingdom, 1890–1913.

them; and, in one case, the total workforce, male and female, in a weaving factory came out on strike because of a change in managers. The skilled and supervisory grades of workers in the industry did not strike with the same frequency as the women, and they generally did not become directly involved in the women's strikes.

Mill strikes were usually initiated by spinners and the factory strikes by weavers. Most of the women's strikes involved workers in one firm, and could number anything from 14 to 500 strikers. There were, however, a small number of strikes which involved most of the firms in the town, and most classes of worker such as happened in 1892, 1893, 1895, 1899, and 1906. In these cases the number of strikers was between 20,000 and 35,000.[55] Spinners and weavers were equally prone to strike. Weavers initiated 40 of the disputes and spinners 60 of the 103 recorded strikes. The vast majority of the disputes were either directly or indirectly related to wages; 39 strikes were either against wage reductions or for increases and 34 related to bad material, with a further 30 related to working conditions, attempts to speed up work, and victimization. Strikes over poor material were also related to wages. For 'bad material' made it difficult to maintain customary earnings, as well as intensifying the work-load. The fact that the disputes of Dundee working women centred on wage demands is not surprising, given that their wages were so low and so many of them were bread-winners.

The success and issues of the disputes were usually related to the state of trade. In periods of depression the workers were usually engaged in battles to resist reductions in wages but there were also strikes against bad materials, or alterations in working conditions. There were several strikes of this nature between 1890 and 1895, the most significant of which was the 1893 general strike against a reduction of 5 per cent. The strike originated at Tay Works in the Scouringburn district and it was here that the most violent scenes were witnessed:

---

[55] Annual Reports by the Chief Labour Correspondent on Strikes and Lockouts in the United Kingdom, 1890–1913.

On Monday at 6 o'clock . . . the employees who had agreed to stand
by the resolution assembled outside the gates, and amused themselves
by hooting at their fellow workers who felt it their duty to continue
at their work. Before breakfast the strikers numbered 500, after
breakfast 2,000 . . . It was observed that many of the younger
workers, both male and female, had come provided with wooden
laths. The 10 o'clock whistle began to sound and as the shrill notes
were heard a few antistrikers made their way towards the entrance.
They were immediately set upon by those armed with sticks, and
ran the gauntlet under a shower of hearty blows.

At the same time they were loudly hooted and subjected to remarks
of a far from complimentary kind. In this way, about 100 workers,
chiefly men found their way in.[56]

On this occasion it appears that most sections of the
workforce were affected by the reduction, including the male
tenters, calenders, dressers, etc., and yet their distaste for strikes
still prevented them from joining the struggle. The employees
succeeded in gaining a compromise which limited the reduction
to 2½ per cent. There were, however, incidences of groups
of workers, or individual workplaces, which successfully
resisted the imposition of any reduction at all, such as in 1894
at Dudhope Works where the women struck against a reduction
of 10 per cent whilst the men in the various departments refused
to take part in the protest and seemed prepared to accept the
new regulation.[57]

The years 1895 till 1906 saw a levelling out of the depression
and were characterized by a low rate of profitability but very
little unemployment. Most disputes concerned attempts to gain
increases in wages, with varying degrees of success. There were
a number of strikes which assumed the proportions of a general
strike. The most significant of these was the 1895 strike for
an increase, which ended in defeat. It is perhaps testimony to
the efficacy of Dundee's textile workers' industrial action that
the 1895 strike was defeated because, for the first time in the
history of the trade, employers combined in an association,
collective action and unanimity ensuring success.

In February 1906 the favourable state of the jute industry
encouraged the executive of the DMFOU to submit a request

⁵⁶ *Dundee Advertiser*, 5 May 1893.   ⁵⁷ Ibid., 3 Mar. 1894.

to the employers for a 5 per cent increase. They were no doubt prompted by the prevailing mood of discontent which signalled the likelihood of the operatives taking action into their own hands and striking. The request was a response to pressure from the workers and an attempt to forestall any general disturbances in the trade. The statement issued to the employers by Williamson illustrates the conciliatory approach of the union and the desire to pre-empt strikes:

In no sense is it put forward as a demand. The Mill and Factory Operatives' Union was organized for the purpose of preventing strikes, and any workers who take matters into their own hands and leave their employment, thus causing serious mischief to their fellow-operatives, are acting entirely contrary to the wishes of the union.[58]

The exhortations not to strike were issued in vain and the discontent was exacerbated when the workers learned of the refusal of the employers to concede the 5 per cent, with 6,000 operatives on strike within two days of the employers' declaration. Although the action was initiated by spinners and shifters, who were on time wages and tended to be lower paid than the piece-workers, the dispute rapidly spread to include all classes of the female workforce. Williamson's response to the employers' intransigence was to negotiate for an increase for the lower-paid workers which he justified as securing higher wages for the underpaid, whether they were spinners or piecers, weavers or winders. Williamson lamented that the concession had not been given before 'irresponsible' workers had taken matters into their own hands, but he was to have even greater cause for censure when the winders, reelers, and weavers rejected the settlement and elected to remain out.

The piece-workers remained resolute in spite of constant attempts by Williamson to persuade them to return while negotiations continued. The efforts of the Trades Council too were directed at reaching a compromise, whereby the lowest paid would receive a 10 per cent increase, the highest paid 2½ per cent, and the bulk of workers something between the two extremes. The piece-workers were adamant that the 5 per cent should be given 'all round'.

---

[58] *Dundee Advertiser*, 23 Feb. 1906.

Much was made in the Press of the hostility and friction between the time workers and the piece-workers. The piece-workers' refusal to accept the terms of agreement was interpreted as an attempt by higher-paid workers to maintain differentials and preserve their privileged position. However, the wages of weavers were subject to a great deal of variability, as breakages, broken time, etc. affected their earnings. To some extent the weavers' earnings were also dependent on their own abilities and skill, so that the range of earnings was considerable. They therefore felt fully justified in taking advantage of the recent prosperity to augment their income, and never resorted to arguments about maintaining differentials.

The dissatisfaction with Williamson's handling of the dispute and his repeated attempts to force them back to work prompted a deputation from the women to approach the Trades Council to seek support for their claim. This initiative represented the seeds of a new union, and, with the aid of a variety of organizations which included the Dundee Social Union, the Independent Labour Party, and the Women's Trade Union League, it was to blossom in the formation of the DDUJFW.

Undoubtedly the driving force behind the establishment of the union was Mary MacArthur, Secretary of the Women's Trade Union League, the successor to the Women's Protective and Provident League. She addressed a number of meetings where she urged the necessity of forming 'a union based on practical Trade Union lines',[59] and cast aspersions on Williamson and his union, claiming the chairman should be a servant of the union, not a boss, and remonstrated with the workers for being 'too long content to bow their necks under the yoke of their employers'.[60]

By 8 March most of the workers had reluctantly returned to work having been encouraged by the Trades Council to insist on the appointment of a conciliation committee. At Grimmond's 2,000 workers remained obdurate and John Reid, of the Trades Council, and Mary MacArthur agreed to accompany a deputation of women to the management, who refused to

[59] *Dundee Advertiser*, 9 Mar. 1906.
[60] *Telegraph and Post*, 9 Mar. 1906.

meet with them. They were subsequently persuaded by Reid and MacArthur to return to work.

The legacy of defeat was the establishment of the DDUJFW, which seemed to represent a break with the 'sham' unionism of Williamson, whose organization was dismissed as a benefit society. The willingness of the workforce to embrace the principles of true unionism was seen as heralding the end of the era of low wages and total subjugation of the workers to the will of the masters and the end of rash strikes, and therefore was seen as a watershed in Dundee textile workers' history. This was an exaggerated representation of the previous history of the workers' struggle and an over-optimistic view of the capacity of the union to effect change or influence Dundee's jute workers.

The union was instituted on 13 March 1906. Its foundation meeting was chaired by Robert Stirton of Dundee's Trades Council and addressed by Mary MacArthur, who recommended affiliation to the General Federation of Unions, to ensure they would have funds to support them in the event of a dispute. A provisional committee was elected to deal with the preliminary work and a proposal to exclude married women from office rejected. Mary MacArthur, whilst opposing the motion, deprecated married women having to work in the mills and intimated that she favoured a policy of increasing men's wages to enable them to support their wives at home.[61] A provisional committee of 25 were elected, composed of 15 women and 10 men, but there is little evidence to indicate the number of married women serving, although it is certain that there was at least one.[62]

The initial membership of 3,000 increased to 4,252 within six months, and was to stabilize at this figure until 1910 when there was a rapid increase until by 1913 it had reached approximately 9,264.[63] There are few details of the ratio of either men to women in the organization or the ratio of spinners to weavers. However, the circumstances of the foundation of the union would make it probable that weavers predominated,

[61] *Dundee Advertiser*, 14 Mar. 1906.
[62] DDUJFW, Executive Committee Minute Books, 13 Mar. 1906.
[63] Ibid., *passim*.

although this theory is somewhat undermined by the claim of the Secretary in 1911 that 75 to 80 per cent of those employed in the spinning department of Cox Brothers were union members.[64]

In the early years of the union, women outnumbered men by at least 2 to 1, but the policy was changed to exclude skilled men, who had organizations specifically for their trade, thus ensuring the greater preponderance of women in the union, until the years immediately preceding the First World War.[65] The composition of the committee varied but normally women were in a majority of 3 : 1.

The union was very much under the tutelage of John Sime, who was President until December 1907 and then organizer and Secretary thereafter. The manner of his appointment as organizer highlights the close links between the union and the Women's Trade Union League, and, more particularly, the influence which Mary MacArthur exercised over the committee. Sime had been dismissed from his position at Grimmonds and, at a special committee meeting called by Mary MacArthur, she proposed that he should receive the wages he had earned at Grimmonds. She also offered to be present at the general meeting to present the case to members.[66]

In its formative years, Mary MacArthur played a central role in organizing the union and was constantly in correspondence with its officials throughout the period. In December 1906 a committee meeting was held at her request, where she dispensed a wealth of advice on how to recruit members which included a bonus scheme for collectors and the proposal that they should engage the services of Mrs Marland Brodie of the Women's Trade Union League, for organizational purposes.[67] Although the DDUJFW did not affiliate to the League until May 1907, Mary MacArthur frequently addressed their public meetings and on occasions the general meetings of the union.

During a strike at Gilroy's in 1907, she was instrumental in setting up a strike committee and persuading the union to donate some of its funds, although the majority of the women

[64] SIC MS 66/11/10/28.
[65] DDUJFW, Executive Committee Minutes, 30 May 1910.
[66] Ibid., 20 Dec. 1907.   [67] Ibid., 21 Dec. 1906.

were not in the union. She also led a procession of the strikers in a march to Gilfillan Hall where she addressed them and urged them to join the union.[68] Relations with the rival DMFOU were not so cordial. Williamson's union continued to attract about 5,000 members, which equalled the numbers of the DDUJFW, and therefore their combined membership figure embraced between 25 and 30 per cent of Dundee's textile workforce. In recognition of its presence, the DDUJFW approached Williamson's union and suggested the formation of a joint council. However, after only one year's existence, the DMFOU withdrew and could not be persuaded to reconsider their decision. In order to embarrass Williamson, the correspondence between the two unions over the joint council was published in the Dundee Press, and relations between the two were further aggravated.[69]

This had been preceded by an even more embittered encounter, which involved several rejoinders concerning the relative merits of the two unions. John Sime accused Williamson of acting independently of the joint council and behind its back thereby jeopardizing unity and solidarity. His dismissal of the union as a benefit society because of the 'ridiculously' high benefits paid was certainly indicative of the irritation of Sime's union at what was considered unfair competition[70] in the struggle to recruit.

Unlike Williamson's union, the DDUJFW was represented on the Trades Council by four delegates and seems to have maintained an active and interested presence in Trades Council affairs. There is little evidence of a high degree of political content at any level of the union's organization, although it did affiliate to the Labour Representation Committee in 1907, entitling them to two delegates at the annual general meeting of the organization. In 1913 at a general meeting, the committee were charged by a Mr Hugh Clark with being a clique of the Labour Representation Committee and the ILP.[71] The union also seems to have been involved in the rising level of militancy and political discontent in the pre-First World

---

[68] DDUJFW, Book of Press Cuttings.
[69] DDUJFW, Copy Letter Book (undated correspondence).
[70] DDUJFW, Book of Press Cuttings.
[71] DDUJFW, General Meetings Minute Book, 30 Oct. 1913.

War years, and in July 1912 two delegates were appointed to a conference of trade union, Labour, and Socialist organizations held in Dundee 'with a view to consolidate the Scottish Political Movement'.[72] A number of resolutions were passed supporting women's suffrage and in 1906 the union sponsored a suffrage meeting in Dundee addressed by Helen Fraser, the Scottish organizer of the Women's Social and Political Union,[73] but this appears to have been the height of their involvement in this sphere. The union passed several resolutions in support of women's suffrage, including a resolution condemning the imprisonment of suffragettes who had demonstrated in the House of Commons.[74] However, there was dissension within the committee of the union over forging closer links with the WSPU and an invitation to send a delegate to a WSPU conference in the Gilfillan Halls in Dundee was left to lie on the table.[75] Support for women's suffrage was not unanimous within the committee with some of the male members arguing in favour of the adult suffrage position. Even after the Labour Party had changed its policy to opposition to any proposed extension to the franchise which did not include women, some male members of the committee remained intransigent in their advocacy of adult suffrage.[76]

The weight of the committee's business revolved around fairly mundane matters, involving the minutiae of organization. A perennial problem was the concern to recruit new members and, to this end, a variety of schemes were devised to induce collectors to boost recruitment. These ranged from increasing the commission fee of collectors to prizes for collectors who enlisted most new members. The importance placed on boosting membership and the collection of dues resulted in a fairly rigorous screening process of those who applied for these posts and consequently discussions about suitable applicants occupied a great deal of time. The Committee displayed a reluctance to discuss policy matters, on several occasions deferring discussion of shorter hours because of the more pressing question of payment of dues.

---

[72] DDUJFW, Executive Committee Minutes, 16 July 1912.
[73] Ibid., 6 Apr. 1906.   [74] Ibid., 23 Oct. 1906.
[75] Ibid., 25 June 1907.   [76] Ibid., 7 Jan. 1913.

Accidents and complaints about working conditions were usually dealt with by writing a letter to the Factory Inspectorate or the individual employer and the matter was rarely pursued by the union, unless further action was taken by the employees.[77] There were a few cases of victimization of members of the union who had either taken part in a strike or encouraged recruitment. The committee's policy was usually to pay benefit or full wages whilst ensuring the person obtained alternative employment. This action was often accompanied by a letter of complaint to the employer concerned. One such letter to Grant and Baxter's in 1909 indicates the union's anxiety to be seen as responsible and moderate:

We have a complaint from Maggie Hutton, weaver, who was in your employment up to last Saturday 20 February when she was dismissed from your services. Mr Davidson informed her that her services were dispensed with because of the part she took in the strike in your works on Friday 4 December 1908.

As a matter of fact she was strongly opposed to the weavers striking before asking an interview with the members of the firm and it was only when the remainder had decided to cease work that she threw in her lot with them.[78]

The union's grievance procedure and strike policy was embodied in a rule imposed by the Secretary of the union and passed at the 1907 Annual General Meeting and read:

That members locked out through action by non-members are entitled to benefit. Any member of the union striking or inciting others to strike or causing any trouble to arise between employer and his workers, without first having laid their grievances before the union committee, forfeits all claim either to strike or lock-out benefit.[79]

The constant references to the state of trade and the acknowledgement that it would have to be taken into account, coupled with its attitude to strikes, indicates that, in many respects, the DDUJFW subscribed to the same philosophy as the established unions of skilled workers. However, the general economic climate and the particular state of the jute trade generated an increasing number of disputes and the committee

---

[77] DDUJFW, Copy Letter Book, *passim*.   [78] Ibid., 22 Feb. 1909.
[79] DDUJFW, Executive Committee Minutes, 28 Mar. 1907.

was forced to adopt a pragmatic approach to the question of lock-out and strike benefit. If it had adhered dogmatically to the rule book, no doubt membership would have declined dramatically as the union membership would seem to offer no tangible benefits.

The union rarely initiated strikes and its role in a dispute was often restricted to that of an intermediary or a dispenser of benefits. It could perhaps be argued that the union did contribute to the successful prosecution of a strike as it frequently gave financial assistance in the form of a reduced rate of benefit to those non-union members who undertook to join when the dispute was over. The union played a major role in at least two important disputes, in that it succeeded in enhancing its reputation and its intervention influenced the manner in which the disputes were resolved. The most significant of these disputes was a seven-week-long struggle by piecers and shifters at Victoria Spinning Company, where the employers had decided to dispense with a squad of thirteen workers, and increase the wages of those left by 1s. per week. According to one commentator the women had chosen a most inopportune time and were therefore likely to be defeated: 'The workers could scarcely have chosen a less opportune time as the mill has been working short time for the past few weeks, and trade generally is said to be very slack. It is expected that the dispute will be quickly ended.'[80]

Of about 300 or 400 strikers only 20 were union members.[81] None the less the committee decided to pay 5s. per week to non-members who joined the union, subject to weekly review by the committee. Repeated compromises were proposed by the employers, but adamantly rejected by the women. The DDUJFW gave their financial support to the strikers, accompanied their deputations to management, campaigned for the dispute to be referred to arbitration, regarding it as a great victory when they managed to persuade the women, in the face of opposition, to resume work once the employers had agreed to arbitration.[82]

[80] DDUJFW, Book of Press Cuttings, 17 Aug 1909.
[81] DDUJFW, Executive Committee Minutes, 31 Aug. 1909.
[82] Ibid., 20 Sept. 1909.

The 1911 strike in Cox Brothers illustrates the role typically performed by the union, where the dispute involved its members. The firm had proposed to dispense with a shifter and helper from each squad in the spinning departments. Once the decision had been implemented, the women consulted the union, who intimated to a packed gathering of the workers that the decision on what was to be done was in their hands. The women unanimously decided to strike, whereupon the union proceeded to issue a financial appeal and lobby Dundee notables to hasten a settlement of the dispute.[83]

As the DDUJFW was in its infancy in the pre-war years, its central concerns were with the problems of implantation and recruitment. This struggle for acceptance was often the underlying motive in pursuing a particular course of action. It therefore often fastened on issues or particular disputes to support if it was felt that they would provide a fillip to membership numbers. Similarly, the union was often prompted to declare support for an issue or to take an initiative if discontent was generalized and events seemed likely to slip out of their control. For these reasons John Sime called a meeting of the Dundee Standing Joint Industrial Committee and explained why he felt such a meeting was necessary: 'The feeling of unrest is rising high among the workers and all around we are met with indication or tendency towards upheaval and we must take some steps to allay if possible this feeling.'[84] The committee reluctantly decided to request a 5 per cent increase, 'because circumstances were driving us to this course and by asking for an increase and fixing a date we might keep the people in check for a time'.[85] In a resolution later submitted to the Press, they warned the workers against any attempts at striking, maintaining that strikes 'do not much forward their interest'.

The union was not only interested in courting the textile workers, they were also anxious to be recognized by the employers and have their role as negotiators accepted and collective bargaining established in the trade. Thus they were

[83] DDUJFW, Executive Committee Minutes, 17 Dec. 1922.
[84] Dundee Standing Joint Industrial Committee, Minute Book, 5 Sept. 1913, DARC.   [85] Ibid., 15 Sept. 1913.

more likely to approve a resolution of a dispute which involved this recognition and enhanced their prestige and reputation with the employers. A protracted dispute in 1911 which involved a claim for 5 per cent was resolved by the employers' committee and the union committee communicating via intermediaries, who included the local Member of Parliament and the Lord Provost. The employers' offer of 2½ per cent was accepted 'because the terms offered convey recognition of our union, and provide for the mutual discussion and probably friendly settlement of future disputes'.[86]

Dundee was not unaffected by the general upsurge in militancy in the immediate pre-war years, and membership of the DDUJFW accelerated to a peak of 8,560 in February 1914.[87] More significantly the union had to cope with an increasing number of strikes which were initiated at the workplace, and a workforce who were less amenable to arguments persuading them to return to work whilst negotiations were conducted.

Despite the existence of two major textile unions, it was still the case that the mainstream of Dundee jute workers' action occurred outside the folds and influence of formal organizations. In a letter to the management committee of the General Federation of Unions, Sime outlined the case for the union receiving Federation benefits for what he considered would be an inevitable general strike. He noted that, because there was a boom in the jute trade, 'general gossip among the workers' indicated that there would be a strike before long as 'strikes, general and sectional, take place at the will of the unorganised workers'.[88]

Between 1906, when the DDUJFW was formed, and the First World War, there were twenty-one officially recorded disputes in the jute industry, although, as has been suggested, the actual number was higher than this.[89] The issues involved in the disputes covered the range of industrial grievances, but in the years 1908 to 1911 disputes over working conditions were

---

[86] DDUJFW, Executive Committee Minutes, 14 Apr. 1912.
[87] Ibid., 14 Feb. 1914.
[88] DDUJFW, Copy Letter Book, 20 Jan. 1912.
[89] Annual Reports on Strikes and Lockouts, 1906–14.

more common and in the two or three years before the war claims for wage increases predominated.[90]

The years 1908 to 1911 were difficult ones for the jute industry as the competition from India became more acute and its share of the world market declined. The employers' attempts to cut costs by intensifying the utilization of labour resulted in speed-ups and productivity schemes which were vehemently resisted by the workers. By contrast the pre-war boom, which began in 1912, ushered in two or three years in which claims for wages increases dominated the industrial scene. Strikes over wages in the immediate pre-war years tended to be more successful than the strikes over working conditions in the earlier period. This was undoubtedly due to the buoyant state of the industry and the demand for labour.

It has been argued that the upsurge in militancy throughout Britain between 1910 and 1911 was not restricted simply to economic grievances, but was a product of a more generalized disenchantment with and resentment towards social and political conditions. Although the prevailing orthodoxy emphasizes the absence of a coherent political challenge to the social order, there is evidence of a climate of discontent which narrowly transcended economic demands.[91] In Dundee this was reflected in 'indignation meetings' organized by various political groups and the labour movement to protest about a number of issues, including rising rents.[92] The employers responded to the crisis by reorganizing their association and also ensuring that it took account of 'all subjects connected with the welfare of their workers, such as the housing of the poorer classes which was not satisfactory in Dundee'.[93]

There were also impressive displays of solidarity across industries. In 1911 there was a general strike of carters and dockers for a minimum wage. The locked-out jute workers,

[90] Annual Reports on Strikes and Lockouts, 1906–14.

[91] The major proponent of the 'crisis' school, which argues that there was a fusion of industrial, political, and social grievances which threatened the stability of the political and social order, is S. Meacham, in 'The Sense of an Impending Clash: English Working Class Unrest before the First World War', *American Historical Review*, 77(5) (1972). See Ch. 7 for a discussion of local political activity in this period.

[92] DDUJFW, Executive Committee Minutes, 21 Jan. 1912.

[93] *Dundee Year Book*, 1912.

thrown idle by the dispute, expressed their solidarity with the strikers by joining their demonstrations and whole-heartedly embracing their cause. The *Dundee Advertiser* carried an article on the dispute which featured a photograph of mill girls with the caption 'A bevy of millgirls making a triumphal march along Dock Street'.[94] In recognition of this support the carters and dockers pledged to give any assistance they could in future disputes involving jute workers, and indeed only two months later they offered to black the goods of a particular firm where there was a strike.

The DDUJFW's moderation and its inclination to look to outside agencies to resolve industrial problems partly reflected changes which were taking place within the Women's Trade Union League, to which the Dundee union was affiliated. It also reflected the desire of the union for recognition by the employers and to establish formal collective bargaining procedures. There was therefore a reluctance to call strikes, except when pressure from operatives forced their hand. For this reason most strikes involving union members continued to be initiated by rank-and-file members at their workplace, although some of these strikes subsequently obtained union support; and, of course, the 'unorganized' majority persisted with their well-established pattern of wildcat strikes.

It has been argued that action which lacks an institutional form or basis is destined to be ephemeral and of little historical significance.[95] However, this need not involve accepting the contention that the spontaneous strikes of Dundee's textile labour force were a product of its weakness or disunity. The nature of the jute industry was such that for most of its pre-war history there was a shortage of labour. It obviously had to endure periodic bouts of unemployment but they were of very little significance in the sense that they were not protracted. The spontaneous strike, generated and extended by word of mouth, could be an effective weapon when there was a seller's market for those workers whose labour was in demand and whose lack of skill could otherwise have ensured their easy replacement.

---

[94] *Dundee Advertiser*, 23 Dec. 1911.
[95] E. J. Hobsbawm, *Primitive Rebels* (Manchester University Press, 1959).

The spread of disaffection during the strike of 1906 typified the manner in which strike action was generated:

> In the present labour trouble history repeated itself, inasmuch as matters were precipitated by that section of the operatives described by the union executive as 'thoughtless', leaving their places, and thus precipitating the struggle that it has been the effort of the union to avert since first the agitation for a five per cent advance of wages was begun . . .
>
> At Tay works, the great spinning and weaving establishments of Messrs Gilroy Sons and Company, there was also a gathering of malcontents who 'demonstrated' according to the accepted fashion. The general body of hands seemed undecided, but most of them in the end filed past the porter's lodge. At the dinner hour, however, evidently impressed by the knowledge of what was going on elsewhere, their ranks were largely augmented.[96]

Although protracted disputes were not unknown, the short lightning strike was more common. The brevity of the disputes mean that the backing of an organization which could provide financial assistance was not so necessary as for a lengthy strike. The jute workers had proved themselves capable of organizing and co-ordinating action on numerous occasions and, therefore, union membership may not have seemed to offer any substantial benefits. The absence of permanent trade union organization should not necessarily be interpreted as meaning that workers were lacking the faculty of effective organization, for, given the objective conditions of the jute industry, it is doubtful that formal trade union organization could have achieved more than the informal patterns of mobilization.

The spontaneous mode of resistance seemed most appropriate to a workforce lacking the industrial muscle derived from skill or workplace authority but whose labour was often in high demand and indispensable to the production process. Decisions to strike were usually taken at the workplace, although doubtless their resolve was buttressed by informal discussions with workmates in their leisure hours. There was rarely recourse to formal meetings and the usual pattern, after the seeds

---

[96] *Dundee Advertiser*, 24 Feb. 1906.

of discontent had been sown, was for someone to say: 'We're no goin' in. Are you goin' in? Naebody's goin' in!'[97] The absence of a central organization capable of co-ordinating action did not seem to detract from their ability to generalize the action, as disaffection rapidly spread within the work and to other works, in the streets and amongst the community generally.

Mass pickets were typically employed to persuade workers to join a strike and, although their inducements were usually confined to shouting and jeering, occasionally more violent methods were resorted to.

The spontaneous action of the women could equally be interpreted as a deliberately conceived weapon rather than a reflection of irrationality or confusion. It maximized disruption by being unpredictable and, as a display of united action, could also serve to heighten the self-respect and self-regard of the women and fuel the communal solidarity of the mill and factory.

There was little evidence of women electing a committee or leadership to organize their disputes, although there usually emerged from each strike a number of women who were particularly indefatigable in their efforts to muster support for the action. During a strike at Cox's in 1911, *Glasgow Forward* referred to the zealousness of one of these anonymous organizers:

The Girl with the 'Green Felt Hat' deserves special praise. She has proved herself a born organiser, leading the strikers in all their frolics during the first week, arranging processions etc., but when want was making itself felt, some serious work had to be done, she proved herself a veritable Trojan, leading the amount collected every week, even going to the International Football Match at Glasgow, only to be refused admittance.[98]

Although there was rarely an identifiable leadership, the manner in which strikes were initiated, spread, and enforced was also coherent and organized, and is testimony to the power of the communal basis of solidarity. The unskilled nature of the work performed by the majority of the jute workers, and the consequent lack of any organizational apparatus which

[97] Interview with Mrs MacDowall.   [98] *Glasgow Forward*, 1 Apr. 1911.

included rules regulating apprenticeships, did not mean that there was little basis for the development of group solidarity. Their shared experience both in and out of the workplace could provide a basis for united action, which was as powerful as that derived from craft autonomy, skill, and pride in one's work.

To understand the form and character of the Dundee women's industrial militancy, it is necessary to take account of much more than their economic experience at the level of the workplace. The organization of the jute industry, its labour process, and the structure of authority relations in the home, in work, and in society generally, all provide part of the explanation.

As has been illustrated, the division of labour and authority in the workplace paralleled conventional patriarchal family relations and this was reinforced by a definition of skilled work which reflected gender divisions and patriarchal authority. However, the absence of a family economy in the jute industry meant that the supervisory role of the small number of men was not sustained or buttressed by family ties which might have confirmed its legitimacy, facilitated the subordination of the women, and guaranteed their quiescence.

Although the spontaneous nature of the strikes could be seen as a rational and instrumental response to the objective conditions of the jute industry, it could also be interpreted as an assertion of independence from the control of both employers and to some extent male-dominated trade unions. The unpredictable nature of the action might have been equally important as a declaration of their autonomy and a reminder to their employers that they could not exercise unfettered control over their workforce. In his evidence to the Labour Commission on the state of the jute industry the Reverend Williamson doubted whether conciliation boards would meet with any success in the trade as:

It is not easy to know what to do with women. They are governed by impulse . . . all at once, without notice 50 or 100 of them are in a state of rebellion, and it requires someone to come in just to advise them, for as a rule neither master, manager nor any other official can get anything from them.[99]

[99] Royal Commission on Labour, *The Employment of Women*, C. 6894 (London: HMSO, 1893).

This defiance could equally be directed at the organized labour movement. The constant complaints of the trade union movement that the women's action was 'hasty' or 'ill-advised' are testimony to the difficulties they encountered when attempting to exercise a restraining influence. At a meeting of the Dundee Trades Council in 1899 which condemned the strike action of the jute workers a motion was passed recording sympathy with the unions 'in the predicament in which they found themselves owing to the rash acts of individuals over whom they had no control'.[100]

It was not only the manner in which strikes were unleashed but the tone of the protest which encapsulated a spirit of resistance and defiance. Strikes were often characterized by behaviour and gestures which challenged patriarchal authority by ridicule and teasing. A favourite ploy of strikers was to visit the Cowgate, the business haunt of the employers and merchants, and indulge in catcalling and heckling. The conscious intention of the strikers was to puncture the dignity of these prominent members of Dundee society by subjecting them to public ridicule and mocking. Invading the territory of the manufacturers and indelibly imprinting their presence on the scene was yet another way of challenging their masters' authority and asserting their independence, so that for a brief period the terms of the relationship were determined by the workers. An account of such an invasion in 1906 is a typical illustration of how this was enacted:

Strikers invaded the Cowgate . . . 'in a twinkling', a circle, the diameter of which extended from the Queen's Statue to the portals of the shelter was formed, and a couple of score of shrieking, shouting spinners spun round in the gyrations of jingo ring . . . ere long Panmure Street was thronged from end to end by an uproarious crowd of lassies. Number gave them the boldness and they made a rush for the shelter, in which for the most part millowners seeking to escape personal allusion and recognition had taken refuge . . . A hooting band made a rush for the last door, but the police, who acted with commendable discretion intervened and the portals were closed.[101]

---

[100] *Dundee Advertiser*, 8 Sept. 1899.
[101] Ibid., 27 Feb. 1906.

It was commonplace for the strikers to carry effigies of particular employers who had aroused their wrath and to dress up in a comic manner for their parades and demonstrations through the streets. The style of dress adopted was also a way of ridiculing patriarchal authority as they often donned men's hats and on several occasions a few of the women wore policemen's helmets.

The hilarity and dancing and singing which invariably accompanied women's strikes sharply distinguished them from men's industrial action, which was altogether a more sober and serious affair. A demonstration of men in 1909 against unemployment displayed a marked reluctance even to march in procession along the street as they felt it might do more harm to their cause than good.[102] The character of women's strikes bore a striking similarity to their leisure activities and commentators often noted how a strike amongst women took on the aspects of a public holiday or carnival, with fun and high spirits the order of the day. They usually roamed the streets in bands or paraded them in processional order singing popular music-hall songs and dancing 'jingo ring'.

The demonstrations were not only carried on during working hours, they frequently spilled over into the evenings with crowds of women converging on the high streets and indulging in what was usually described as 'unruly' behaviour. Parading up and down streets with workmates, who were invariably leisure time companions, and engaging in banter with other groups, was an integral part of 'play', especially for the younger unmarried girls, and could almost be described as a form of street life. It was surely no accident that the behaviour of women on strike should be analogous to their leisure activities for it was the only time they were free from direct control and supervision. Leisure involved self-expression and fun, which the daily grind at work denied them, and, by stamping their strike action with the flavour of their lesiure time, they could recapture it as their own time. Although their action had quite definite and specific objectives, it also assumed a symbolic significance. It was a flight from work, a collective expression of defiance, however temporary, and, by imbuing it with a

[102] *Dundee Advertiser*, 17 Aug. 1909.

sense of fun, they underscored the fact that they were
expropriating this time from the masters and repossessing it
themselves.

However, subverting male authority was clearly a central
part of women's actions and, by using ridicule, embarrassment,
and sexual impropriety, they turned sexual divisions into an
effective weapon which left the victims of their *badinage*
emasculated and without redress. The converse of the
dominance and pervasiveness of male power was the submission
and deference of women, who were expected to have respect
for this power and to conform to their culturally prescribed
gender roles, which were largely determined by men. Therefore,
not surprisingly, women's resistance symbolized a rejection of
male control and dominance by subjecting them to ridicule and
mocking, thus demonstrating disrespect, whilst, by breaching
the codes of modesty and flaunting sexual differences, they
denied men's power to control their behaviour.

The organized sections' references to the state of their trade
and their quest for respectability reflected acceptance of the
permanence of existing social arrangements. The informal
organization of Dundee women and their culture displayed a
subversive disrespect for authority, but it also reflected a
fatalistic acceptance of class divisions and inequality as part
of the natural order of things. This view is expressed in the
Jute Mill Song written by Mary Brooksbank, a Dundee jute
worker:

> Oh dear me, the warld's ill divided,
> Them that work the hardest are aye wi' least provided,
> But I maun bide contented, dark days or fine,
> But there's no much pleasure livin' offen ten-and-nine.

The weapons of teasing and ridicule may have brought
authority to the point of exasperation, but they were highly
unlikely to topple the edifice of capitalism. Although the
ebullience and gaiety of strikes were important aspects of the
pattern of resistance, they were manifestations of an essentially
defensive culture where primacy was placed on fun and high
spirits as a means of escaping from the drudgery of work.
Whatever the inadequacies of the ideology developed by the
jute workers for the purpose of mounting a significant challenge

to capitalism, it is important to stress that it was oppositional and that resignation or non-committed compliance to the social order did not signify complete submission.

The labour process of the jute industry and the social structures of the locality displayed certain features which may have fuelled working women's militancy; for example, the pattern of migration into the city contributed to population instability and, coupled with the accompanying disruption of kinship relations, had the effect of dislocating conventional family authority relations. Similarly, conventional family authority relations had no analogue in the workplace, in contrast to Lancashire's workplace authority structures. Dundee's social structure may have been unique, but the widespread evidence throughout Scotland of women's workplace militancy suggests that in this respect it was not an aberration.

6. Women and Trade-Unionism, 1890–1914

BETWEEN 1890 and 1914, more women were drawn into the formal structures of trade-unionism, due largely to the formation of trade unions aimed specifically at the recruitment of women. However, it was still the case that the majority of women workers remained outside the ranks of the trade union movement and the perennial problem was sustaining union organization amongst women once it had been implanted. Although there is little evidence that women workers displayed hostility towards these organizations, the fact that they remained outside the fold of trade unions which were provided specifically for them requires some explanation, particularly when women did not display any reluctance to engage in collective action to achieve their demands.

Although the trade union organization of women fluctuated between 1890 and the First World War, one enduring feature was the continued existence of the Women's Protection and Provident League, which was the organizational residue of the years of heightened industrial conflict and trade union growth. The inaugural meeting of the League in 1888 was sponsored by the Glasgow Trades Council and supported by leading academics and clergy[1] and till the end of the century it was the focus of women's trade-unionism in the west of Scotland.

Paradoxically, at a time when the aspirations of the labour movement were directed at independent working-class representation, the organization of women workers was under the tutelage of middle-class philanthropists, many of whom were implacably opposed to the political aspirations of organized labour. However, the one sphere where the two groups maintained a dialogue, took concerted action, and indeed where labour was happy to surrender the initiative to philanthropic elements was in the trade union organization of

---

[1] See Ch. 3.

women. The view of women as helpless creatures who were suitable objects for charitable enterprise was shared by those sections of the middle class who were interested in social policy and by organized labour. The Reverend A. C. Laughlin, who was Organization Secretary of the Scottish Council for Women's Trades, wrote in its annual report:

Few realise until they try to remove them the grave and disheartening difficulties which beset any attempt to organise women's labour. To begin with, the idea of uniting as a precaution of mutual defence is a novel one to the woman worker and there are few if any leading spirits amongst them who will agitate them to combine for a reformation of the serious abuses so often characteristic of their occupations.[2]

It was, therefore, a common conception of women workers as weak and powerless which provided the basis for co-operation between two groups who were in other ways pursuing different and sometimes antagonistic goals.

Of the constellation of voluntary and philanthropic groups which existed in the 1890s, the WPPL and the SCWT occupied a central position. Not only were they the focal point of issues specifically concerned with women, but, as they drew their membership from such diverse sources as trades councils, the Churches, academic institutions, and socialist parties, they provided virtually the sole terrain for the development of links with a number of organizations which were otherwise discrete.

The WPPL was based in Glasgow and its activities centred on the city and its outlying areas, although there are examples of its influence spreading to other areas, in the west and east coasts and to Edinburgh, where a tailoresses' branch and a typographical branch were established. The leading positions of the League and its governing organs were dominated almost exclusively by individuals from other organizations rather than by working women themselves. Although the trade unions played an active part in the establishment of the League and encouraged its work, it was essentially a mixed-class organization with the middle and upper classes dominating. Professor William Smart of Glasgow University was for a time

[2] SCWT, *Seventh Annual Report, 1901–1902*, SRA, 18.

214   *Women and Trade-Unionism*

Honorary President, as was A. J. Hunter, a Glasgow bailie, and the President of its Executive Committee was Mr George Galloway, President of the Glasgow Trades Council.[3]

The structure of the League superficially resembled the arrangement of orthodox trade unions, in that the basic unit of organization was the branch. Each branch was composed of women who worked in a particular trade and it was the members of the branch who elected the President, Vice-President, Secretary, Treasurer, and branch committee. In addition provision was made for a central branch, a miscellaneous grouping of those whose trade was not organized into a branch.[4] At this point the organization of the League departed significantly from the established pattern sanctioned by the official trade union movement. The rules of the WPPL included the institution of a League Council 'consisting of persons taking an interest in the objects of the League'.[5] The functions of the Council was to assist in the work of organization and to act as a board of arbitration and appeal when invited to do so by the Executive Committee, the governing body of the League. The Council was also entitled to have four of its members on the Executive Committee, which made most of the central decisions affecting the League including whether or not to negotiate over the regulation of wages, hours, and conditions. Decision-making was concentrated in the upper echelons of the League, thus heavily weighting the balance of power in favour of the middle classes, who predominated at that level.

The primary function of the League was to encourage the trade union organization of women, but by the turn of the century its emphasis focused more on organizing women to secure legislative change in order to improve their conditions. The reports of the League and the Glasgow Trades Council indicate that its success in organizing women workers followed a pattern of rapid fluctuations with years when trade organization was virtually moribund. The peak year for membership appears to have been 1893–94 when the League had eleven members

³ WPPL, *Annual Report, 1897*, SRA.
⁴ WPPL, *Rules, 1894*, SRA.
⁵ Ibid.

affiliated to the Glasgow Trades Council,[6] including delegates from branches of tailoresses, handkerchief hemmers, tobacco pipe-finishers, and weavers and winders. Thereafter the WPPL maintained a precarious existence and between 1895 and 1897 could not muster any delegates to the Trades Council from its branches. There was a modest revival in 1897 in both membership and activity but by the beginning of the century momentum had petered out and the annual reports of the Glasgow Trades Council fail to mention any affiliations from the League.

The evanescence of the organizing work of the WPPL did not mean that the League ceased to exist but merely that it shifted the emphasis of its work to agitation for legislation and that working women formed an ever decreasing proportion of its membership. Given the composition of the WPPL it is not surprising that its philosophy was governed more by philanthropic concern than by aggressive trade-unionism. Its sister organization in England recognized this orientation and was inclined to regard the work of the Glasgow WPPL as akin to a Friendly Society rather than a bona fide trade union.[7] The decline of its trade union work might therefore be viewed as a natural progression for an organization which was never fully committed to the principles of trade-unionism and the independent activity of working women but whose involvement in that sphere was interpreted as an adjunct of philanthropic endeavour.

One offshoot of the League's trade union work was the formation in 1893 of the National Federal Council for Women's Trades, a federation of labour bodies, with a collective membership of 101,200 consisting of 16 trades councils and 35 other societies, including men's unions in trades employing women, women's unions, and societies representing women's industrial and social interests. The function of the NFCWT was to publicize women's issues, and to co-ordinate and liaise with any groups who professed an interest in the work of the federation and whose support and expertise could be drawn on to give muscle to their campaigns. However, perhaps the most significant achievement of the League was

[6] GTC, *Annual Report, 1893–94*, SRA.
[7] GCWT, *First Annual Report, 1895–96* (Glasgow: GCWT, 1896), SRA, 223–5.

the formation in 1894 of the Glasgow Council for Women's Trades, which in 1900 was renamed the Scottish Council for Women's Trades. The SCWT was the organizational expression of the League's policy of concentrating on legislative action and propaganda work. The WPPL and NFCWT and the SCWT were the central bodies in a network of organizations which were characterized by cross-representation, formal affiliations, and overlapping personnel.

Although the three bodies were organizationally distinct, they did work in conjunction with each other and drew on the same pool of people for their membership. Margaret Irwin, who had been Organizing Secretary of the WPPL, resigned her post to take up the secretaryship of the SCWT, although she still maintained an active presence in the League and was a member of its Executive Council. Officials of the League were usually members of the various committees of the SCWT, whilst the SCWT Council was represented on the Central Executive of the NFCWT.[8] These formal affiliations were buttressed by the overlapping membership of the three organizations, most of which was drawn from the Church, academic institutions, and a variety of voluntary organizations. This dense and expansive network of cross-representations was augmented by their affiliation to a number of social, political, educational, and philanthropic bodies, and mutual representation on their respective committees.

The SCWT made a concerted effort to enlist the support of what they termed 'other sections of the women's movement' in their legislative campaigns and maintained a policy of liberal co-operation with the burgeoning charity and voluntary organizations of the period.[9] The seventh Annual Report of the SCWT noted with satisfaction that a number of its members sat on school boards, parochial boards, and the committees of the Glasgow Union of Women Workers, the Charity Organization Society, the Association for the Return of Women to Local Boards, etc. They were particularly self-congratulatory about their connection with the GUWW, which was essentially a pressure group of middle-class women directed at extending

[8] GCWT, *First Annual Report, 1895–96* (Glasgow: GCWT, 1896), SRA.
[9] SCWT, *Seventh Annual Report, 1901–1902*.

women's influence and employment in public life. This was largely because the affiliated societies of the GUWW included practically all the associations in Glasgow engaged in social and philanthropic work for women and the SCWT would be able to draw on 'the sympathy and influence of many women who [had] not hitherto had this subject brought so directly before them'.[10]

The SCWT was spawned by the WPPL Executive Council's decision that the scope of its work should be extended and developed 'on lines that would include other means for remedying the difficulties and grievances of working women in addition to that of trade organization'.[11] The SCWT became the fulcrum of the organizations devoted to improving the industrial conditions of women workers, concentrating on legislative solutions, whilst the WPPL functioned as its organizing wing. Apart from the representatives from labour organizations, the SCWT's membership was avowedly middle class and included a smattering of titled individuals. The Countess of Aberdeen was Honorary President and the membership of over 100 in 1904 included a number of academics, notably Professor Edward Caird, Master of Balliol, William Smart of Glasgow, and a cluster of Churchmen.[12]

The structure of the SCWT reflected its priorities, being divided into three departments: a Department of Enquiry, which was responsible for investigating and reporting on the conditions of employment among women and children; a Department of Organization, to promote the formation of Women's Trade Unions; and a Parliamentary Bills Committee, to promote legislation in the interests of women and children. The thrust of the SCWT work revolved around its investigative department, which produced a spate of pamphlets and reports of women's work and conditions. These included a report on the problem of home work among women; an inquiry into the conditions of employment amongst charwomen, washerwomen, and cooks; and a report on women's work in the tailoring, printing, and textile trades. The purpose of the reports, which

[10] SCWT, *Seventh Annual Report, 1901–1902*, 19.
[11] GCWT, *First Annual Report, 1895–96*, 5.
[12] SCWT, *Seventh Annual Report, 1904–05*.

218 Women and Trade-Unionism

were based on the careful and systematic investigations of Margaret Irwin, was to build a cast-iron case for legislative action to regulate women's wages, hours, and conditions. The statistics-gathering and investigative work were supplemented by numerous delegations and trade union conferences to muster support for their campaigns.

The SCWT worked in closest harmony with the labour movement over the anti-sweating campaign but it never wavered from its policy of engaging the support of the wealthy and philanthropic. One of its early ventures was to try to get seats for shop assistants because of 'the terrible strain imposed on delicate women and girls of standing on their feet throughout the long, weary hours they were on duty'. It was considered that the most effective way of achieving this was if an appeal to leading shopkeepers was signed and issued by influential women who were large buyers. The SCWT reported that the matter was 'very heartily taken up by Lady Helen Munro Ferguson who sent out very widely among leading firms a circular—signed by her, and by the Duchess of Montrose, and other well known ladies'.[13]

The organizing work of the SCWT had initially been conceived as assisting the trade union work of the WPPL, but gradually the latter's functions were incorporated and modified into the SCWT. This arose out of the failure of the League to make substantial headway in organizing working women and the decision that their efforts should be directed at obtaining legislative change to improve industrial conditions. The SCWT still continued to liaise with trade unions and trades councils and frequently addressed meetings called by unions to organize women. Between 1898 and 1899 Margaret Irwin paid three visits to Edinburgh to address meetings at the invitation of the Typographical Association and other societies and, as a result of her efforts, a union branch of women engaged in the printing trades was formed. In Dunfermline she assisted in the formation of an affiliated branch of the Scottish Mill and Factory Workers' Federal Union, whilst she acted in an informal advisory capacity to the Alva and Tillicoultry textile unions.[14]

---

[13] GCWT, *First Annual Report, 1895–96.*
[14] GCWT, *Fourth Annual Report, 1898–99.*

On a number of occasions the SCWT intervened in disputes
involving women to try to hasten a settlement. During a strike
of the pipe-finishers' branch of the League, a deputation from
the SCWT visited three of the leading employers and succeeded
in obtaining an increase for the women. Usually the prime
concern of the SCWT was to bring the dispute to a close and
then perhaps try to resolve the grievance. It rarely pursued an
aggressive or militant policy and never countenanced using the
strike as a weapon. In the pipe-finishers' dispute, the deputation
emphasized that their success had been in ending the dispute,
and the rise of wages was viewed as a bonus which rounded
off the success of their efforts.

The SCWT did not challenge traditional ideas of separate
sexual spheres nor did they wish to violate women's prescribed
roles. It was accepted that women occupied a separate sphere
which was closely identified with the home and the family,
and that women's involvement in industry was an inevitable
and undesirable consequence of the low wages of men. When
Margaret Irwin addressed a conference of tailors, she prefaced
her remarks by stating that women would not be in the trade
'if men were paid what they should be but since they were,
the men should make the best of the situation [and] organize
the women'.[15] Although there were references to the objective
conditions which inhibited trade union organization amongst
women, there was a general acceptance of the idea that women
were unorganized because they were docile and apathetic. The
Reverend Laughlin, the Organizing Secretary of the Council,
maintained that one of the major obstacles to organizing
women was that they worked for 'pin money' and 'under these
circumstances the amount earned is not of prime importance'.[16]
In his view an additional impediment was the fact that most
women workers were marking time until they embarked on
their true vocation of marriage. The consequence of these
factors had the effect of inducing women 'to dumbly acquiesce
in the prevailing state of things—inadequate pay, unduly long
hours, and insanitary surroundings, and they refuse, or at all
events look askance, at efforts to agitate (which the very fact of

[15] SNAOT, *Twenty-Second Annual Report, 1898*, NLS.
[16] SCWT, *Seventh Annual Report, 1904–05*.

joining a union implies) for their removal, and the general elevation and upraising of their class'.[17] Whatever explanations were afforded, the confluence of opinion was that women themselves were responsible for both the state of their wages and the weakness of their trade union organization. At a public meeting in Glasgow held to extend trade-unionism amongst women, the contributions of Lady Mary Murray, Professor G. A. Smith, and Robert Smillie of the Miners' Federation all emphasized the fact that 'the lack of effective organization of the women workers is largely due to their own apathy'.[18]

Women were very much regarded as the weak link in the chain of labour organization, because they allowed themselves to be used as cheap labour. There was obviously genuine concern to improve the conditions of women workers, although this was often allied to a desire to improve their moral, social, and intellectual condition. One cannot underestimate the efforts of individuals like Margaret Irwin, who devoted a lifetime to attempts to improve the lot of working women. However, the SCWT did not challenge long-standing assumptions about the nature of the sexual division of labour nor connect 'the traditionally low wage of women' to her domestic role. Although it was acknowledged that a woman's domestic burdens made it more difficult for her to attend meetings to fulfil the minimum requirements of trade union membership, the pattern of her exploitation in the workplace and the assumption that women should earn less was never seen as conditioned by her role in the family. Women were still identified primarily in relation to the family, even when they were engaged in full-time labour, and the prevailing ideology of the prior importance of men's work was never questioned. Therefore, the SCWT tended to view the 'problem' of women workers from the perspective of the men and to advocate solutions which confirmed women's inferior position in the labour market. Their concern was directed as much at protecting men's wages and work from 'the disorganized competition' of women as it was to strive to improve the conditions of women.

[17] SCWT, *Seventh Annual Report, 1904–05.*
[18] WPPL, *Annual Report, 1897.*

The question of organizing women produced a variety of proposals which ranged from establishing separate unions for them to incorporating them into the men's unions as either equal or subordinate members. Whatever scheme was projected, cognizance was always taken of the prior rights of the male workers and was underpinned by what would best serve their interests.

The spokeswoman and the driving force behind the SCWT, Margaret Irwin, who was its Organizing Secretary throughout its forty-four years of existence, was the only daughter of Captain James Irwin of Broughty Ferry. She was educated at Queen Margaret College, Glasgow, and spent some time as a student of Glasgow School of Art and St Andrews University where she obtained a degree.[19] Despite her close ties with labour organizations and her devotion to the cause of women workers, she never really broke with the traditions of middle-class philanthropy. Her political philosophy was more liberal than socialist and she did not display any great enthusiasm for the trade union movement's goal of independent labour representation. In industrial affairs she was equally moderate, favouring conciliation and compromise and regarding strikes as 'uncivilized'. Nevertheless, she maintained a cordial relationship with both the Glasgow Trades Council and the Scottish Trades Union Congress. In 1897 the STUC altered a Congress Standing Order to enable the SCWT and the WPPL to send delegates to the Congress[20] and, certainly until the First World War, Margaret Irwin was usually among the SCWT's delegation. She was unanimously elected Secretary of the first STUC and at the second Congress she was presented with a silver tea service in recognition of her work for the Scottish labour movement.[21] This loyalty to Margaret Irwin is particularly pertinent as her appointment as Assistant Commissioner on the Royal Commission on Labour (Women's Employment) was regarded with disfavour by some sections of the British labour movement.[22]

[19] *Glasgow Herald*, 22 Jan. 1940, Obituary Notice, Margaret Irwin.
[20] S. Lewenhak, *Women and Trade Unions* (London: Benn, 1977), 105.
[21] STUC, *Report of the Second Annual Congress, 1898*, NLS.
[22] GTC, *Annual Report, 1893–94*.

Relations between the STUC and Margaret Irwin were not always cordial and there were areas where her lack of commitment to class politics created tensions and rifts between her and the union movement. Although she was a member of the STUC's Parliamentary Committee, and for a time its Secretary, she was criticized for her lack of commitment to the Eight-Hour Bill and for her failure, in her annual report, to give prominence to the committee's efforts to promote independent labour representation.[23] She was an active campaigner for women's suffrage and a firm believer that women should receive the vote on the same basis as men. This commitment was reinforced by her belief that legislation was necessary to remove the grievances of women workers and therefore women should have some say in the making of the laws. Although, at their first Congress, the STUC gave support to a motion proposed by Margaret Irwin for equal franchise for women, they reversed this decision at their next conference in favour of universal adult suffrage. Their argument was that, since the franchise was based on a property qualification, the vote of the upper and middle classes would be strengthened if it was extended to women on the same limited basis. In opposing the motion for universal adult suffrage, Margaret Irwin argued that it was a tactical question: 'They were all in favour of a large extension of the suffrage, but they did not think that the best way of bringing that about was to introduce the thick end of the wedge first.'[24]

However, there can be no doubt that Margaret Irwin's priorities were dictated more by her commitment to women than by her loyalty to any class-based organization. She was certainly sympathetic to the general principles of trade-unionism and more particularly to championing the cause of women workers, but this concern was underpinned by a philanthropic philosophy which denied the fundamental conflict between capital and labour. She saw no contradiction in arguing that middle-class women should be enfranchised to allow them 'a direct vote in the making of the laws which

---

[23] Lewenhak, *Women and Trade Unions*, 106.
[24] STUC, *Report of the Second Annual Congress, 1898*.

so seriously affect them'[25] when the laws she was referring to related to industrial conditions of working-class women. In time the philanthropic strain in her philosophy eclipsed her commitment to working through the institutions of labour, and the mainspring of her life's work, the desire to improve the conditions of women, was expressed through works of charity. She was instrumental in securing reform for the improvement of housing conditions of women workers in potato lifting, fish curing, and fruit gathering, and, at Blairgowrie in Perthshire, she ran a fruit farm where women could work 'under ideal conditions'.[26]

Althought the SCWT was a good deal more than Margaret Irwin, she embodied the mentality and philosophy of the organization. The SCWT had been drawn into co-operation with the organizations of labour as a means of improving the moral and intellectual life of women workers so that they would be better equipped to help themselves instead of relying on others. Trade unions were valued for their 'civilizing' functions and for the contribution they could make, not only to moral elevation but to promoting the efficiency of labour. The retreat of charity work was an inevitable result of the increasing polarization between labour and the progressive middle classes. The industrial, political, and social conflicts of the pre-war years brought to the surface the fundamental differences between the aspirations of the SCWT and the labour movement. As it became evident that the classes could not be reconciled by the mediation of sympathetic middle-class philanthropists, the SCWT, acknowledging its irrelevance in this scene, elected to devote its energies to philanthropic work outside the organizations and institutions of the labour movement.

The activities of the Glasgow WPPL and the SCWT were paralleled by the efforts of the London-based Women's Trade Union League to organize in Scotland. The WTUL, like the Glasgow WPPL, was an offshoot of the English WPPL, which had been founded by Emma Paterson in 1874.[27] The change

[25] STUC, *Report of the First Annual Congress, 1897.*
[26] *Glasgow Herald*, 22 Jan. 1940, Obituary Notice, Margaret Irwin.
[27] See Ch. 3.

of name in 1891 coincided with a shift in policy as the new WTUL shed its provident aspect and concentrated more on trade union organization. Clementina Black was appointed Secretary of the WTUL and Lady Dilke the Chairwoman, and a scheme was devised whereby any union which admitted women could affiliate to the League for ½*d.* per year per female member. Although the WTUL and the Glasgow WPPL never came into direct conflict, they tended to have different activities and it was fairly clear that the English-based League saw itself fulfilling a different role from the Glasgow organization. The WTUL was anxious to be accepted as a bona fide trade union rather than an organization of middle-class philanthropists. At a meeting in Glasgow in 1892, held under the auspices of the Glasgow Trades Council, Lady Dilke made it clear that the purpose of organizing women was to enable them to be self-supporting so that they could be free from middle-class patronage and improve their conditions by independent activity. She urged them to do away 'with those ladies and gentlemen who wanted to manage them for their own ends. Use these if found useful, take their money and use them as servants . . . Put these people on one side. Let the women take care. They were quite as independent as the men.'[28] This was perhaps intended as a side-swipe at the Glasgow WPPL, which was holding a meeting that same evening in another hall in Glasgow. Certainly a proposal that the two meetings should combine fell through and the comment of the *Women's Trade Union Review*, the official organ of the WTUL, was that this was to be expected 'seeing the considerable difference existing in the character and the work of the two societies'.[29] If there was an absence of co-operation and joint activity between the two organizations, there was also little animosity. Amongst those on the platform of the Glasgow WPPL meeting was Clementina Black, the Secretary of the WTUL. Although the WTUL had its fair share of middle-class activists, they were individuals who were more committed to the labour movement and less influenced by the mentality of charity organizations than the members of the Glasgow WPPL. Therefore, the

[28] Reported in the *Glasgow Herald*, 7 Sept. 1892.
[29] *WTUR* 7 (Oct. 1892).

WTUL would be reluctant to associate with an organization so reliant on middle-class patronage, lest they be tarred with the same brush and lose credibility with the trade union movement.

Until the early years of the twentieth century, the WTUL combined the goal of trade union organization of women with attempts to secure legislative reform. In the latter sphere it claimed to be instrumental in obtaining the 1895 Factory Act, the 1904 Regulation of Conditions of Home Work Act, and the Shop Hours Act of 1906.[30] However, it devoted much time and energy to trade union organization and it is a mark of its success and tenacity that a London-based organization was able to penetrate not only beyond the border, but beyond the large urban centres, and establish unions in small towns and country districts.

Although in 1892 the League claimed that the bulk of its work outside the provinces was carried on in Lancashire, Yorkshire, and the west of Scotland, by 1897 it had built up a base throughout Scotland and could claim affiliated unions in Aberdeen, Edinburgh, Glasgow, Ayr, Paisley, and many east coast towns. Textile unions figured prominently in the League's membership in the border burghs, who belonged to a number of separate organizations.[31] The League also claimed to have assisted in the formation of the Tillicoultry Textile Workers' Union and the Carnoustie Factory Workers' Union. However, organization was by no means confined to textile workers and, by the beginning of the twentieth century, the League's membership, reflecting the widening sphere of women's employment, included women in the service and white-collar sectors. By 1903 the League could boast affiliated unions of shop assistants, warehousemen, and clerks in Aberdeen[32] and Edinburgh, and in 1906 an organizing tour resulted in the formation of branches of the National Association of Telephone Operators in Dundee and branches of the National Society of Telephone Employees in Aberdeen and Glasgow.[33]

[30] Lewenhak, *Women and Trade Unions*, 81.
[31] WTUL, *Twenty-Third Annual Report, 1897*, SRA.
[32] WTUL, *Twenty-Ninth Annual Report, 1904*.
[33] WTUL, *Thirty-First Annual Report, 1906*.

The WTUL was able to boost its membership by dint of vigorous organizing campaigns, which included sending speakers and organizers throughout the country. In 1891 the autumn tour of the League visited Kirriemuir, Forfar, Aberdeen, Alva, Kirkcaldy, and Edinburgh,[34] and the Secretary's tour in 1906 involved a week's organizing in Brechin as well as addressing meetings of most of the affiliated unions in Scotland.

In spite of these effects, it was still the case that the vast majority of women workers were untouched by trade union organization and, although the League was often able to set up separate women's societies, they rarely lasted any length of time.

The stated claim of the WTUL was to free working women from the yoke of middle-class patronage and to encourage their independent organization. However, the unintended outcome of their policies was to substitute the work of professional organizers for the activity of rank-and-file women. Strikes were certainly given more support than organizations such as the Glasgow WPPL had been willing to give, but they were rarely celebrated as examples of class solidarity or class action but rather viewed as potential recruiting grounds for the League's societies. It was obviously desirable that any expression of discontent or raw anger be given direction and deposit some organizational residue, but the League seemed to regard implantation of the organization as primary. They were likely to take over the reins of a dispute and it was usually League organizers who negotiated with employers and attempted to secure settlements. Women were often chastised for going on strike too soon or too often and for placing the organization in jeopardy. If trade union organization was deemed not to be robust enough to cope with a confrontation, strikers were counselled to return to work rather than to mobilize more support and attempt to galvanize other workers and workplaces into action. It was therefore not surprising that the League was usually unable to sustain any union organization which emerged from these struggles and that, once a League organizer left a locality, there followed a rapid disintegration of the union.

---

[34] WTUL, *Thirty-First Annual Report, 1906.*

Much of the League's dynamism was provided by Mary MacArthur and there is little doubt that WTUL organization was given a fillip with her appointment as Secretary in 1903. She was born in 1880 in Glasgow, the daughter of a prosperous draper and, by the time she was 15, the family had settled in Ayr.[35] She worked for a time as a bookkeeper in her father's firm and her initial encounter with trade-unionism was the product of accident rather than design or any deep-seated commitment to its principles. The local Conservative newspaper asked her to write a satirical piece on a meeting organized by the Shop Assistants' Union, but the scheme backfired and she returned from the meeting totally converted to the aims of the trade union movement, as she later commented: 'I went to a meeting at Ayr to write a skit on the proceedings. Going to scoff, I remained to pray. I became impressed with the truth and meaning of the Labour movement.'[36]

By 1902 she had been elected President of the Scottish National District Council of the Shop Assistants' Union.[37] As a result of the close links the Scottish group had with various socialist societies her trade-unionism became fleshed out with socialist politics and she, in time, joined the Independent Labour Party. It is a measure of the WTUL's limited influence in Scotland that Mary MacArthur was unfamiliar with its work when Margaret Bondfield of the Shop Assistants' Union proposed her for the post of the League Secretary in London.

Her enthusiasm and organizational skills injected the League with new vitality. She proclaimed that it was necessary to seek women workers out rather than to expect them to come to the League. Although the WTUL had a policy of organizing public meetings, speaking tours, etc., under Mary MacArthur's secretaryship this was supplemented by a more informal approach, and factory gate meetings and distributing leaflets and handbills became regular features of the League's activities. In an address to the American Women's Trade Union League, she explained the process of organizing for a meeting:

---

[35] M. A. Hamilton, *Mary MacArthur* (London: Leonard Parsons, 1925), 6.
[36] Ibid. 7.   [37] Ibid. 14.

Bills were printed, asking such elementary questions as: 'Do you want higher wages?' 'Do you want shorter hours?' followed by several big query marks, and then we say, 'If you want these things, come to our meeting.' We had a number of tickets printed, 'Admit bearer to social evening and conference at such and such a hall. Complimentary ticket, Reserved.' At the end, 'No seats reserved after 7.45.' With these bills and tickets we go to the factories. We are careful beforehand to find out something about the conditions at the factory. It is no good talking generalities to a number of girls who are rushing out of factories to get meals. It is no good talking about human welfare or the future of the race. They will not understand. You have got to talk about why they should be fined twopence or threepence a week or why the employer does not pay for the thread. These small things interest them more. We find out the special grievance in the factory; we get a chair, and somebody gets up on it and two people stand around with the complimentary tickets. You begin: 'Why are you paying for whalebone?'. 'Do you think you ought to have thread found?'. Of course they are interested. Then we talk. We don't open with long speeches but short and to the point. We tell something briefly, about conditions in the well organized trades, and say: 'if you want to hear more, come to the meeting to-morrow night. It will be very crowded, but we've got a few tickets. If you come early you will get a seat.' Of course there is a frightful scramble for the tickets.[38]

This kind of effort obviously stimulated trade union organization amongst women but the League encountered a perennial problem of, once having recruited the women, holding on to them. Although Mary MacArthur recognized the necessity of an organization directed specifically at women workers, she regarded it as a temporary expedient which stemmed from their organizational weakness. Her frequently quoted observation was that 'Women are badly paid and badly treated because they are not organized and they are not organized because they are badly paid and badly treated'.[39] To her, women workers were the same as men, with the same problems and the same grievances, and they required the same solutions for resolving them. If there was a difference between men and women, it was quantitative rather than qualitative.

Women were more difficult to organize because they were badly paid. The solution, therefore, was to raise their wages. The catch was that this required organization. She never acknowledged that women's work experience was qualitatively different from men's or that it required a special approach which took account of the fact that the sexual division of labour in society patterned and conditioned both women's experience of waged labour and their response to exploitation. Campaigning around women's low pay and bad conditions was obviously the central issue, but, by diagnosing it as the root of the problem, rather than as a manifestation of the wider problem of women's inequality in society generally, the League never tackled the other issues which related to women and which gave to their working life its special characteristics.

Frustration over the League's inability to sustain union organization amongst women led to the formation in 1906 of the National Federation of Women Workers. The purpose of the NFWW was to provide a national organization open to all women who were not admitted to the appropriate union in their trade. It was felt that by affiliation to a central body the women would gain a sense of solidarity and overcome the demoralization and isolation which characterized their trades. The WTUL and the NFWW maintained close links, in that Mary MacArthur remained Secretary of the WTUL whilst assuming the position of President in the new NFWW, and the League was also represented on its executive. By the end of 1906 the NFWW claimed to have over 2,000 members and seventeen branches in Scotland and England. Women were always urged to join a men's trade union where it existed and when they were eligible, and affiliation to the NFWW was advocated only when there was no alternative. The Federation was affiliated to both the Trades Union Congress and the General Federation of Trade Unionists. By 1908 it claimed to have two million trade-unionists behind it and funds of over £250,000.[40]

The Federation was not only more firmly based in the working-class movement than any other organization which

---

[40] Quoted in M. A. Hamilton, *Mary MacArthur* (London: Leonard Parsons, 1925), 56.

was involved with organizing women, it spoke in the language of aggressive trade-unionism and appealed to a sense of class solidarity. The benefits of trade-unionism were couched less in terms of moral or spiritual uplift than in terms of realizing the collective strength of the working class. Through the columns of the *Woman Worker*, the Federation's newspaper, Mary MacArthur appealed to women to join trade unions: 'Organization gives courage and a new strength. By means of organization the dumb can speak, the public can be aroused, the employers approached, factory laws enforced. Parliament compelled to move and freedom slowly won.'[41]

Unequivocal support was given to the demand for equal pay and as always this was guided by a concern to promote working-class unity. Trade-unionism was seen as a vehicle for creating co-operation between men and women workers by cutting across and transcending sex differences. In appealing to male trade-unionists to support equal pay it was argued that failure to do so weakened class solidarity and undermined the potential strength of the whole labour movement:

No justice can be imposed upon women that will not in the end re-act disastrously upon men. Take one instance. Woman was never welcomed in the industrial arena. The man wage-earner watched her entrance sullenly. He resented her intrusion into spheres of work and activity in which he had previously held unchallenged sway. He tried to close the door of his trade in her face. And sometimes succeeded. He did close the door of his Trade Union. Women got no encouragement, no help to make a stand for equal wages for equal work. What happened? . . . They became unwittingly the instruments whereby the wages of men were lowered. The problem of their competition grew more and more acute, until at last the men recognised the folly of this Mrs Partington policy. Now every intelligent Trade Unionist is glad to help in the work of organizing women workers.[42]

Support for equal pay was therefore couched in terms of the protection of men from unfair competition, as much as the right of women to equal pay. Indeed support for equal pay, minimum wages, and the anti-sweating campaign was always framed in terms of their wider social benefits, rather than

[41] *Woman Worker*, 19 June 1908.   [42] Ibid., 12 June 1908.

simply the benefits to women workers. These demands were the indirect means of shaking out of the labour market married women and those workers whose low wages threatened to pull down the general rate. As Barbara Hutchins argued: 'the extension of employent under fair conditions will benefit the sweated workers not only directly, in so far as they themselves obtain employment under those conditions, but indirectly, as the payment of fair wages to the men employed would lessen the competition for work by married women'.[43]

The anti-sweating campaign, whilst referring to the physically debilitating effects on women of working in unhealthy conditions, focused on the 'undermining of family life by the degradation of the home into a workshop'.[44] These concerns were stoked by contemporary fears about the falling birth-rate and the health and national efficiency of the race, which also underlay demands for state support for motherhood and family allowance.[45]

Although there was sympathy with the aim of the suffragettes to extend the franchise to women, the *Woman Worker* chose to align itself with the labour movement and support universal adult suffrage. In 1909 Mary MacArthur became Honorary Secretary of a new society, the People's Suffrage Federation, which took the view that 'If the House of Commons is to represent the people truly, every man and woman must have the vote independent of property and tenancy.'[46] Again this policy stemmed from a commitment to class politics rather than feminism but it was also a reflection of Mary MacArthur's philosophy that to treat women differently or to identify them as having special needs would undermine the solidarity between men and women which she was so anxious to promote. As her biographer claimed, 'She had far too sure a belief in the comradeship of the sexes to be a feminist.'[47]

[43] B. L. Hutchins, 'Homework and Sweating: The Causes and the Remedies', Fabian Society Tract, No. 130 (London: Fabian Society, 1908).

[44] Mrs Sidney Webb, 'Women and the Factory Acts', Fabian Society Tract, No. 67 (London: Fabian Society, 1896).

[45] Sidney Webb, 'The Decline in the Birth-Rate', Fabian Society Tract, No. 131 (London: Fabian Society, 1913); A. Davin, 'Imperialism and Motherhood', *History Workshop Journal*, 5 (Spring 1978).

[46] *Woman Worker*, 27 Oct. 1909.

[47] Hamilton, *Mary MacArthur*, 202.

In the years leading up to the First World War, the Federation became the focus of women's unionism in Scotland. The Glasgow WPPL and the SCWT had more or less ditched their organizational activities and sunk their efforts into obtaining legislative reform, which left the field open for the WTUL and the Federation to work in tandem. In Glasgow in 1910, the Federation had one branch of 250 and another of cardboard box makers with a membership of 200. Branches of the League or the Federation had also been set up in Paisley, Johnstone, Dundee, and Hawick.

The period of 'labour unrest' between 1910 and 1914, which resulted in an upsurge of trade union growth, was reflected in the membership of the Federation and the League. By 1911 the NFWW had appointed Kate McLean and Agnes Brown as full-time officials of the union in Scotland,[48] and for the first time the Federation had a delegation to the STUC's conference in Dundee.[49] Branches of the Federation continued to sprout up in the aftermath of a dispute and in this way branches were established in Neilston and Kilbirnie. Organizing campaigns were still a feature of the Federation's work and eight separate branches with a total membership of 1,500 were established in Alexandria in 1911, after a vigorous recruiting drive. They were joined by branches in Dalry, Kilwinning, Airdrie, and Larkhall, which were formed in the same year.[50]

Although both the WTUL and the NFWW never abandoned their trade union work, increasingly they looked to Parliament rather than trade union action to promote changes in industrial life. Mary MacArthur's priorities became the anti-sweating campaign and, allied to it, the campaign for wages boards and a minimum wage. At the end of 1908 she surrendered the editorship of the *Woman Worker* so that she could more completely devote her energies to these issues.[51] Increasingly her time was taken up with parliamentary questions and agitation around legislation rather than around organization. This necessarily meant that activity focused more on lobbying

[48] WTUL, *Thirty-Sixth Annual Report, 1911*.
[49] STUC, *Fifteenth Annual Report, 1911*.
[50] WTUC, *Thirty-Sixth Annual Report, 1911*.
[51] Hamilton, *Mary MacArthur*, 75.

influential and prominent individuals than on mobilizing mass action: 'every day of her life she had to draft questions, scan the columns of Hansard, follow proceedings upstairs, in committee, and on the floor of the House. Very soon, she became a familiar figure in the lobbies.'[52]

Mary MacArthur had always recognized the need for political action and her trade union work was always informed and influenced by socialist politics. She had never been a revolutionary socialist but rather had envisaged the transformation of society as the product of a gradual accretion of reforms. But increasingly her politics became less rooted in a commitment to class action and more influenced by notions of inter-class co-operation. This may have been a product of her association with the WTUL, whose leadership was still dominated by the middle classes, or of her commitment to legislative reform, which involved lobbying MPs of all parties and seeking support from all sympathetic sections of the community. Certainly her biographer claimed that:

The Trade Union League itself was an object lesson in social co-operation. Its members belonged to all parties . . . They came from all classes though the middle class decidedly predominated. Differing on many points, they came together for practical work. With them in mind, tirades against the bourgeoisie became unreal: an idle interruption of the task. If, in her early, slap-dash enthusiasm, she had been inclined to despise the members of the Executive, associations with such women as Lady Dilke and Miss Tuckwell, in whom wide culture was a spur to, not a brake on, an intense and unremitting devotion to the cause of the less fortunate, taught her much.[53]

The turn to legislative work also sprung from the League's conception of women workers as essentially weak and powerless. When Mona Wilson resigned from the secretaryship of the League in 1903, the committee agreed that they had to find an organizer who would rouse the 'underpaid and helpless women workers', although it seemed a task which was 'well-nigh hopeless',[54] whilst Lady Dilke spoke of 'the joy of knowing that by our efforts we have brought the feeble, the

[52] Hamilton, *Mary MacArthur*, 44.   [53] Ibid. 43.   [54] Ibid. 27.

ignorant and the lonely to feel that they are not alone'.[55] Yet women workers had demonstrated time and again by their willingness to strike that their discontent and anger could erupt into a display of collective action which demonstrated a potential for struggle and solidarity. If that potential was not harnessed to the institutions of labour and given organizational form, perhaps it was as much because of the nature of trade-unionism as with the 'weakness' of the women.

There can be no doubt that the League performed pioneering work in the trade union organization of women. Frequently, in Scotland, this was done with the co-operation and assistance of the male trade union movement. However, the sustained work of agitation and the day-to-day minutiae of organization were shouldered by the WTUL and the NFWW. They recognized that the double burden of women and their domestic role made it more difficult to become involved in trade union affairs and presented obstacles not encountered by male workers. More significantly they recognized the need for special organizational apparatus and propaganda directed specifically at women. However, they made no attempt to tackle the conditions which created these difficulties and were content to confine their concerns within the traditional boundaries of trade union issues rather than push for particular reforms which would benefit women workers. For example, they made no demands around the question of women's reproductive role such as birth control, maternity rights, and child care facilities. This contrasted with the approach of the Russian women socialists to organizing women. In an interview in *Woman Worker* in 1909 Alexandra Kollontai argued that, to organize women successfully, it was necessary to address questions which specifically affected them and mentioned that maternity rights was one of the issues which they had taken up.[56] Similarly, the Confédération Générale du Travail, the French union, had considerable success in recruiting women by addressing such issues.[57]

[55] Hamilton, *Mary MacArthur*, 76.
[56] *Woman Worker*, 19 May 1909, 469.
[57] Patricia Hilden, *Working Women and Socialist Politics in France 1880–1914* (Oxford: Clarendon Press, 1986), ch. 6.

Most of the leadership of the League accepted the view that married women's work outside the home was undesirable, that they had no inalienable 'right to work', and that their proper sphere was the home. Married women's presence in the labour force was, for the middle-class members of the League, a flaw in capitalism, a manifestation of a temporary breakdown in social organization which could be remedied without the transformation of the social structure; whilst for the socialist women in the League, like Mary MacArthur, it pointed up the inefficiency and the brutality of capitalism. Part of the struggle for socialism was to ensure that woman could more properly perform her 'natural' role by ensuring that husbands earned enough to support their wives and children, at home and in comfort.

It is therefore not surprising that there was no onslaught on the ideology of domesticity and separate sexual spheres. However, adherence to this ideology, which conceived of women as primarily dependants, militated against the WTUL campaigning on the right of single women, who had to support themselves, to work for the same wages as men, and from organizing to facilitate employment for the many women with dependants, who needed to work. For many married women work was a financial necessity and either a permanent or an intermittent part of their life, yet the League did not extend the range of trade union issues to encompass policies which would make it easier for women with children to remain in employment. There was a recognition by these unions that organizing women required different strategies, and, in this sense, they provided a more supportive institutional framework for women workers. However, men's primacy in the labour market was never questioned and this was reflected in both the ideology and the organizational practice of these organizations, whose strategic concerns were shaped by the dominant strand of male trade-unionism and the familial ideology of the broader working-class movement.

Working-class women may not have consciously sought to challenge these views and undermine the ideology of separate spheres. However, the experience and the economic necessity of working engendered a more pragmatic acceptance of this ideology amongst working women. The response of the female coalpickers of Lanarkshire to charges that their work was 'most unsuitable for women' was probably typical of many working women. They claimed that they 'did not dislike the work, and in any case there was nothing else in Blantyre that they could turn their hands to'.[58]

There were some women who were more assertive about their right to work, and who consciously challenged the domestic ideal and sought economic independence, such as the Edinburgh printer who chastised John Wheatley, a leading member of the Independent Labour Party, for his support for legislation to exclude women from the pit-brow: 'Woman no longer believes her one niche in life is motherhood, she longs to do her share of the world's work to assist in its education, add to its store of literature, art and science.'[59]

The stance of the 400 Edinburgh women compositors to the male union's claims for a ban on further recruitment of female labour most clearly captures the ambiguities in women's modified perception of men and women's position in industry. The women issued their own memorial arguing that:

we, as representing a large number of the women compositors of Edinburgh, feel that a question affecting a considerable body of women should not be settled without these women having an opportunity of giving expression to their views.

That while recognising that the men have had a real grievance in that some firms have employed an unfair proportion of young girls at apprentice wages, or nearly so, *we women* regard it as a great injustice that one of the main skilled industries open to Edinburgh women should be closed against them.

That *we women* feel the fact that women have been employed in Edinburgh as compositors for nearly forty years gives women a claim on the business. That up to the time in Edinburgh, the monotype machines have largely, if not chiefly, been operated by women, and that women have proved themselves entirely competent to work these machines, so that it seems a great hardship that women should be debarred from working at them in future.

That since we have realised the position of women in the printing trade is seriously threatened, *we women* have been trying to organise

[58] Quoted in Royal Commission on Labour, *The Employment of Women* C. 6894, vol. 23 (London: HMSO, 1893), 186.
[59] *Glasgow Forward*, 30 Sept. 1911.

ourselves with a view to securing justice for ourselves and for the women who may in future desire to practise the business of compositors or monotypists.

That in view of the foregoing consideration we ask you . . . to urge the Masters' Association to delay any decision hurtful to the interests of women compositors until the women's case has been given full consideration.[60]

The 'We Women' memorial clearly cannot be read as an aggressive assertion of women's right to work and to an equal place on the industrial stage. Rather the use of the term 'injustice' conveys a sense of special pleading and an implicit recognition that men had a greater eligibility to work. None the less the tone of the memorial also suggests that the female printers subscribed to the belief that, where women had carved out a niche for themselves in industry, they should be allowed to occupy it, unassailed by the proprietorial claims of male trade-unionists.

Whatever the contradictions and ambiguities surrounding women's paid labour, women workers did not seem to share the view of them as weak and powerless as they continued to strike and argue their case vociferously and publicly. As previously, the women workers who took collective action to redress their grievances usually went on strike without the formal sanction of trade-unionism. Indeed the pattern of women's strikes from the beginning of the twentieth century indicates that the majority of disputes involved non-unionized workers, although union organization was often established during a strike, or in the wake of one.

The history of industrial relations in the early years of the twentieth century until the First World War is dominated by the years 1910 to 1914, which are commonly referred to as the period of 'labour unrest'. There are a number of competing interpretations of the significance of this period.[61] However,

[60] Quoted in C. Cockburn, *Brothers* (London: Pluto, 1983), 156.
[61] See R. Holton, *British Syndicalism, 1900–1914* (London: Pluto, 1976); E. H. Phelps-Brown, *The Growth of British Industrial Relations* (London: Macmillan, 1959); H. Pelling, 'The Triple Industrial Alliance in 1914', *Economic History Review*, 24(1) (1971); R. Price, 'New Unionism and the Labour Process', Paper delivered to the German Historical Institute Conference (May 1981), in W. Mommsen and G. H. G. Hubung (eds.), *The Development of Trade Unionism in Great Britain and Germany, 1880–1914* (London: Allen and Unwin, 1985).

238 Women and Trade-Unionism

the officially recorded statistics indicate an upsurge in industrial struggle which far exceeded the dimensions of the period of 'New Unionism', twenty-five years earlier.[62] The number of strikers, strike days, and stoppages was substantially above the peaks recorded in any previous year and this was accompanied by an unprecedented increase in the number of trade-unionists which surpassed the achievements of 1889-91 in absolute if not relative terms.[63]

The pattern of women's strikes in Scotland for this period does not indicate such a marked increase in the scale of industrial struggle, but this can partly be attributed to the lacunae in the officially compiled statistics which are a record of 'Principal Disputes' and which concentrate almost exclusively on disputes in the major textile industries in which women worked. Given the diversification of women's employment by the beginning of the twentieth century, the number of strikes is certainly underestimated. Newspapers carry many reports of strikes during this period which do not appear in the official statistics but which were often protracted and involved substantial numbers of homeworkers. This included strikes of women woodyard workers in Bo'ness, bleachworkers in Neilston, bleach- and dyeworkers in Cowdenbeath, cardboard box makers in Glasgow, sailcloth workers in Edinburgh, and textile workers in Kirkcaldy.[64] Although this underrepresentation in the officially recorded disputes was not specific to women's strikes, it is possible that the problem of omission was more acute for their strikes. Reporting of strikes was not obligatory, but left to the voluntary co-operation of the involved parties. As women strikers were often not represented by a union, and as many of the strikes were lightning affairs, they may not have regarded them as worthy of official notification, even if they satisfied the official inclusion criterion of 300 or more working days lost.

The unreliability of the official statistics obviously imposes limitations on the generalizations which can be made about

---

62 R. Hyman, 'Mass Organisations and Militancy in Britain: Contrasts and Continuities, 1888-1914', Paper delivered to the German Historical Institute Conference (May 1981), in Mommsen and Hubung (eds.), *The Development of Trade Unionism in Great Britain and Germany*. 63 Ibid. 11.
    64 *Glasgow Forward*, various issues, 1910 and 1911.

TABLE 6.1. *The pattern of women's strikes, 1890–1913*

Year[a]	No. of strikes which included women	Average length (days)	No. of women
1890–1[b]	8	n/a	n/a
1892	9	8.2	n/a
1893	5	5.4	n/a
1894	14	7.4	4,728
1895	10	3.3	33,163
1896	23	3.3	2,799
1897	19	6.5	2,319
1898	14	9.9	1,313
1899	13	8.4	35,962
1900	10	22.9	1,679
1902	7	8.0	1,278
1903	6	28.0	1,124
1904	2	6.5	600
1905	4	4.8	3,267
1906	5	6.0	22,450
1907	10	20.5	6,953
1909	3	27.7	603
1910	3	11.3	2,062
1911	8	20.6	5,582
1912	11	18.8	42,591
1913	13	26.0	4,689

n/a = not available.
[a]No strikes recorded in 1901 and 1908.
[b]The sources for these statistics were local newspapers.
Source: Annual Reports by the Chief Labour Correspondent on Strikes and Lockouts in the United Kingdom, 1892–1913.

strike statistics during this period. However, it is possible that they can still reveal broad trends in strike patterns. The incidence of officially recorded stoppages of women workers in the years 1911, 1912, and 1913 is certainly greater than the previous nine years with the exception of 1907; but, during the last decade of the nineteenth century, there were a number of occasions when the number of strikes far exceeded the peaks of the period of 'labour unrest' (Table 6.1).[65] However, the statistics do reveal that women's strikes in the immediate pre-war years were on average longer and involved greater numbers

[65] Annual Reports by the Chief Labour Correspondent on Strikes and Lockouts in the United Kingdom, 1892–1913.

than the years from 1892 till 1910. In 1912 there were 42,591 women strikers and an aggregate of 800,710 strike days lost compared with the previous peak of 35,962 and 302,000 strike days in 1899, which was largely attributable to one strike in Dundee (Table 6.1).[66] This pattern reflects the general trends exhibited by the rest of the industrial workforce of larger and more protracted disputes between 1910 and 1914.[67] There were three major issues involved in the disputes of women workers: straightforward wage demands, bad material, and resistance to the intensification of work pressure, with wage demands predominating. In 1912, 9 out of 11 disputes related to wage demands and, in 1913, 10 of the 13 recorded stoppages were for wage increases.[68] The most striking contrast with the previous twenty years was the fact that disputes over wages were generally for increases rather than against reductions and the issue of union recognition first emerged in 1910. Strikes resisting the intensification of work pressure, changed working arrangements, or disciplinary issues were a constant feature in the years between the two explosive phases of collective struggle. However they predominated in the 1890s and declined in significance in the early years of the twentieth century.

In very general terms the contours of women's strikes corresponded with the dominant pattern, in that they were protracted and involved large numbers of workers. However, one of the distinctive features of the labour unrest was the unofficial nature of many of the disputes, which led an official of the Board of Trade to observe that there were 'more differences between the men and their leaders than between the latter and employers'.[69] Given that the majority of women were not members of trade unions and indeed were on occasion striking for trade union recognition, their strikes could not be described as 'unofficial' or related to growing dissatisfaction with existing practices of collective bargaining.

The general economic context of the unrest was the threat to British capital from the growth of foreign competition and

---

[66] Annual Reports by the Chief Labour Correspondent on Strikes and Lockouts in the United Kingdom, 1892–1913.

[67] Hyman, 'Mass Organisations and Militancy in Britain', 12.

[68] Annual Reports on Strikes and Lockouts, 1892–1913.

[69] Quoted in K. Burgess, *The Challenge of Labour* (London: Croom Helm, 1980).

the adoption by British employers of a number of diverse strategies in order to maintain profits. One consequence of this trend was a sustained period of falling real wages from 1900, which provoked widespread discontent over living standards and accounts for the predominance of wage disputes in the unrest. There were, however, a complex range of factors underlying the upsurge of militancy in this period, and so it is not possible to specify a universal source of the disputes. Women's strikes had more to do with wages and working conditions and union recognition than did the minority of disputes concerning workers who were resisting the steady encroachment of machinery and the erosion of traditional craft skills and controls. Women had rarely exercised any control or autonomy within the labour process; therefore, their struggles could not be characterized as part of a generalized struggle for workers' control arising from the defence of existing craft prerogatives and controls at the point of production.

Women continued to demonstrate that when they embarked on collective action they injected it with a spirit of fun and gaiety not normally displayed by striking men. One particular strike of Kirkcaldy textile workers in 1911 embodied all the ingredients that were commonly associated with the disputes of women workers. The weavers had struck in support of nine members of the newly formed union who had been dismissed after a number of demands had been presented to the company which included a 20 per cent wage increase, recognition of the union, and no victimization:

The organisation of the strikes consists in roll-call meetings, street parades, picketing the works, and in breakfast, dinner and evening meetings at factory gates and in halls, with the object of extending the strike to other firms and industries. The picketing is done with such wholehearted enthusiasm as to be joyously exhilarating. Parties of strikers meet the blacklegs at the gates and 'sing them home' from work. Naturally there is some hooting too and not a little badinage is thrown at the police who shamefacedly walk arm in arm with the blacklegs to protect them 'from the fury of the mob'.[70]

[70] *Forward*, 21 Oct. 1911.

During the course of this dispute fifteen of the strikers were fined for 'disorderly conduct', receiving a tumultuous reception from the Kirkcaldy townsfolk when they returned from their trial. The strike was eventually won by the women and, according to the correspondent in *Glasgow Forward*, it was their example which inspired other workers in the town to organize and fight for wage increases. It was claimed that, since the women weavers' strike, an increase had been sought and granted in every factory in the district, policemen and tramwaymen had received a substantial weekly increase, and a number of union branches had been established among the previously unorganized workers. The article concluded: 'Public opinion in Kirkcaldy says "We owe it to our women folk".'[71]

It is difficult to quantify precisely the impact of women's strikes in the period of labour unrest, but it does seem clear that their disputes contributed in no small measure to the escalation of militancy in the immediate pre-war years. There were also a small number of strikes which were qualitatively significant in terms of the Press coverage which they received, the support they elicited from the broader labour movement, and their wider ramifications. A more detailed analysis of these disputes may provide insights into the specific context of unrest, the attitudes and aspirations of the women, and the role and relationship of various labour organizations to these struggles.

The first of these disputes took place at the thread mills of R. F. & J. Alexander and Co. at Neilston, part of the Coats combine, on May 1910. It stemmed from an initiative from the management to reduce piece-rates and speed up machinery in the copwinding department of the mill.[72] Given assurances by management that they would be able to maintain their wages by producing more, the women gave the scheme a trial but struck when they discovered that they could only produce the same quantity as before, resulting in a drop in earnings from about 12s. 9d. to 11s. per week. This move by management seems to have been part of an overall strategy to reduce costs in the face of competition and shrinking markets, as several other departments had already had their rates reduced and the

---

[71] *Forward*, 30 Dec. 1911.   [72] Ibid., 4 June 1910.

initial demand of the 120 strikers was for parity with the Clark
Company thread workers in Paisley.

From an early stage in the dispute various flanks of the labour
movement mobilized to support the strikers. The National
Federation of Women Workers drafted in an organizer to assist
the women,[73] the Glasgow Trades Council sent representatives
and organized financial aid,[74] and the Social Democratic
Party immediately held a public meeting on the dispute.[75]
Indeed it was the presence of what management deemed to
be 'outsiders' which occasioned the escalation of the dispute
and extended it to the rest of the workforce. Members of the
NFWW, such as Esther Dicks and Kate McLean, and the
Glasgow Trades Council had been instrumental in establishing
a branch of the NFWW in the factory and represented the
women in negotiations with management. When the demand
for parity with the Clark's works was presented, the directors
refused further negotiations with anyone other than the girls
themselves. This provoked the other departments in the factory
to strike in sympathy with the copwinders and for recognition
of the union. The Coats management responded by locking
out the entire workforce.

From this point, the character of the dispute transformed
from a relatively peaceful, pedestrian affair to a turbulent and
hostile display of collective defiance. The target of the women's
anger was primarily the manager of the works, although
managers of particular departments and the mill itself did not
escape unscathed.[76] The *Paisley Daily Express* reported that
'further scenes of an exciting nature' had taken place in
connection with the strike:

On Wednesday evening the force of about 30 police were unable
to cope efficiently with the crowd, fully 5,000 strong (mainly window
breaking). The manager of the turning shop has since Monday been
a marked man and his house, which is situated near the mills, has
been a target for many missiles. He has, however, now taken safety
in flight (the windows of the mills are all more or less shattered).[77]

[73] *Forward*, 4 June 1910.
[74] GTC, Minutes, 28 May, 1 June, and 8 June 1910.
[75] *Forward*, 4 June 1910.   [76] *Paisley Daily Express*, 7 June 1910.
[77] Ibid., 10 June 1910.

The dispute continued with frequent demonstration and marches to the accompaniment of singing, dancing, and banner waving. Mass meetings were held afternoon and evenings, addressed by an array of representatives from the labour movements of Glasgow, Barrhead, and Paisley. The highlight of the dispute was a demonstration which marched from Barrhead all the way to the manager's house in Fotheringay Road, Pollokshields, where an 'indignation meeting' was held at the rear of his house.[78] The demonstration was about 2,000 strong and was composed of both men and women. According to one male participant the demonstration displayed the usual traits of high spirit and good humour.

It can be understood that to lead such a disorderly, undisciplined horde of young girls to whom the thing was more of a joke than anything else [they were carrying effigies of the manager which were intended to be burned] was by no means an easy job . . .

The march, with a great banging of tin cans and shouting and singing pursued its noisy way from Neilston to Pollokshields where the respectable inhabitants were thoroughly disturbed.[79]

There appear to have been no direct attacks on the manager himself in contrast to an earlier episode in the dispute when he had to seek refuge in the booking office of the railway station to avoid a hail of missiles thrown by angry strikers.[80] The strike was successfully resolved in the women's favour and they returned to work having gained parity with the workers of Clark and Co. in Paisley. A concert was held to celebrate the resolution of the dispute, presided over by the President of the Glasgow Trades Council. The women expressed their appreciation to the men and women of the trade union movement who had assisted them by presenting them with gifts followed by a song extolling the virtues of the NFWW, its organizer, Esther Dicks, and the benefits of union membership.[81]

There were a number of features of the dispute which coalesced to activate the labour movement to support the

[78] *Paisley Daily Express*, 11 June 1910.
[79] An account given by James MacDougall, an associate of John McLean's, quoted in N. Milton, *John McLean* (London: Pluto, 1973), 49–50.
[80] *Paisley Daily Express*, 7 June 1910.   [81] Ibid., 11 June 1910.

women. Many of the strikers were between 15 and 18 years of age and their youth, combined with the heavy work of the mill, underscored the inhumanity and brutality of industrial capitalism which were common themes of socialist attacks. The bulk of an article in *Glasgow Forward* by John McLean of the Social Democratic Party was a tirade against the hypocrisy of Christians and the brutality of capitalism, which 'crushes innocent girlhood merely for the sake of money'.[82] The youth of the girls highlighted their vulnerability and so confirmed the stereotypical image of women workers as essentially weak and helpless creatures who were 'sheepishly downtrodden'.[83]

Most of the girls lived in localities near the mills, but the majority were drawn from the mining village of Nitshill, which had a highly integrated community with strong labour traditions. It has been suggested by an associate of John McLean that the strike was initiated by the daughters of socialist miners from Nitshill and that it was these same miners who sought out McLean and the SDP to organize the girls.[84] Whatever the veracity of this account, the claim that it was McLean who was responsible for contacting the NFWW probably owes more to the traditions of hagiography than to the truth. McLean certainly wrote to the Glasgow Trades Council requesting their support for the girls' strike committee, but both they and the NFWW had already rallied to their cause.[85] The fact that demonstrations were able to attract up to 5,000 participants when the number of strikers approximated 1,700 indicates that the strikers were able to draw on the support of existing institutions of labour organizations in the locality, buttressed by the networks of family and community loyalties.

The nature of the dispute, resistance to the intensification of work pressures, and a reduction in labour costs, particularly in a climate of falling real wages, did much to generate support for the strike. For McLean and the SDP, versed in the tenets of Marxist economics, it represented in extreme form the strategy of employers increasingly to subordinate labour to capital when profits were squeezed by intense competition,

---

[82] *Forward*, 4 June 1910.
[83] Ibid., 18 June 1910.
[84] Milton, *John McLean*, 49.
[85] GTC, Minutes, 11 June 1910.

246 Women and Trade-Unionism

McLean warned that 'Unless the firm is beaten on this occasion, section after section will be scientifically bled by the employers.'[86] He exhorted the amalgamation of unions 'not only to fight the Capitalists but to help overthrow the capitalist system that enables a few owners of land and capital to unscrupulously rob young and old alike'.[87] Similarly, the dispute was interpreted by the ILP as 'a struggle against the power and arrogance of Capitalism'.[88] The women themselves seemed to perceive the struggle in terms of self-assertion as much as economic grievance. As one woman voiced: 'We will eat grass before we will be beaten this time.'[89]

This defiance seemed to have been fuelled by the treatment they had received from management, which included a reference to the women as 'a lot of dirty Scottish pigs'.[90] This might explain why the management of the firm were the targets of abuse and violence in the course of the strike. This suggests that, although the immediate demand of the strike was a narrowly economic one, it was underlaid by a desire to retrieve some vestiges of self-respect and dignity, which, for so long, the women had been denied. The intervention of the SDP was partly fortuitous as they appeared to have a branch in the area and had been engaged in considerable propaganda work. However, they considered it an ideal opportunity to use the dispute as a platform to propagate socialist ideas, to broaden the basis of the dispute, and to argue for the necessity of a political movement to transform the economic and social organization of society: 'It would never have done had we let slip such a fine opportunity to drive home the Socialist moral to the Nitshill girls on strikes, and to the villagers generally.'[91]

In spite of the efforts of the SDP, there is little to suggest that the experience of their struggle convinced the women and girls of the necessity of political remedies to redress their grievances, although it was claimed by McLean that the SDP had a huge turn-out for one of their public meetings held at the outset of the strike and that they had 'temporarily captured the hearts and minds of the people'.[92] It was the refusal of

[86] Forward, 4 June 1910. [87] Ibid. [88] Ibid., 25 June 1910.
[89] Ibid., 18 June 1910. [90] Ibid., 11 June 1910.
[91] Ibid., 4 June 1910. [92] Ibid.

the employer to negotiate with their union representatives which led to the escalation of the dispute, and as the song which they sang at the victory celebration indicates, it was the process of unionization and the recognition accorded the union by the employers which seemed to palliate their grievances and restore their dignity and self respect.

> All the nice girls are in the Union
> All the nice girls wear its badge
> But there's something about the union
> Some fools don't understand
> But when on the strike list
> And on the sick list
> When we get the seven and six
> They will spark around Miss Dick
> Let us join! Let us join!
>
> (Sung to the tune of 'Ship Ahoy')[93]

Therefore, one can only speculate on the validity of the claim by an SDP supporter that 'a great mass of virgin minds received a favourable impression of their first real contact with Socialism',[94] as it appeared to be the material benefits of unionization which attracted them.

The longest recorded strike of women workers in the pre-war years was the networkers' strike in Kilbirnie, Ayrshire, which lasted from early April 1913 until September of the same year. The local economy of Kilbirnie centred on thread mills and net-making and was dominated by the firm of W. & J. Knox and Company.[95]

The strike originated among the 'treadle jumpers' in the six net-making factories in the town. These were the women who worked the looms but this also involved 'jumping' on the treadles so that they had to 'work with our whole faculties from start to finish'.[96] One woman claimed that she 'jumped' 1,240 times while making a net and as she made three nets a week she estimated that she jumped from nine to ten miles a day.[97] There seems to have been a general recognition that the work was particularly arduous and the women themselves often

---

[93] *Forward*, 16 July 1910.
[95] *Forward*, 14 June 1913.
[97] Ibid.

[94] Quoted in Milton, *John McLean*, 50.
[96] Ibid., 7 June 1913.

referred to their job as 'hard' or 'fatiguing', although for the women a positive feature of the work was that it was clean. They were piece-workers who earned between 12s. and 15s. per week although their earnings were frequently less because of breakages and time lost over breakdowns in machinery.[98] The strike originated over a demand for an increase of 6d. per net and initially involved 160 to 170 of the 200 'jumpers' in the six factories, with the 200 women who worked in the steam section of the factory joining the strike after a few weeks. Commentators remarked on the solidarity and determination of the women despite the fact that their sole source of financial support came from their own street collections. However, within a short time a variety of trade union and socialist organizations had rallied to the women's cause to the extent that *Glasgow Forward* commented that 'hordes of agitators have poured into the town'.[99] Most of these 'agitators' were there at the request of Kate McLean, the Scottish organizer of the NFWW, who had undertaken the task of organizing support for the strikers. The Glasgow Trades Council sent speakers to factory gates to appeal for donations,[100] the Parliamentary Committee of the Scottish Trades Union Congress played a role in the resolution of the dispute, and some fifty speakers addressed mass meetings in the town. The women also enjoyed considerable local support from the men and women in the surrounding areas. In the sixth week of the strike a procession and rally was held, which according to *Forward* was

the greatest Labour demonstration in the industrial history of Ayrshire in support of strikes. There was a march of trade unionists from surrounding districts. 4,000 marched to Beith and a mass meeting of about 10,000. . . . Strikes in Kilbirnie are akin to village carnivals—everyone takes part in them. . . . Mothers with babes in their arms walked the 6 miles ungrudgingly in the cause of justice, while four brakes conveyed the older women about 80 of whom took part in their first labour demonstration . . . Boys in fancy costume collected for the strike fund, and these with the cheerful costumed strikers, gave to the procession an appearance of joy and rebellion that could not have pleased the employers.[101]

---

[98] *Forward*, 7 June 1913.
[100] GTC, Minutes, 11 June 1913.

[99] Ibid., 10 May 1913.
[101] *Forward*, 10 May 1913.

Kilbirnie was a small, tightly knit community and within one family it was common to find the young women working in the net works or thread works, and the men of the house employed in the iron mines and steelworks of nearby Glengarnock. It appears that family loyalties and trade union solidarity fused to provide a bedrock of support for the women's strike. One newspaper report noted that when six of the strikers had to go to Kilmarnock to be tried for intimidation, which amounted to verbal abuse of blacklegs, they were accompanied by 'About sixty sympathisers, including pipers and the night-shift workers from Glengarnock'.[102]

Four of the women were found guilty and fined, and on their return to Kilbirnie the whole town turned out to welcome them. It was claimed that the charge of intimidation had the effect of generating more support for the strikers. Not all the women in the factories went on strike and there was a handful of blacklegs who, according to oral evidence, were the daughters of 'Knox's licks', that is, the male overseers and gatekeepers in the factory.[103] These women had to run a gauntlet of abuse and derision from the strikers, who constantly harassed and badgered them with taunts of 'scab' and 'blackleg'.

The small number of skilled men in the factory, such as the hecklers, who were already unionized, were sympathetic to the women's demands, but did not come out on strike, although they were eventually locked out by the employers. Enumerators' rolls suggest that the skilled men in the net works tended not to have female relatives in the factory.[104] Perhaps not having the spark of family loyalty to fuel support for the strikers accounts for their reluctance to translate their sympathy into action solidarity. Their actions were certainly in keeping with skilled men throughout the textile industry, who rarely struck in support of women, although they may on occasions have been in sympathy with their aims.

Patriarchal authority as well as family loyalty seems to have been an important factor in determining the course of action of the strikers. When one firm offered their workers an increase,

---

[102] S. Howitt, 'The Kilbirnie Networkers' Strike 1913', dissertation, University of Strathclyde, 1988, 13.   [103] Ibid.
[104] Ibid.

the other factories reopened their works in an attempt to break the strike. Although the ploy was unsuccessful, newspaper reports claimed that women and girls mobbed and assaulted male workers on their way to and from work, as they had allowed their daughters to restart work.[105]

At an early stage in the dispute, the issue of union recognition became the focal point of the women's grievances in the face of the refusal of the employers to negotiate with women's trade unions. The unionized men in the factories, the hecklers, held a meeting with the employers to request that they recognize the women's union but were given short shrift by the employers, who argued that 'too many paid agitators had been in town for them to grant recognition'.[106] The women themselves attributed the entrenched position of the employers to their reluctance to deal with women's unions, and one striker maintained that 'The employers would give in were it not necessary for them to recognize the Union', and went on to warn them 'the sooner they learn to negotiate with our trade unions the better'.[107]

The most intransigent of the employers was the firm of W. & J. Knox, whose economic dominance of the district was so great that they were referred to as 'lords' by the local people. Their business and property interests included the local thread mills, most of the net-making factories, the local gas supply, house property, mansions, and a fifteen-mile strip of land between Kilbirnie and Greenock.[108]

Knox's was part of the Linen Thread Company, an amalgamation of leading thread companies formed in 1898 in response to increasing competition and marketing difficulties.[109] The three principal firms which formed the core of the composite Linen Thread Company were William Barbour and Sons of Hilden, Lisburn, Northern Ireland, Finlayson, Bousefield and Company Ltd. of Johnstone, and W. & J. Knox of Kilbirnie.[110] The official company history claimed that the

---

[105] S. Howitt, 'The Kilbirnie Networkers' Strike 1913', dissertation, University of Strathclyde, 1988, 13.

[106] *Forward*, 21 June 1913. [107] Ibid., 7 June 1913.

[108] Ibid., 31 May 1913.

[109] R. Sinclair, *The Faithful Fibre: A History of the Development of the Linen Thread Company* (Glasgow: Linen Thread Co., 1965). [110] Ibid.

firms involved in the merger were representative of enlightened employers who distinguished themselves in a century of great personal enterprise.[111] Certainly the Finlaysons seemed to favour encouraging self-help amongst their employees, persuading them in 1861 to set up a co-operative society[112] and in the 1870s advocating that 'some intelligent working men' be elected to the burgh council.[113] The Barbours established a wide range of welfare and social provisions for their employees including building a village at Hilden with semi-detached cottages standing in their own grounds, a primary school built in 1875 and another built in 1912, dental and eye-testing clinics for children, a community hall, a children's playground, and a village sports ground.[114] The paucity of reference to the Knox family's contributions may be indicative of little paternalistic endeavour on their part, although it was claimed that the family 'enjoy the closest contact with the mill personnel'.[115] Reference is made to 250 houses which were built by the company; however, it is likely that in keeping with Victorian paternalism these would have been to accommodate the male skilled grades of workers, such as hecklers. There is therefore little evidence to indicate that the Knox family dominated the town either culturally or socially as there seems to have been an absence of the usual panoply of paternalistic employers in the sense of extensive social and leisure provisions. They built a William Knox Institute for their workforce, 'out of gratitude for all that Kilbirnie has done for them', as *Glasgow Forward* ironically noted.[116]

The changing social, political, and economic climate of the 1890s and the early twentieth century may have served to weaken the influence of the Knoxes and drive a wedge between employers and employees.[117] The industrial militancy of the immediate pre-war years, the growing influence of socialism over the working class, and the constant threat of foreign competition no doubt had some effect on employer and employee relationships. One indication of this polarization

[111] R. Sinclair, *The Faithful Fibre: A History of the Development of the Linen Thread Company* (Glasgow: Linen Thread Co., 1965) ch. 5.　　[112] Ibid.
[113] Ibid.　　[114] Ibid.　　[115] Ibid.　　[116] *Forward*, 7 June 1913.
[117] P. Joyce, *Work, Society and Politics* (London: Methuen, 1980), Epilogue, deals with the decline of paternalism of the late 19th and early 20th cents.

252 Women and Trade-Unionism

was the fact that the Knox family transferred their political loyalties to the Tories as a consequence of Lloyd George's land taxes, and were therefore part of the flight of wealth from the Liberal Party which occurred in the late nineteenth and early twentieth centuries.

The economic dominance of the Knox family, coupled with what may have been increasing social, cultural, and political differentiation, partly explains the widespread support the strike elicited in the district. Although there is no reference to the Knox family or property being the direct targets of abuse or violence, there clearly was considerable animosity towards them and their conspicuous wealth. The strikers often justified their claim for more money by alluding to the wealth of the Knox family. One striker argued that millionaires would hardly be bankrupted by an increase of £35 in the weekly wage bill: 'Some of them spend that amount when they go for a cruise on the Mediterranean. If they can afford to maintain a fleet of motor cars, not to speak of other luxuries, they can easily afford to give us an increase.'[118] The list of shareholders in the Knox firm reveals that, of the six members of the Knox family mentioned, five were resident at Kilbirnie at three different addresses.[119] Therefore, the visibility of their wealth when contrasted with the meagre wages paid to the women probably did much to heighten an awareness of economic inequalities and sharpen the sense of material deprivation.

The demands made by the strikers for more money and recognition of their union were often expressed in terms of gaining equality with men. However, the basis of their claim for 'twice the pay' rested on the arduous nature of their work, which one of them described as 'not work for women, but for men'.[120] They justified their claim by arguing that if men were employed as 'treadle jumpers' they would receive twice the pay.

The women who worked the steam section of the factory and who operated steam power machines earned 6s. to 12s. per week compared with 21s. per week earned by the men who worked the same machines at night. These women claimed that, as the men produced the same amount of work as the

[118] *Forward*, 7 June 1913.   [119] Ibid., 14 June 1913.
[120] Ibid., 7 June 1913.

women, the women should get an increase. This theme of equality with men running through their claim was perhaps stoked by the employers' refusal to recognize women's unions, which gave a feminist edge to the dispute, evinced by the comment made by one striker, and given general assent, 'Wait till we get a vote,'[121] and the perhaps hopeful remark by the correspondent in *Glasgow Forward* that the strikers were 'keen suffragists, and for the most part Socialists too'.[122]

There were certainly no references made by the strikers to the necessity of a revolutionary transformation of political and economic structures, nor was there any challenge to the right of property or profit, provided it did not interfere with workers' right to a 'fair wage'. However, the arguments of the strikers, which were couched in the language of socialist economics, indicate an acquaintance with the economics of capitalist manufacture and an awareness of the source of profit, which may be attributed to a schooling in the socialist economics of the ILP. The women informed a *Forward* correspondent that there was little chance of their increase bankrupting the employers as they were claiming:

Bankruptcy! I don't think! Why, it is said they get from £1 to £3 per net. Suppose we average the price at £2. We make three nets a week. That's £6 for making these nets, we get an average pay of let us say 14/-. That leaves the employers with £5 6/- profits from each worker. There are 400 networkers which means that our employers make £2,120 from our labour every week. No doubt they have material to buy, machinery and factories to maintain but that cost won't absorb all the profit.[123]

Their familiarity with this branch of economics may have stemmed from the socialist propaganda they were exposed to in the course of the dispute from a variety of creeds including the syndicalists and the ILP. *Forward* claimed that as a result of the strike a branch of the ILP had been formed in the town and sales of both their newspaper and the *Daily Citizen*, the official newspaper of the Labour Party, had increased.[124]

The widespread support which the strike elicited from the broader labour movement derived from the fact that the strikers

[121] *Forward*, 14 June 1913.   [122] Ibid.   [123] Ibid., 7 June 1913.
[124] Ibid., 17 May 1913.

were primarily young girls involved in heavy work. As with the Neilston strike, it was the image of women as helpless victims in need of protection which dominated the rhetoric of the labour organizations. Once again women were held up as exhibits in the case against industrial capitalism. George Barnes, the Labour MP for Blackfriars, addressed an open-air meeting of the strikers and gave a clear indication of how he would like to have seen the issue resolved in the long term: 'As to the place of women in the industrial system he was one of those old-fashioned enough to believe that the women should be taking care of things at home instead of going into factories.'[125]

The strike was resolved after twenty-one weeks, with the women obtaining an increase, which, although less than the initial demand, was regarded as a victory, and, significantly, they also won the recognition of their union. Although the women did not struggle alone, they played a prominent role throughout the dispute as well as in its resolution. The negotiating committee was headed by Kate McLean of the NFWW, but it also consisted of six networkers, who subsequently became union delegates in the six factories.[126]

The impact of the strike had a number of wider-ranging repercussions, some of which had a lasting influence on the face of labour and trade union organizations in the area. In addition to the formation of a branch of the ILP and the creation of a permanent socialist presence in the district, a number of men's trade unions increased their membership. The NFWW enrolled almost 1,000 new members, and the dispute sparked off a number of claims from other workers for increases which had Kilbirnie 'seething with discontent'.[127] Perhaps most significantly the strike generated an unprecedented level of support and solidarity. It contributed significantly to the mobilization of labour in the area on a class-wide basis rather than a purely sectional one, with steelworkers, miners, and non-wage-earning members of the community

[125] Howitt, 'The Kilbirnie Networkers' Strike 1913', 11.
[126] Ibid. 18.
[127] *Forward*, 31 May 1913.

participating in the women's demonstrations, and the striking women giving their support to the disputes of other workers.[128]

It was women workers who initiated the strike at Singer Manufacturing Works, Clydebank, in March 1911, a strike which has been depicted as one of the most significant episodes in the pre-war history of the Clyde because of the role of the Industrial Workers of Great Britain. The strike originated among women in the cabinet polishing department over an attempt by management to increase their work-load without extra payment. The women in this department were immediately supported by the majority of the 3,000 women employed in the factory, and within a couple of days the dispute had spread to other departments although the small section of skilled and unionized workers were slower to respond to the call for a total stoppage. The dispute received such widespread support in the factory because it was the culmination of several years of grievances centring on deskilling, the substitution of labour by machines, speed-ups, increased supervision, and a host of what the workforce referred to as 'petty tyrannies'.

The Singer plant employed over 12,000 workers and incorporated the most up-to-date production and labour management techniques. It was fiercely anti-union, only reluctantly recognizing two of the craft unions in the plant, the Scottish Typographical Association, and the Amalgamated Society of Engineers.[129] Attempts had been made to form a union for the unskilled and semi-skilled workers in the industry during the 'New Unionism' period in the late 1880s,[130] but it succumbed to the 'dirty tricks' department of management, who employed a 'spy' to acquire information on the union.[131]

The ILP newspaper, *Glasgow Forward*, detailed the pressures which the workforce had been subjected to:

---

[128] A demonstration of those on strike at Nobel's Explosive Company in Ardeer was attended by a contingent of the Kilbirnie networkers, *Glasgow Herald*, 24 May 1913.

[129] GLHW pamphlet, *The Singer Strike, Clydebank 1911* (Glasgow: Clydebank District Libraries, 1989).

[130] Ibid.   [131] Ibid.

In many of the departments foremen stand with watches in their hands timing the men and girls so that the maximum amount of labour can be exacted from the operatives in return for the minimum wage. In one department especially, a foreman has been nicknamed 'Crippen' because of his timing propensities. The watch is seldom out of this individual's hand. Wages are not reduced collectively. In Singer's, the wages of two or three are broken today, a few others tomorrow, and so on until the workers have been reduced, and the game of Scientific Reduction begins once more.[132]

In the two or three months preceding the women's strike, there had been three disputes in different departments involving speed-ups, work intensification, and disciplinary procedures.[133] These disputes were resolved in the workers' favour and undoubtedly bolstered their confidence and militancy, which was expressed in the snowballing membership of the Sewing Machine Group of the IWGB, which had been established in the factory in 1910.

It is significant that, having capitulated to similar demands from the male workers, the employers refused to redress the grievances of the women polishers. This was recognized by the strike committee, who interpreted it as typical of management's maltreatment of women workers. There is a suggestion in the strike committee's manifesto that the explanation for the differential treatment meted out to women was their defencelessness. In arguing the case for collective bargaining, the committee illustrated the disadvantages of the system advocated by management: 'the firm contend that in the event of a dispute the individuals only directly concerned have a right to negotiate with them. In most cases this would mean only one individual and that perhaps a girl who, it will be seen, would be at a considerable disadvantage.'[134] It may have been the case that management hoped to nip in the bud the workforce's new-found militancy by picking off the section they perceived as the weakest, but it could also be interpreted as a particularly hostile reaction provoked by the defiance of those who were expected to be more submissive to managerial authority.

---

[132] GLHW pamphlet, *The Singer Strike, Clydebank 1911* (Glasgow: Clydebank District Libraries, 1989).   [133] Ibid.   [134] Ibid.

Although the claim of the women in the polishing section was not entirely eclipsed, the central demand of the strikers became to establish the principle of collective bargaining for the unskilled and semi-skilled workers in the factory. The women participated fully in the strike and had delegates on the 200-strong strike committee and representatives on the delegations to management. However, they were outnumbered 3 : 1 by male strikers and the dispute was never really defined as a strike of women workers in popular consciousness. In the annals of labour history the Singer strike has acquired its prominence because of its association with syndicalism, whilst contemporary commentators and the Singer management themselves were convinced that it was fomented by socialist agitators. In justifying their refusal to accede to the demands of the strikers, the manager of the factory claimed: 'it was all a matter of public interest. We are fighting a public battle when we oppose the Socialist teaching which is at the bottom of the whole business.'[135]

The IWGB had established a branch in the factory the previous year and, through sustained propaganda work, the distribution of leaflets and pamphlets, and lunch-time factory gate meetings, they claimed to have built up to a membership of 1,500,[136] although membership was confined to a handful of the forty-one departments of the factory. However, the IWGB had little influence on the outbreak of the dispute, although they perhaps played a role in extending the strike to all departments, not merely by their presence, but by dint of their patient propaganda work. Their influence on the strike committee and on the course of the strike was limited as the committee was comprised of five representatives from the forty-one departments. The spokesmen for the workforce were at pains to stress the representative nature of the committee and its independence from an 'outside body', boasting that 'fully one half of the committee is non-unionist and anti-socialist'.[137]

---

[135] *Clydebank and Renfrew Press*, 4 Apr. 1911.

[136] From Singer Sewing Machine Group, IWGB, 'The Kilbowie Strike and its Lessons', quoted in R. Challinor, *The Origins of British Bolshevism* (London: Croom Helm, 1977), 101.

[137] *Forward*, 8 Apr. 1911.

There was certainly little evidence of syndicalist doctrines having an impact on the disputes, as the slogans and the demands of the strikers were confined to the specific issue of union recognition and general exhortations for solidarity. One demonstration of the strikers displayed a number of banners with slogans such as 'No surrender', 'Unity is strength', and 'Wha sae base as be a slave?'[138] The limited objectives of the strikers were stressed by a succession of speakers at a rally on Glasgow Green who disclaimed any desire on the part of the workers 'to hamper the operations of the firm', claiming their objective was to stop the 'alleged tampering with the normal wage, of which the case of the polishers' wage was a concrete example'.[139]

The initial upsurge of defiance and enthusiasm quickly evaporated in the face of management's tactics of conducting a referendum of the workers appealing to strikers to return to work and promising that grievances would be carefully investigated and any 'ascertained injustice would be rectified'. The success of this tactic is perhaps a measure of the uneven consciousness of the workforce and the limited influence of syndicalist ideas on the strikers, whose slow drift back to work was the signal for large-scale victimizations by Singer management. Those blacked included sixty ILP members, over twenty members of the Socialist Labour Party, and some members of the Social Democratic Federation. The aftermath of the strike also witnessed the dissolution of the Clydebank branch of the SLP and the collapse of trade-unionism in the factory.[140] There were, however, some positive developments emerging from the strike in that at least two of the women who took a leading part in the strike, Fanny Abbott and Jane Rae, played an active part in Clydebank's labour movement after the strike, joining the ILP and participating in the political life of Red Clydeside and the anti-war movement.[141]

The demand for union recognition which emerged in many of the women's disputes, although this issue may not have sparked off the disputes, suggests a need to modify the

---

[138] *Clydebank Press*, 4 Apr. 1911.   [139] Ibid., 27 Mar. 1911.
[140] GLHW, *The Singer Strike, Clydebank 1911.*
[141] Ibid., app. 2, oral testimony of the family of Jane Rae and Fanny Abbott.

characterization of this period as signifying an impatience with orthodox trade-unionism. Strikes by women and other non-unionized workers, which were a significant feature of the labour unrest, often involved a demand for trade union controls rather than a rejection of them. Similarly, there is little indication of syndicalist-inspired action even in the Singer dispute where the IWGB played a significant role. However, neither can these disputes substantiate the view that political and industrial struggles were discrete. Not only were political activists involved in industrial struggles, but it was often the experience of industrial struggle which politicized a community. At both Kilbirnie and Neilston, branches of political organizations were established in the wake of the unrest, and in Clydebank, where the defeat of the Singer strike led to demoralization and the dissolution of socialist organizations, individual women who had taken an active role in the struggle, such as Fanny Abbot and Jane Rae, went on to play a leading role in socialist politics.

The demands for union recognition or wage increases or the protests against speed-ups and tighter discipline may have been primarily instrumental. However, the disputes of women illustrate that underlying basic material grievances there were more intractable issues relating to dignity, self-assertion, and self-respect. Employers seemed particularly intransigent and hostile to trade union recognition for women, which perhaps reflected a desire on their part to have unfettered control over their women workers. One of the assumed advantages of employing women lay in their imputed docility, and trade unions represented the interference of 'outsiders' who might intrude on what was conceived of as a personal if not patriarchal relationship between employers and women workers and usurp employer power. Inherent in this conception of women workers was the contradictory view of them as malleable and tractable creatures who could be easily manipulated but who were also subject to irrational behaviour and impulses which needed tight controls. Therefore, whilst employers tended to oppose unionization of women workers where there had been no history of strikes or resistance, they tended to welcome trade union intervention as a means of exerting discipline and constraint on women workers who had displayed a persistent tendency to engage in disruptive industrial action, particularly if there already existed established collective bargaining procedures with groups of male workers within the same workplace.

The language of the struggles illustrates that, for unorganized workers, unionization was part of a protest against the pervasive authority and control of employers and therefore one means of asserting their independence and self-respect. In this sense these strikes could be interpreted as signifying deep-seated social discontent and a sense of class antagonism. However, the strikes also illustrate that, whilst more than material grievances were at stake, they were easily palliated, employer recognition of unions usually being sufficient to defuse the situation.

Despite the limitations of their challenge, women workers' contribution to the explosion of militancy in the pre-war years confirms the need to revise the view that the difficulties in organizing them into trade unions were rooted in their apathy, weakness, and conservatism.

7. Women and Working-Class Politics, 1900–1914

DESPITE the challenge of the Labour Party in the pre-war years, the Liberals still held sway in national electoral politics. It should be emphasized, however, that the national franchise was extremely limited: only about 60 per cent of adult males were enfranchised, and of course no women had the vote. In Scotland the Labour Party was even less successful than south of the border in winning parliamentary representation. This was partly because there was no electoral pact with the Liberals and three-cornered contests were therefore more common, and partly because Labour contested fewer seats in Scotland.[1]

At local level political life could assume a different hue and socialist politics and ideas often had an altogether more flourishing and vigorous existence, even if this was not always translated into electoral success. Local elections, municipal school boards, and parish councils were frequently contested and occasionally won by committed socialists of different creeds. By 1914, there were only two Labour MPs in Scotland, but there were about 200 labour representatives across a range of local government bodies. There was a flowering of socialist or more broadly labour organizations, which spearheaded a number of campaigns attracting widespread popular support among the working class. The broader social issues around which socialists campaigned ranged from the housing question and unemployment to school meals and the medical inspection of schoolchildren. In the early years of the twentieth century a new socialist culture was created, which found organizational expression through the formation of Clarion Clubs, socialist Sunday schools, rambling clubs, socialist orchestras and choirs, and a plethora of political education classes.

[1] I. G. C. Hutchison, *A Political History of Scotland 1832–1924: Parties, Elections and Issues* (Edinburgh: John Donald, 1986), 253.

The socialist movement could be loosely divided into two ideological camps: one whose intellectual roots were in early utopian socialism and radical liberalism, which has been termed 'ethical socialism'; and one whose intellectual touchstone was the writings of Karl Marx, which has been referred to as 'scientific socialism'.[2] In Scotland the major representative of ethical socialism was the Independent Labour Party, the most influential of all the socialist organizations in Scotland. The Marxist tradition was represented by the Social Democratic Federation, which in 1909 became the Social Democratic Party, and the Socialist Labour Party, although in terms of membership these organizations were tiny. Despite differences in political ideology and strategy, socialist politics were characterized by fluidity of ideas and membership. There was a dense and interlocking network of labour organizations and activists, and an absence of rigid divisions between socialist organizations, which engaged in a continuing dialogue with each other.

The common denominator for each of these organizations was the emphasis which they placed on education and propaganda as a means of disseminating their ideas, and frequently they shared political platforms in order to do this. The reputedly sectarian SDP was equally involved in this socialist current, with John McLean's lectures on history, Marxist economics, and public speaking attended by socialists of a variety of persuasions. Even the courses for women co-operators and their speakers' classes, which were held under the auspices of the politically moderate co-operative union, were taught by McLean.[3] The public meetings organized by the Clarion Scouts and the ILP were addressed by speakers drawn from the wide spectrum of left-wing politics, and were attended by hundreds, whilst socialist literature was widely distributed by the Reformers' Bookstall and the Civic Press.[4] Frequent overtures were made by the SDP to the ILP to amalgamate and form a United Socialist Party, and this

---

[2] See S. MacIntyre, *A Proletarian Science* (Cambridge University Press, 1980), for an elaboration of the political philosophies of these two strains of socialism.

[3] SCWG, *Twenty-Second Annual Report, 1914*, Scottish Co-operative Society, Shieldhall, Glasgow.

[4] W. H. Fraser, 'The Labour Party in Scotland', in K. D. Brown (ed.), *The First Labour Party* (London: Croom Helm, 1985), 47.

willingness to engage in debate created a number of common forums. The emergence of industrial unionist and syndicalist organizations, although officially opposed by the ILP and SDP, attracted a number of their members and created another terrain for socialists from different organizations to work alongside each other free from the sectionalism and sectarianism which frequently characterized industrial and political initiatives.

Clearly socialist politics and propaganda reached a wide audience and, more importantly, political activity involved a broader constituency than the formal membership of the different socialist organizations. Therefore, the lack-lustre performance of labour candidates in electoral politics belied the fact that at local level there was a vibrant network of socialist organization, propaganda, and agitation.

What was novel about working-class politics during this period was the extent to which some of the political associations of the labour movement attempted to involve women in political activity. This was more true of the ethical socialist wing of the movement than of the Marxist wing, which neither attracted many women to its ranks nor set up separate organizations to recruit them. The Scottish Co-operative Women's Guild and the Women's Labour League, which was effectively the women's section of the Labour Party, were formed chiefly to introduce the principles of co-operation and labour politics to women, whilst the ILP contained a fair contingent of women in its ranks.

The ILP, which after 1906 was the dominant organization of the labour coalition in Scotland, displayed many of the political traits of radical liberalism, and indeed is often portrayed as the heir to liberal traditions, particularly in its prime target for vilification, landlordism. The continuities between liberalism and the ILP's ethical socialism were not only restricted to the land question, but evident in its strongly moral and ethical tone, its association with non-conformism, and its emphasis on education as the means of moral and social elevation.[5]

Although the ILP was virulently anti-capitalist in its rhetoric and invoked the vision of a socialist commonwealth as the

[5] MacIntyre, *Proletarian Science*, 56.

solution to poverty, oppression, and suffering, its specific proposals for reform were limited and pragmatic.[6] Its economic analysis of capitalism identified the key problem as inefficient purchasing power as a result of the disproportion between production and consumption, and there was an implicit belief that British capitalism could be made more efficient by the eradication of parasitic elements such as landlordism and state regulation of the economy.[7] Given the emerging current within liberalism of commitment to state-sponsored social reform, the ILP's faith in state intervention as a panacea was another strand of its politics which was not dissimilar to the more radical elements of liberalism.

The ILP's belief in the neutrality of state institutions led to its policies centring on an electoral strategy which sought to colonize both local and national political institutions with the representatives of labour organizations. The ILP, alone of the socialist groups, supported the extension of the franchise to women on the same basis as men. Although little was done in the way of active support or promoting a campaign for women's suffrage, the issue of the 'Woman Question' was given extensive and sympathetic coverage in the pages of *Glasgow Forward*, which was effectively the voice of the ILP. The ILP's stance on women's suffrage may have been one reason for its relative success in attracting women to the organization. However, more significant was its political strategy, which was succinctly outlined in a *Forward* editorial:

To us in a democratic country, the realisation of socialism consists in the continuous hum-drum application of a principle day to day and week to week in the workshops of Parliament, Town, Country or Parish Council, Trade Union, Co-op Society, and every form of associated effort the object of which is to promote human and social well-being and not the profits and aggrandisement of the proprietary classes.[8]

The ILP's involvement in a wide range of projects and in many forms of associational life which were outside the

[6] MacIntyre, *Proletarian Science*, 162.
[7] D. Howell, *British Workers and the Independent Labour Party, 1888–1906* (Manchester University Press, 1982), 349.
[8] *Glasgow Forward*, 30 Jan. 1909.

boundaries of conventional politics ensured that socialist politics reached a broad layer of the community whilst simultaneously widening the appeal of the ILP by injecting its politics with immediacy and local relevance. The ILP placed greater premium on social and political struggles than on industrial struggles and correspondingly there was more focus on the locality as the centre of agitational work rather than the workplace. Campaigning on issues current in local politics such as housing, rents, unemployment, and education and an emphasis on the importance of grass-roots involvement was a feature of ILP political practice. It was also willing to engage in direct and radical struggles of an extraparliamentary nature and to foster organizations of local democracy such as ward committees and tenants' defence associations.[9]

Thus a hallmark of the ILP was its involvement in a range of issues and diverse political forums, and a willingness to cast the net of its educational and propaganda work to include women, who were regarded as political assets rather than liabilities. Keir Hardie had articulated this view in 1894 when he suggested that the Scottish Labour Party should select women as candidates for school board elections.[10] This approach not only attracted women members but drew many more women into the ambit of political activity than formally joined the organization. Although women rarely appeared as candidates in elections or as office-holders in the ILP's local party structure, they were acknowledged party stalwarts in the humdrum but essential business of electioneering. *Forward* commented of Labour's narrow defeat in the municipal elections for Glasgow's Kingston ward that 'the women have worked like Trojans on behalf of Councillor Jackson'.[11]

The ILP did not have a separate women's section, but many of its women members joined the WLL, which established its first Scottish branch in Glasgow in June 1908[12] and within the year had a membership of 130,[13] including 'the best

   [9] J. Smith, 'Labour Tradition in Glasgow and Liverpool', *History Workshop Journal*, 17 (Spring 1984).
   [10] J. Smyth, 'Labour and Socialism in Glasgow, 1880–1914: The Electoral Challenge Prior to Democracy', Ph.D. thesis, University of Edinburgh, 1987, 217–18.
   [11] *Forward*, 9 Nov. 1912.
   [12] *Woman Worker*, 26 June 1908.   [13] Ibid., 4 Sept. 1909.

working women in the ILP'.[14] In order to harness women to
the socialist cause, the WLL established political education
classes in a number of wards where women voters were
'brought together in a homely way to learn the meaning of the
labour movement'. Many of the ILP and WLL women were
working class. However, few of them seem to have been wage-
earners, and overlapping membership of trade unions and
political organizations was restricted to a tiny handful of
women such as Kate McLean, the Scottish organizer of the
NFWW and a member of the ILP, and Agnes Pettigrew,
Secretary of the Shop Assistants' Union and active in the WLL
and ILP. This seems to have been the product of a conscious
recruitment policy which was directed at housewives. For
the League regarded enlisting women wage-earners as 'the
supplementary side to the interesting of the working wives and
mothers in our cause'.[15]

The largest of the working-class women's organizations,
the SCWG, was not only aimed at housewives, but more
particularly at the wives of better-off sections of the working
class. According to the SCWG's first historian and former
President, Mrs Buchanan, its original purpose was to enable
'the women of the Co-operative movement to meet together
in friendly converse and by so doing, help to break the
monotonous existence of even a comfortable home'.[16] The
SCWG had the biggest membership of the constellation
of women's labour organizations, growing from an initial
membership of a few hundred in 1892 to 12,420 in 1913.[17]
The primary objective of the Guild was to promote the
principles and ideals of co-operation amongst the women and
to train them 'to take their place in the home, in the social
circle and in the Co-operative Society'.[18] In the early years of
the Guild, the emphasis was very much on women's role as

[14] *Woman Worker*, 8 Sept. 1908.
[15] Ibid., 3 July 1908. The usage of the term 'working wives' is indicative of the
belief that women's domestic work was of equal value and should be equally esteemed
as waged work.
[16] A. Buchan, *A History of the Scottish Co-operative Women's Guild, 1892–1913*
(Glasgow: Scottish Co-operative Wholesale Society, 1913), 64.
[17] SCWG, Annual Reports, *passim*.
[18] SCWG, *Fourteenth Annual Report*, 1906.

homemakers, and the content of their education courses reflects a concern with training women in domestic skills. Topics for discussion and lectures in the branches included home management, personal hygiene, and food and drink, as well as practical classes in laundry work, flower making, and cookery.[19]

However, during the early years of the twentieth century, the Guild gradually extended the scope of its activities, including affiliation to the Labour Party at a time when its English counterpart declined to join,[20] and campaigning vigorously in the 1910 general election. However, this politicization was still accompanied by a staunch commitment to Sabbatarianism, a belief that crime and poverty were the product of intemperance, and the conviction that the Christian home was the corner-stone of a civilized society.[21] Guildswomen were encouraged to 'acquaint themselves with social questions such as the housing of the poor and the drink question'[22] and in 1910 this trend was incorporated into Guild policy when a resolution was passed arguing that 'the time has now arrived when women should take a deep interest in social and civic questions and calls upon the Central Council to organise meetings, prepare papers and addresses for the purpose of bringing the importance of citizenship before the Guild'.[23] Guild branches campaigned vigorously on a number of issues, including medical inspection of schoolchildren, school meals, minimum wages for co-operative employees, anti-credit trading, opposition to the use of the tramway profits for the relief of rates, and equal concessions for working women travelling on public transport.[24] By 1912 there was a discernible shift in their educational work towards wider political and social questions such as Poor Law legislation, municipal and school board work, labour exchanges, and sweated labour, although domestic concerns were maintained with the inclusion of lectures on 'Flannelette and its Dangers'.[25]

[19] SCWG, *Fourth Annual Report, 1896*, 'Branch Notes'.
[20] *Woman Worker*, 3 July 1908.
[21] SCWG, *Sixteenth Annual Report, 1908*.
[22] SCWG, *Fifteenth Annual Report, 1907*.
[23] SCWG, *Eighteenth Annual Report, 1910*.
[24] SCWG, *Annual Reports, passim*.
[25] SCWG, *Twentieth Annual Report, 1912*.

A concerted effort was made to get women co-operators elected on to a wide range of committees. From its inception, the Guild actively campaigned for women's involvement in local government politics, and in 1894 it was represented on the committee of an association formed in Glasgow to promote the return of women to local government boards.[26] The Guild also campaigned tirelessly to get women on to the committees of the co-operative movement itself. By 1911, eight guildswomen were on the boards of management of co-operative societies and fourteen on educational committees,[27] and eventually the Guild won the right to delegate representation on local Labour parties.[28]

Women co-operators were exhorted to regard themselves as 'a worker, a missionary for the cause of women's progress', and to support 'all questions especially relating to women'.[29] Consequently, there was a strong feminist strand within the Guild, which was the first and most persistent advocate amongst the socialist and labour groups for the extension of the parliamentary franchise to women.

As early as 1893 the Guild sent a petition to the Government in favour of women's suffrage and consistently passed resolutions at annual conferences in favour of votes for women. The Guild was the only working-class women's organization to affiliate to a suffrage society, having delegates on the committee of the non-militant West of Scotland Suffrage Society. Although the Guild rejected the militant tactics of the Women's Social and Political Union, their commitment to women's suffrage was unflinching and they also rejected the adult suffrage position adopted by the Labour Party as 'not at all favourable to the wants and wishes of our association'.[30]

The efforts of the Guild to develop the organizational skills of its members and instil confidence by holding regular public-speaking classes fructified during the legendary 1915 Rent

---

[26] SCWG, *Second Annual Report, 1894*.
[27] SCWG, *Nineteenth Annual Report, 1911*.
[28] Smyth, 'Labour and Socialism in Glasgow', 231.
[29] SCWG, Minutes of the Quarterly Meeting of the Guild, 8 June 1901, Scottish Co-operative Society, Shieldhall.
[30] SCWG, *Thirteenth Annual Report, 1905*.

Strikes when individual members of the Guild took leading roles.[31] The strike seems to have originated in South Govan, part of the area covered by the Kinning Park Women's Guild, which was in fact the first co-operative guild to be established in Scotland. According to the historian of Kinning Park Co-operative Society, the strike began with the decision of Kinning Park members to withhold demanded rent increases.[32]

Therefore, in the pre-war years, women were gradually creating a role for themselves within the broad labour movement. However, the organizations which sought to recruit women to the socialist and co-operative movement shared a common conception of women's role as bound up with domesticity and a common conviction that social roles should be sexually differentiated. Women were invariably related to in their capacity as homemakers, and were addressed as the 'wives, sisters, and sweethearts of male workers'.[33] Women's involvement in politics and wider social questions was premissed on the belief that it would develop their qualities as homemakers as well as infusing political life with the 'purifying and elevating' influence of women. Similarly, the SCWG sought to introduce women to the principles of co-operation with the aim of making them 'better wives, better mothers and better members of society'.[34] During the 1915 Rent Strike organizing meetings were held in local halls on weekday afternoons, as it was assumed that the women involved would be housewives.[35]

The SCWG defined woman's province as the home and her primary duties and responsibilities as being to the family. However, the Guild maintained that this should not preclude women from participation in public life, arguing that 'the hand that rocked the cradle was directed by a brain that notwithstanding she had to be the wife and mother and responsible for the home, was yet able to spare the time and the will to help her sister worker'.[36]

[31] Smyth, 'Labour and Socialism in Glasgow', 232.
[32] P. Dollan, *Jubilee History of the Kinning Park Co-operative Society* (Glasgow: Kinning Park Co-operative Society, 1923), 42; Smyth, 'Labour and Socialism in Glasgow', 232, states that this claim is corroborated by local Press reports.
[33] *Woman Worker*, 12 June 1908.
[34] SCWG, *Fourteenth Annual Report, 1906*.
[35] Smyth, 'Labour and Socialism in Glasgow', 338.
[36] Buchan, *History of the Scottish Co-operative Women's Guild*, 13.

Moreover, it was argued that political life would be enriched by women's contribution as they possessed a number of valuable qualities, both moral and practical, which derived from their role as homemakers and mothers. Mrs Buchan, President of the Guild for several years, argued that guildswomen were more conversant with the 'inner workings of the movement' than the men, as their role of 'Chancellors of the Exchequer' in the home imbued them with the root principles of co-operation;[37] whilst in a lecture on 'Women's Influence, and the Decay of Home Life', a Mr Miller stressed women's 'ability for special service whenever tenderness, love and sympathy were required'.[38] Woman's role in the co-operative movement and her relationship to it was viewed as an extension of her role in the family: 'the existence of a branch of the Guild in connection with a cooperative society should be a guarantee that, in that society there is a strong refining influence, leading the society to cooperative idealism, as the mother leads her husband and children in the right direction.'[39]

For male co-operators the particular virtues which women possessed were regarded as ideally suited to the role of moral campaigner and it was believed their major contribution to the movement would centre on schemes for the 'moral and social elevation of the poorer members' of society and 'the elimination of Sin and Crime'.[40]

Guildswomen did not predicate their public role solely on the basis of the duties of citizens, but also on the rights, and they stressed the advancement of women as citizens as much as the responsibilities of women to the co-operative movement. Their tribute to Queen Victoria on her death succinctly captures the Guild's conception of women's role: 'Her vigilant attention to public affairs, her conscientious discharge of the difficult duties of her position, the tender affection which characterised her in the capacities of wife and mother, enshrined her in the heart of every woman in her wide realm.'[41] The SCWG's belief in women's unique qualities which derived from motherhood

[37] SCWG, *Seventeenth Annual Report, 1909.*
[38] SCWG, *Sixteenth Annual Report, 1908.*
[39] Buchan, *History of the Scottish Co-operative Women's Guild*, p xi.
[40] SCWG, *Ninth Annual Report, 1901.*   [41] Ibid.

fuelled their feminism. References to women's special nature were used as a means of asserting their moral superiority and as a justification for their entry into public life, and did not imply social subordination or women's confinement to the domestic sphere.

The ILP and the WLL, which was dominated by ILP women, had a similar conception of the role of women, basing their case for women's enfranchisement on the superior and distinct moral attributes of women and the enrichment to political life which their involvement would entail. Sexual equality was defined as the recognition of the equal value of motherhood and the centrality of the home and the family to the health of the nation: 'First let our citizenship be recognised, and we are on the only safe and sure road to the enthronement of motherhood equally with fatherhood as the guiding principle of our national life. Then will woman, the mother and homemaker, set about her benificent work in the land, unhampered no longer "unofficially".'[42]

The destruction of the home and the undermining of the importance of the family was regarded as the product of unfettered capitalism and an index of its brutality, whilst the task of defending the home and the family was assigned to the socialists and incorporated into the working-class struggle. Defence of the family was interpreted as the defence of the 'natural' sexual division of labour, which located women in the home. By drawing women into the labour force, capitalism was regarded as violating the natural order of things and destroying the 'natural' qualities of women. In an article fulminating against the extent of married women's work in Dundee and deriding a scheme for the provision of day nurseries, Tom Johnston, the Editor of *Forward*, asserted: 'The husbands stay at home dry nursing, the women go out to earn wages. What an inversion of civilisation! What a damning indictment of capitalism!'[43]

Therefore, whilst the ILP alone of the early twentieth century labour movements displayed an active commitment to the 'Woman Question', its definition of feminism involved elevating the status and role of mothers and reasserting the ideology of

---

[42] *Forward*, 16 Jan. 1909.   [43] Ibid., 19 Oct. 1912.

separate sexual spheres. Women were not to be denied a public role but they were to be restored to the domestic sphere and withdrawn from the labour force in order that they might more effectively carry out their primary role as carers and nurturers.

The ILP's preoccupation with women's role as mothers was to some extent a reflection of contemporary concerns with 'the health of the nation' as well as a commitment to sexual equality and the rights of women. Labour League women and ILP socialists shared a common conception with official opinion of the pivotal role of the mother in the health and welfare of the future generation and subscribed to the philosophy that the greatness of the nation was linked to the quality of family life.[44] Whereas medical and official bodies tended to deposit the responsibility for infant welfare with the mother and strove to promote improved child care by advocating greater maternal efficiency, Labour League women were more likely to advocate environmental solutions and social reform, for example, blaming the quality of the milk supply for infant mortality rather than bad maternal habits.[45]

Although the ILP's definition of feminism was conceived in terms of women's role as homemakers, it was sufficiently broad to encompass a conception of equality and freedom based on the economic freedom of women and their emancipation from the drudgery of housework. It was envisaged by Johnston that within a generation of women acquiring the vote:

we shall have demands by married women that they shall be paid wages for indoor work, payment to be fixed and regular, and made direct to them by their husband's employers. That payment to continue during maternity. In short the economic freedom of women. The women will demand less unnecessary home work. She will see the advantages of Cooperative housekeeping. She will see that if several families clubbed together to form a hotel company, they will live cheaper, economise in the cooking and save the present useless wastage of coal fires and harassed feminine labour by having common dining halls and the cooking done by professional cooks.[46]

[44] J. Lewis 'The Social History of Social Policy: Infant Welfare in Edwardian England', *Journal of Social Policy*, 9 (1980), 477.   [45] Ibid.
[46] *Forward*, 19 Nov. 1910.

The provision of communal facilities was advocated as a means of consolidating the family, rather than undermining it, and as a way of providing the condition for women to develop to their full potential as homemakers. The ILP did have a vision of their new Socialist Commonwealth, which involved the transformation of family life and the role of women. However, it was a vision which was still grounded in the ideology of domesticity and the complementarity of gender relations. An editorial in *Forward* argued that when women got the vote 'Where man has rigged a scaffold and a gas pipe, women will plant a flower . . . the inevitable tendency will be . . . to drastic Housing and Temperance legislation.'[47] The introduction of women into politics and public life was viewed as a means of democratizing and humanizing society by incorporating the particular qualities of women, developed by virtue of their roles as wives and mothers:

Soon for the first time, we shall set abuilding that new society, built on a true Democracy, and which absorbing as it must, the finer woman feelings, and the social spirit, gives to Humanity its one last hope of rearing on Earth that happy, joyous free life, for which we have struggled and yearned down the centuries.[48]

By addressing women primarily as homemakers, organizations such as the SCWG, the WLL, and the ILP endorsed the view of separate spheres, albeit in a modified version. The particular formulation of this ideology was conceived in terms of broadening women's public role and social responsibilities, rather than restricting them. Moreover, the success of these organizations in involving women in labour politics demonstrates women's receptiveness to political issues which related to their concerns and which were important materially and politically to their daily lives. There were, however, difficulties in reconciling notions of the distinct and innate nature of men and women and the complementarity of gender roles with a belief in complete equality between the sexes. Despite the formal commitment to equality, in practice the interpretation of separate spheres frequently connoted the dependence and subordination of women. In political life this could mean that

[47] *Forward*, 19 Nov. 1910.   [48] Ibid.

women were confined to a separate and auxiliary role. In an article urging men to undertake propaganda work and distribute socialist literature from door to door, a woman ILP supporter argued:

Our men can do this good work if they only care. I know that if our Branch don't begin soon it won't be my fault. Because I will 'sway' the Branch into doing it. And you can bet your saucepan that my husband gives his hour per week to the cause instead of wasting his time arguing about impossible theories. Now then, you women readers, begin to 'nag' your husbands into doing some useful propaganda work for Socialism.[49]

Despite the rhetoric of the ILP, the fragility of its commitment to women's rights and equal status was evident in its reluctance to select women as candidates in elections. Although women were nominated for school boards and parish councils before 1914, they were never selected to contest the more prestigious and politically important town council elections as they had been in England and Wales.[50] Whilst the ILP made much of its belief that women were a necessary and integral part of the struggle for socialism, a *post mortem* in *Forward* of socialists' poor showing in 1909 local elections suggested that 'The Socialist movement has never been the success it might have been because it neglected the women.'[51] Socialist men were berated for their hypocrisy and the fact that their day-to-day practice diverged considerably from their formal commitment to equality:

The average socialist believes theoretically in the equality of the sexes, but he sheds that belief along with the mud from his boots when he crosses the threshold of his own door. In practice he does not admit that his wife has any other sphere than that of cleaning pots and pans and cooking steak and potatoes. Social questions are beyond the grasp of her intelligence.[52]

Ironically, in the same article which stressed that women were political assets and allies, socialists were constantly defined as

[49] *Forward*, 1 Apr. 1911.
[50] Smyth, 'Labour and Socialism in Glasgow', 217; Irene Sweeney, 'Municipal Politics and the Labour Party: Glasgow, 1909–1914', undergraduate dissertation, University of Strathclyde, 1986.
[51] *Forward*, 13 Nov. 1909.   [52] Ibid.

men: 'Socialism demands all that any man has to give . . . the public expect more from a socialist than from any other man . . . every socialist must be better than other men . . . There is no propagandist so effective as the man who lives a clean and noble life.'[53] Another article which was critical of the limited franchise underlined the fact that 5,500,000 men were disfranchised, no reference being made to the far greater number of women excluded.[54]

Male co-operators were even more entrenched and overt in their hostility to the full and equal participation of women in the movement. An early report of the SCWG lamented the 'prejudice still strong in some quarters against women taking their share in the work of the movement'.[55] Mrs Buchan, a President of the Guild, was nominated thirteen times before she succeeded in being elected to the Board of the St George Society in 1910.[56] The circumscribed public role accorded to women is confirmed by the observation of a leading co-operator and ILP supporter that it was not 'considered good form for women to appear on the platform at co-operative or other working class meetings'.[57]

Women's role was ascribed equal value and they were accorded recognition of the part they could play in the regeneration of society, but the view that women should be nurturers and men providers, and the assertion of innate male and female differences was never questioned. Essentially women's place in the labour movement was based on their status as wives and mothers, and, whilst this drew many women into political activity and extended their public role, it was in a way which reinforced existing gender divisions, confirmed the home as the natural domain of women, and ultimately limited their choice of social roles and their opportunities.

The Marxist wing of the labour movement was less successful in attracting women to its organizations. The Social Democratic Federation is usually depicted as a sectarian and dogmatic organization which was isolated from the mainstream

[53] *Forward*, 13 Nov. 1909. [54] Ibid., 12 Feb. 1910.
[55] SCWG, *Fourth Annual Report*, 1896.
[56] K. M. Callin, *History of the Co-operative Women's Guild: Diamond Jubilee, 1892–1952* (Glasgow: Scottish Co-operative Society, 1952).
[57] Dollan, *Jubilee History of the Kinning Park Co-operative Society*, 48.

of the labour movement. However, the SDF in Scotland could not be accused of isolationism as they participated fully in the socialist culture of the pre-war years, due largely to the efforts of John McLean to reach the widest possible audience with his education classes. McLean, the leading light of the SDF, also rejected the mechanical version of Marxism prevalent at the time, which minimized the role of working-class organization and activity in effecting change. In Scotland, therefore, the SDF had a greater impact on the Scottish working class by dint of its educational and propaganda work than it did south of the border, although its membership was still tiny and restricted mainly to skilled workers.

The SDF had little to say on the specific issue of the 'Woman Question'. Therefore, its conception of women's role and the relations between the sexes can only be inferred from its political diagnosis and its vision of an alternative social and political order. McLean referred only to a socialist future where classes would be abolished and no mention was made of sexual inequalities, the sexual division of labour, or the role of women in a socialist society. However, there is an indication that McLean subscribed to the view that married women's province was the home and not the workplace when he exhorted women strikers in Neilston to form a union: 'We strongly advised the Nitshill lassies to get into a union, and stay in until they got married.'[58]

Further evidence of the SDF's commitment to the family and the notion of the home as the haven of working men from the rigours of competitive capitalism is contained in a speech given by one of their members at a rally in Dundee. Condemning Dundee's industrial system, which employed so many married women, he railed:

A home ought to be the holiest of holies. The man who performed his honest duties ought to be able to say—here is my altar of love, here shall I rest, here shall I withstand the vile temptations . . . of the world . . . But what did they do—went home and gave the baby a bottle—went home and let the wife go out and earn the dollars.[59]

[58] *Woman Worker*, 14 June 1910.
[59] W. Walker, *Juteopolis: Dundee and its Textile Workers, 1885–1923* (Edinburgh: Scottish Academic Press, 1979), 60.

Clearly the political ideologies of socialist and labour organizations and their conceptions of women's role conditioned their responses to women workers and their struggles. The WLL were active in campaigns to alleviate unemployment amongst women, and petitioned Glasgow Council to set up a Women's Distress Committee. However, the League's support for women's right to work was confined to spheres which were regarded as 'women's work', and did not pose any threat of competition to male employment. For example, members of the League devised schemes for training in domestic work and hygiene and elementary sick nursing, the establishment of a municipal workshop, and the creation of 'similarly suitable employment' such as needlework, agricultural field-work, and market gardening.[60]

The ILP could also be active in support of the struggles of women workers, but it was in the women's capacity as victims rather than as a way of developing their capacity for self-organization. Its support was fuelled by the belief that capitalism had plucked these women from their natural territory and stripped them of their natural 'womanly attributes'. George Barnes, an ILP Member of Parliament, addressed the women strikers of Kilbirnie, denounced their employers, and pledged his support for their cause on the basis that it was the iniquities of capitalism which forced them to do 'men's work'.[61]

The ILP also saw their task as establishing the ideal of a family wage as a reality and attacking every example of its violation. It was on this basis that they related to women workers and elicited their support for socialism. There were obviously women workers for whom this policy had great appeal and who were in accord with the ILP's conception of women's role. A letter to *Woman Worker* from a married woman weaver expressed her support for socialism on the basis that:

one of the most cruel and brutal conditions is that which married women have to live under when the time comes when they have to endure that sacred duty which should be the glory of superb womanhood. A mother has to go to the mill up to the time of

60 Special Committee on Relief of Unemployment amongst Women, Minutes, 1 Dec. 1909, E-36-6, SRA.
61 *Forward*, 14 June 1910.

childbirth because her husband's wages will not keep them. Then consider the heartache that mother must endure when she has to take her baby between 5 and 6 o'clock in the morning out to nursery in all kinds of weather. This is the system that brutalizes, instead of bringing out the instincts of motherhood.[62]

There were other women in the socialist movement who adopted a quite different position, who defended women's right to work, and who were critical of the position taken by many trade-unionists and socialists who sought to exclude women from certain occupations. A letter in *Forward*, from a miner, arguing that women should be excluded from pit-brow work, provoked a number of responses from women who denounced the hypocrisy of 'some Labour men' on the question of women's work. It was pointed out that concerns over conditions of work and long hours were rarely expressed about entirely female trades such as domestic service and shop work. One letter accused the writer of 'trying to deprive a decent and hard-working class of industrial workers of their means of livelihood',[63] whilst another curtly concluded that 'the time is past for treating women as irresponsible beings'.[64]

For many women workers, the demand for the right to work and equal pay was based on necessity rather than a challenge to the ideology of the male bread-winners, but the commitment of the ILP to the ideology of separate sexual spheres and the sanctity of the family frequently led them to support sectional trade union struggles to exclude women which failed to recognize this elementary right. An article in *Forward* putting the case of Glasgow pipemakers who were involved in a strike with one of the export employers in the city argued that:

They are not fighting for better wages, nor yet better working conditions, but are compelled to fight for their existence as a trade against the introduction of female labour. The employers are not satisfied with male serfs, they are now employing women, who will have no trade union to protect their interests and who will before the employers are done with them have lost all the attributes of their sex.[65]

[62] *Woman Worker*, 9 Sept. 1911.
[63] *Forward*, 26 June 1908.   [64] Ibid., 16 Sept. 1911.
[65] Ibid., 21 Aug. 1909.

The *Forward* editorial fully supported the action and urged readers to boycott shopkeepers doing business with the firm. The ILP's commitment to a family wage was to a large extent a reflection of the material interests of the ILP constituency, which was drawn from the upper ranks of the working class and the lower middle class.[66] This was similar to many of the ILP policies, which, although generating significant struggles, neglected the material interest of significant sections of the working class. The housing struggles in which ILP activists played a leading part tackled the issue of rents when arguably a more pressing issue was the incredibly high number of evictions in Scotland, a problem which affected the poorer sections of the working class.[67] The demand for a family wage may have been perceived as a sound tactic for combating working-class exploitation, but at the expense of women who were forced to labour for supplementary wages. In this respect the ILP was as sectional and exclusivist as the trade-unionism it so readily dismissed. Consequently, it failed to develop political strategies which embraced all sections of the working class.

The only socialist organization which related to women as workers rather than homemakers was the SLP, whose emphasis on industrial struggle and class unity precluded a conception of an arena of struggle other than the workplace. The SLP were revolutionary socialists who argued that capitalism could not be reformed by electing representatives of the working class to Parliament, and as an alternative advocated building industrial unionism to organize the economic power of the working class. This strategy flowed from an analysis of capitalism which attributed all manifestations of exploitation and oppression to the monopoly of economic power by the capitalist class and which asserted the identity of interests of all sections of the working class, irrespective of occupational,

---

[66] Deian Hopkins, 'The Membership of the ILP 1904–1910: A Spatial and Occupational Analysis', *International Review of Social History*, 20 (1975), 195.

[67] D. Englander, 'Landlord and Tenant in Urban Scotland: The Background to the Clyde Rent Strike 1915', *Journal of the Scottish Labour History Society*, 15 (1981). Englander makes the general point that the labour movement in this period, including the ILP, held the poorer elements of the working class in low regard and often expressed the same attitudes towards these sections as the middle classes.

racial, ethnic, and sexual divisions. Their insistence on the
futility of reforming capitalism, which they argued contributed
to its stability, endowed their socialism with a particular brand
of revolutionary purism which could be dismissive of measures
intended to lessen the hardship of working-class life.

The diagnosis of all problems as class problems clearly
shaped the SLP's attitude to women's suffrage and the more
general issue of women's rights. Although they frequently
proclaimed their belief in the equality of the sexes and women's
social, political, and economic emancipation, they remained
implacably opposed to women's suffrage, arguing:

Socialism is in full accord with the Suffragist movement insofar as
it is a protest against the present social status of women. Socialism
is in accord with the Suffragists' exposure of the contemptible and
superficial arguments of the anti-feminists. Socialism takes no part
in the howl of opprobrium raised against the tactics of the neo-
suffragists, but gives full credit to these women for the energy and
successful organisation with which they are carrying out their plan
of campaign. Finally Socialism also aims at true equality of the sexes
and the end of women's subjection to men.

When all is said, however, Socialism and Suffragism remain at
enmity because of the basic difference in their principles . . . under
the existing system of society any change of laws giving the same
opportunities to women as to men, would only benefit those women
who belonged to the privileged or propertied class in society.
Socialism in fact is a revolutionary movement, Suffrage is a mere
bourgeois reform movement . . . The SLP holds that the Suffragist
movement is of great importance and interest to the women of the
bourgeoisie, but of none to women of the working class.[68]

They buttressed this argument against women's suffrage with
arguments about the misguided belief that acquisition of the
vote would lead to equality:

Women's subjection did not arise from political disabilities—these
disabilities arose from women's subjection. And that subjection from
the first had a distinctly economic basis, sex inequality as Morgan
has shown came into being in the dim past of barbaric ages with the
development of a system of society based upon private property.[69]

[68] Lily Gair Wilkinson, 'Revolutionary Socialism and the Women's Movement',
Socialist, Jan. 1909.   [69] Ibid.

As with other issues, the source of women's subordination and oppression was diagnosed as an economic problem which could only be resolved by the abolition of class society and the birth of socialism. The SLP's analysis of women's subordination drew heavily on Engels's *Origin of the Family, Private Property and the State*, which linked woman's oppression to the development of private property and her subsequent exclusion from public and socially necessary labour.

Although the SLP prescribed the equal access of women to the means of production as the basis of independence and equality, in practice they subscribed to the ideology of a family wage under capitalism, accepting that if women were married their wages would be supplementary to the men's. They attributed this to the fact that married women themselves were content to work for less money because they had other means of support, claiming that single and widowed women 'suffer from the competition of many less helpless wives and daughters whose necessities only force them to aim at supplementary earnings'.[70] This position is a variant on the theme that there are certain groups of workers who are willing to work for lower wages, and ignores the powerful ideological and social factors which determine earnings. For the SLP women's low pay was attributable solely to economic factors, as they regarded the roots of women's subordination as having an economic basis. They therefore neglected the ideological basis for women's oppression and the role of the family in its maintenance.

The SLP were reticent about outlining a detailed blueprint for the new socialist order and despite their constant assertions about the equality of the sexes they gave little indication of how the role of women and men might be transformed by socialism or what constituted equality. They were clearly sensitive to attacks on socialists as anti-family and argued that, whilst it was impossible to predict the detailed results of freedom for women,

this much can be said. If the home in its true sense is an ideal, if monogamy in its true sense is also an ideal, these are ideals which will only be possible of realisation under Socialism. There is nothing in Socialism incompatible with that true home life which Capitalism destroys.[71]

    [70] *Socialist*, Sept. 1909.   [71] Ibid., Oct. 1909.

The crucial issue for the SLP was the abolition of classes through the socialization of the means of production; the question of the family and the roles of men and women were not regarded as central to socialist strategy. Their claim that 'Whatever ideas individuals may hold in regard to [the true freedom of women] can only be more or less of guesswork'[72] indicates that these matters were consigned to the private sphere and subject to individual rather than collective resolution.

The refusal of the SLP to view women as other than members of an oppressed and exploited class whose historic mission was the overthrow of capitalism meant that they did not subscribe to the stereotypical images of women as passive and were quick to acknowledge women's combative quality.

Their rejection of the sectionalism of craft unionism and insistence of the common interest of the working class led them to champion women's right to work in the face of campaigns to exclude 'cheap female labour'. They took Edinburgh compositors to task when they demanded that machine composition be solely undertaken by male union labour, accusing them of being reactionary and divisive:

What economic or social argument can be put forward to justify the claim that the trade is yours? Whatever the justification there may have been in the past when a high degree of ability may have been necessary to acquire and work at the trade, that reason has forever passed away, if it ever was more than a trade guild superstition.[73]

However, their dismissal of reforms which they considered mere palliatives, and their refusal to acknowledge the specific problems of women as distinct from the class question, meant that they did nothing in practice to advance the right of women to work and indeed could be obstructive on this issue. Thus they attacked the Women's Freedom League for advocating maternity benefits because 'the intention of the capitalist is to secure a healthier and more capable community of workers'.[74]

As the issue of women's rights was subsumed under the class struggle, the SLP did not attempt to relate to women workers as women but as wage-earners whose entry into the labour

---

[72] *Socialist*, Oct. 1909.   [73] Ibid., July 1910.
[74] Ibid., June 1910.

force made their interest identical with that of other wage-earners. Therefore, they made no special effort to organize women workers and did not conduct any campaigns based on the specific interest of women workers, such as advancing their right to work. Women were recruited to the struggle for socialism as wage-earners; therefore, all non-wage-earning women were ignored, as were the real differences in the historical experience of diverse sections of the working class.

With the exception of the SLP, the political organizations of the working class in the pre-war years shared a conception of women's role in terms of the domestic sphere and their primary commitment to the home and the family. The housing struggles of the war years, and the campaigns around school meals, the medical inspection of schoolchildren, and a range of issues, are testimony to the fact that this position encouraged a definition of feminism which exploited the potential for the broadening of political consciousness and political engagement within the parameters of the existing sexual division of labour. It also exposes the fallacy of the view that women's participation in the formal economy is a necessary precondition for their political mobilization. However, it demonstrates, too, the political limitations of the familial ideology of the labour movement and the view of women as primarily homemakers. Although this ideology generated political struggles, it reflected and sustained the fragmentation of the working class along gender lines by confirming women's association with domestic labour and reinforcing patterns of job segregation which confined women to a well-defined sphere of 'women's employment'.

The idealization of family life and the central place accorded to women in the spiritual and moral development of the working class were in stark contrast to the serious material disadvantages imposed on those women who did not conform to the stereotype of the woman dependent on the earnings of a male bread-winner and who were forced to sell their labour for a wage which was assumed to be supplementary.

The stereotypical image of women as homemakers treated women as a homogeneous group with identical experiences and needs, and denied the validity of their experience as waged labour. Women's place in the labour movement was based on their status as wives and mothers and there was little attempt to harness them to the struggle for socialism in their capacity as workers or to encourage them to identify or organize as workers. This not only reinforced their marginality in the labour market but contributed to the marginality of working women to working-class politics by failing to recognize them as a potential political constituency.

Conclusion

THE history of women's employment in Scotland from 1850 until the First World War provides strong confirmation of the view that women's subordinate position in the labour market was linked to prevailing ideologies of gender and domesticity. However, the evidence suggests that women's experience of waged labour was mediated by these ideologies and not determined by them. The analysis of the development of the Glasgow cotton-spinning industry demonstrated that decisions about when and how to employ women were contingent on the interaction of a number of variables and could not be explained by one general theoretical model whether it was based on patriarchal ideology, the exclusionary practices of trade unions, or the assumption of any inherent logic of capital to deskill and cheapen costs. Managerial strategies were influenced by wider market conditions, relations between capital and labour, and the kind of technology employed. However, these categories, which are derived from the labour process, are insufficient and partial in their explanatory value and have to be integrated with consideration of the wider social relations outside the workplace, crucially gender ideologies, in order to provide a comprehensive analysis of the structuring of labour markets.

Clearly women's entry into social production did not release them from male domination or replace gender subordination with exploitation as waged labour, but rather their experience as workers was premissed upon their subordination as a gender. Even in a town such as Dundee, where female employment was widespread and many women were the major or sole contributors to the family income, the yoke of patriarchal authority and control hung heavily, defining the nature of their work, earnings, modes of supervision, and codes of behaviour. In Dundee and elsewhere wider social relations penetrated the workplace so that the capitalist labour process was also shaped by the relations between the sexes and not solely by the imperatives of capital accumulation. Therefore, gender relations were constituted in both the workplace and the home. Women's identity as members of a gender was not discarded when they became workers as in practice their entry into production was in part shaped by a domestic ideology which prescribed appropriate roles for women and appropriate relations between the sexes.

The pervasiveness of domestic ideology and the notion of separate sexual spheres, which percolated throughout society, did not mean it was digested in exactly this form by the working classes. It was forged and elaborated by the bourgeoisie, and, whilst providing the touchstone of culturally acceptable gender roles, it was recast by the working classes to make sense of their experience. For the organized minority of the working class who were either in possession of skills or strategically placed in the production process, it was an ideal to be realized. However, the recognition that it could not always be achieved meant that separate spheres were reinterpreted to include work for women, provided it did not encroach on men's province or usurp men's prior rights to work, and was compatible with women's culturally prescribed role. The reformulated version of the separate spheres ideology meant that the critical issue which was contested was the site of female labour rather than its exclusion from the labour market.

Labour historians have drawn attention to the exclusivist practices of Victorian trade-unionism which sought to maintain differentials of skill and earnings within the labour force. They have ignored, however, the ways in which such practices embodied assumptions about gender roles and the familial ideology that women's place was in the home. The notion of the male provider and protector reinforced the claims of skilled, semi-skilled, and unskilled trade-unionists to a prior right to work and their demand for a family wage, which meant that frequently their strategies disadvantaged women workers, even when other sectional policies had been eroded or abandoned. The corollary of the demand for a family wage for men was the conception of women as economic dependants whose earnings did not need to cover their living costs. This contributed to one of the most pressing problems for working women in this period, their appallingly low wages; and yet the response of the trade union movement to a situation which they helped to create was to view women's low pay as a consequence of their inability to organize and as a threat or a problem to be overcome by excluding them from the labour market or at least controlling their entry. Because trade unions related to women as dependants and failed to recognize the ways in which women's gender roles structured their status and experience as waged workers and created many of the problems which they faced in the labour market, they represented in practice the interests of male workers.

Trade-unionists did not always set their face like flint against organizing women, but their support was conditional and contingent. Instances of supportive action by trade-unionists were usually confined to well-defined areas of women's work which did not compete with male labour, and where combination was viewed as an indirect means of moral and social regulation by providing the lever to raise wages and thus dispel the spectre of prostitution. Regulation and control of female labour motivated attempts by male trade-unionists to organize women workers in the same industry or workplace where employers had succeeded in introducing female labour over the heads of male workers. Trade union organization was often advocated as a way of outmanœuvring employers' attempts to use women to undercut and undermine male labour's wages and organization. Alternatively, trade union controls were advocated when non-unionized women in an industry persistently bypassed established negotiating procedures and took independent initiatives which not only had a disruptive effect on production but undermined the legitimacy of workplace trade union organization and threatened the economic interests of the organized men. In these instances support for organizing women was cynically exploited as a means of channelling collective action along more manageable and containable routes. The experience of women workers in this period illustrates that the problems that women faced in the labour market derived from the wider sexual division of labour in society, and that, if trade unions were to represent their interests adequately, the structures and practices of trade-unionism would have had to recognize and challenge these divisions rather than reflect them. This would have involved developing alternative forms of organization and moving beyond the traditional concerns of trade-unionism in order to encompass issues which tackled gender divisions.

Whilst subordination was the keynote of women's labour market position, it is not the full story. Underlying the somewhat bleak general structures lurks a more complex reality which breaks down the gender stereotype associated with over-reliance on general abstract models to explain women's waged work. Although invariably classed as unskilled labour, women workers often possessed genuine skills from which they derived immense satisfaction but which were socially unrecognized. Although women usually had little formal authority in the workplace, their centrality to production and their possession of valued skills, as in Dundee's jute industry, enabled them to exert informal levers of influence, if not legitimately sanctioned authority. Both spinners and weavers in Dundee were responsible for the on-the-job training of new recruits which placed them in a strategic position they were not slow to exploit, particularly when their labour was in short supply.

Women did not always perceive their experience of work as unalloyed drudgery and tedium or as a period of marking time until they could occupy their rightful and proper place in the home as the helpmeet of a husband. Despite the diffusion and force of Victorian domestic ideology, the experience of waged work could generate an ambivalent or even oppositional response to this ideology among women who might not have consciously challenged it but who none the less articulated positive and enthusiastic attitudes to their work. The confine-ment of women to well-defined sectors of the economy where they occupied a subordinate position in the labour force in terms of authority, skill, and pay is indisputable, but this did not mean that work was an arid and negative experience which lacked the compensating skills and status of men's work.

Whatever qualifications are applied to the general theory of women's subordination in the labour market, the history of working women in Scotland demonstrates its limitations as an explanation for their workplace behaviour. The copious evidence of women workers' collective action indicates that one cannot ascribe typical characteristics to women workers which are derived from general models of gender. More recent contributions to labour process debates have restored to labour a key role in the formation of the labour process, and illustrate the contested character of managerial authority. Similarly, women's structural and ideological subordination in the workplace and society did not mean complete submission to patriarchal control and authority. By concentrating on formal trade union organizations, assumptions have been made about women based on their absence from these spheres, as if these areas exhausted all collectivist tendencies. Consequently, the received view of non-unionized women is one of either irrationality and impulsiveness or deference and docility. However, it is clear that the history of women workers is one of struggle and opposition and that they frequently displayed a strong commitment to collective action. This is not to suggest that women's forms of resistance were superior to those of the organized trade union movement or that they displayed a higher level of class consciousness, but to reappraise the view that women represented the most backward section of the working class.

The nature of sexual divisions in society mediated women's experience of class and therefore shaped the form of their class consciousness. It would therefore be a mistake to view the form of working women's resistance in this period as outmoded, anachronistic, or irrelevant simply because it did not conform to the practices of nineteenth-century trade-unionism.

The controls and constraints placed upon every aspect of women's lives derived from a male-dominated culture. Therefore, not surprisingly, women's resistance often took the form of subverting male authority and challenging gender divisions. Women's collective struggles in the workplace, even when they were expressions of economic grievances, displayed an awareness of their common experience and identity as women and as workers. Waged labour, by drawing women together as a gender and as workers, created the potential for them to struggle as both workers and as a gender. Although there is little basis for the unqualified optimism of Engels's prediction concerning the liberating consequences of women's entry into social production, intensification and reinforcement of gender subordination was not the only alternative. Women's entry into waged labour generated struggles which both strengthened their capacity for self-organization and contained implicit challenges to prescribed gender roles.

The nature of women's resistance may be dismissed as a temporary release which did not threaten the basic order of society or undermine the gender of authority relations, but the style of confrontation where emboldened women mimicked and ridiculed patriarchal authority did question and challenge existing gender divisions and the dominance of masculinity. Therefore, their resistance contained an additional dimension to the traditional masculine style of confrontation which left the existing social relations untouched.

In arguing that women's identity as members of a gender was not discarded when they became workers, it is not suggested that their experience of work was undifferentiated and that women were a homogeneous group, but that their experience was mediated through their gender subordination. Nor is it suggested that the process was one way and that ideology shaped work experience. Clearly work-related factors had some impact on women's consciousness and responses. What was decisive for women's (and men's) experience of waged labour and their responses to it was the interaction between social relations and processes within the workplace and those outside.

Historical debate about divisions within the British working class has largely centred on the divisions between skilled and unskilled workers and more precisely between a labour aristocracy of workers and the rest. The concept of the labour aristocracy has recently been subjected to vigorous criticism which has seriously questioned its explanatory value and drawn attention to the fact that its central weakness is that it is too simplistic to capture all the distinctions between British workers in the second half of the nineteenth century. The present study provides further evidence of the inadequacy of an explanation of the social formation of the working class which poses a simple dichotomy between workers and fails to recognize either the complexity of divisions or more profound divisions than skilled versus unskilled. In arguing that gender divisions were central to the formation of the workforce, it is not intended to substitute one polarity for another, but to draw attention to the interaction of class and gender and indeed to the interconnectedness of different elements of the social structure such as the family and the workplace. The orthodox Marxist definition of class which concentrates on the realm of production and economic experience at the point of production has proved inadequate for an understanding of the differential experience of men and women in the labour market. This points to the need for a broader consideration of the social formation and an analysis of the interrelationship of production and reproduction if we are to conceptualize the position of women in the world of work.

Select Bibliography

PRIMARY SOURCES

Manuscripts

Census Enumerator's Schedules, 1891, Dundee Registration District, St Clement's District, West Register House.
DDUJFW (Dundee and District Union of Jute and Flax Workers), Executive Committee Minutes, 1906-15, DARC.
—— Copy Letter Book, 1907-14, DARC.
—— General Meetings Minute Book, 1906-14, DARC.
—— Dundee Standing Joint Industrial Committee, Minute Book, 1912-14, DARC.
DUA (Dundee University Archives), MS 15/46, Wage Records of an Unidentified Jute Mill, 1860-2.
Edinburgh Typographical Society, Copy of an Agreement between the Scottish Typographical Association and Edinburgh Master Printers' Association, Sept. 1910, ACC4068 (127), NLS.
—— Report of a Meeting of Representatives from the Executive Council and the Edinburgh Case Branch, 1911, ACC4008 (124), NLS.
—— Report of Meetings on the Female Question between the Edinburgh Master Printers' Association and the National Printing and Kindred Trades, ACC4068 (124), NLS.
Glasgow Typographical Society, Board of Management Minute Books, 1888-1915, T-GTS1/1/5, T-GTS1/1/6, SUA.
—— Report of the Proceedings between the Master Printers' Association of Glasgow and the GTS, Dec. 1903, T-GTS1/9/5, SUA.
GTC (Glasgow Trades Council), Minutes, Aug. 1858-May 1859, 1910, 1911, 1913, MLG.
National Society of Operative Printers and Assistants, Glasgow Branch Minutes, 1905-1908, TV 331.881(55) Nat., MLG.
Schemes for Relief of Unemployment among Women, Copy Letters to the Town Clerk from Mrs Carnegie and Mrs Nixon, Women's Labour League, 4 Dec. 1909, 13 Dec. 1909, E-36-8, SRA.
SCWG (Scottish Co-operative Women's Guild), Minutes of the Quarterly Meeting of the Guild, 1893-1914, Scottish Co-operative Society, Shieldhall.

SIC (Sidlaw Industries Collection, DUA), contains miscellaneous records of the various firms, principally Cox Brothers and Baxter Brothers, which now constitute Sidlaw Industries.

Special Committee on the Relief of Unemployment among Women, Minutes, Dec. 1909, E-36-6, SRA.

WCE (Webb Collection E), British Library of Political and Economic Science, sects. A, B, C, and D.

Government Publications

Annual Reports by the Chief Labour Correspondent on Strikes and Lockouts in the United Kingdom, 1890–1914 (London: HMSO, various years).

Censuses of Great Britain and Scotland, 1851–1911 (London: HMSO, various years).

Factory Inquiry Commission, 1833, First Report, *Employment of Children in Factories with Minutes of Evidence*, in *Industrial Revolution: Children's Employment, 3* Factories, 20: *1833* (Shannon: Irish University Press, 1970).

First Report of the Select Committee on Combinations of Workmen 1837–38, C. 488 (London: HMSO, 1838).

Half-Yearly Reports by the Inspectors of Factories, 1842–1896, in *Industrial Revolution* (Factories, 6–25; Shannon: Irish University Press, 1970).

Report by the Labour Correspondent to the Board of Trade, Strikes and Lockouts, C. 5809–LXX.703 (London: HMSO, 1889).

Report from the Select Committee on Manufactures, Commerce and Shipping, 1833, in *Industrial Revolution: Trade, 2* (Shannon: Irish University Press, 1970).

Return of the Rate of Wages in the Minor Textile Trades of the United Kingdom, C. 6161 (London: HMSO, 1890).

Return of Wages, 1830–86, C. 1572 (London: HMSO, 1887).

Royal Commission on Labour, *The Employment of Women*, C. 6894 (London: HMSO, 1893).

—— *Fifth Report on Changes in the Rate of Wages and Hours of Labour in the United Kingdom 1898*, C. 8795 (London: HMSO, 1898).

Royal Commission on the Poor Laws, *William and Jones Report*, C. 4690 (London: HMSO, 1909).

Statistical Tables and Reports on Trade Unions, 1887, C. 5104; 1888, C. 5505; 1889, C. 5808 (London: HMSO, various years).

Newspapers and Journals

Clydebank and Renfrew Press, 1911.
Daily Record and Mail, 1912.
Dundee Mill and Factory Operatives' Herald, 1885–9.
Dundee Advertiser, 1875–1913.
Dundee Courier, 1906, 1907.
Dundee Year Book, 1891–1913.
Evening Times, 1885–92.
Glasgow Forward, 1906–13.
Glasgow Herald, 1892, 1897, 1910, 1911, 1913.
Glasgow Sentinel, 1851–76.
Glasgow Weekly Herald, 1879–92.
Govan Press, 1890.
North British Daily Mail 1875–92.
Paisley Daily Express, 1905–10.
People's Journal, 1881, 1922.
Scottish Typographical Circular, 1905–10.
Scottish Typographical Journal, 1911–13.
Socialist, 1908–10.
Woman Worker, 1908–9.
WTUR (Women's Trade Union Review), 1891–1902.
WUJ (Women's Union Journal), 1876–90.

Other Published Material

Bookbinders' and Machine Rulers' Consolidated Union, Trade Circulars and Reports 1872, 1891–1900, MLG.
BREMNER, R. L., *The Housing Problem in Glasgow* (Glasgow: SCWT, 1902).
DSU (Dundee Social Union), *Report on Housing, Industrial Conditions and the Medical Inspection of School Children* (Dundee: DSU, 1905).
Dundee Year Book (Dundee, various years).
GCWT (Glasgow Council for Women's Trades), *1st Annual Report, 1895–96, 4th Annual Report, 1898–99*, SRA.
GTC (Glasgow Trades Council), Annual Reports, 1886–1914, SRA.
IRWIN, M. H., *The Problem of Homework* (Glasgow: SCWT, 1903).
—— *Report of an Inquiry into Women's Work in Laundries* (Glasgow: SCWT, 1904).
—— *Women Shop Assistants: How They Live and Work* (Glasgow: SCWT, 1901).

IRWIN, M. H., 'Women's Industries in Scotland', *Proceedings of the Philosophical Society of Glasgow*, 27 (1895–6).

—— *Women's Work in Tailoring and Dressmaking* (Glasgow: SCWT, 1900).

LC (Lamb Collection), Dundee Public Library, consists of books, pamphlets, paintings, manuscripts, the reports of societies and institutions, and newspaper cuttings. (A. C. Lamb was a local antiquarian.)

LENNOX, D., 'Working Class Life in Dundee for 25 Years 1878–1903', TS, n.d., *c*.1906, St Andrews University Library.

MYLES, J., *Chapters in the Life of a Dundee Factory Boy* (Dundee, 1887).

SNAOT (Scottish National Association of Operatives' Tailors), Annual Conference Reports, 1865–1913, NLS.

SCWG (Scottish Co-operative Women's Guild), Annual Reports, 1893–1914, Scottish Co-operative Society, Shieldhall, Glasgow.

SCWT (Scottish Council for Women's Trades), Annual Reports, 1901–2, 1904–5, 1905–6, SRA.

STUC (Scottish Trades Union Congress), Annual Reports, 1897–1914, NLS.

SMART, W., 'The Housing Problem and the Municipality', *University of Glasgow free lectures* (Glasgow: Adshead, 1902).

WARDEN, A. J., The Linen Trade Ancient and Modern (London: Frank Cass & Co., 1864).

WPPL (Women's Protection and Provident League), Annual Reports, 1875–88, 1897, SRA.

—— *Rules, 1894*, SRA.

WTUL (Women's Trade Union League), Annual Reports, 1891–1914, SRA.

SECONDARY SOURCES

Published Material

ALDCROFT, D. (ed.), *The Development of British Industry and Foreign Competition, 1875–1914* (London: Allen and Unwin, 1968).

ALEXANDER, S., 'Women, Class and Sexual Differences in the 1830's and 1840's', *History Workshop Journal*, 17 (Spring 1984).

—— 'Women's Work in Nineteenth Century London: A Study of the Years 1820–1850', in J. Mitchell and A. Oakley (eds.), *The Rights and Wrongs of Women* (Harmondsworth: Penguin, 1976).

—— and DAVIN, A., 'Feminist History', Editorial, *History Workshop Journal*, 1 (Spring 1976).

ALLEN, D., ' "Culture" and the Scottish Labour Movement', *Journal of the Scottish Labour History Society*, 14 (May 1980).

ALLEN, V. L., 'A Methodological Criticism of the Webbs as Trade Union Historians', *Bulletin of the Society for the Study of Labour History*, 4 (Spring 1962).

ANDERSON, M., *Family Structure in 19th Century Lancashire* (Cambridge University Press, 1971).

ARDENER, S., *Perceiving Women* (London: Mellaby Press, 1975).

BANNISTER, R., *Social Darwinism* (Philadelphia, Pa.: Temple University Press, 1979).

BARRETT, M., *Women's Oppression Today* (London: Verso, 1980).

—— and MACINTOSH, M., 'The Family Wage: Some Problems for Socialists and Feminists', *Capital and Class*, 11 (Summer 1980).

BEECHEY, V., 'On Patriarchy', *Feminist Review*, 3 (1979).

—— 'What's so Special about Women's Employment? A Review of Some Recent Studies of Women's Paid Work', *Feminist Review*, 15 (Winter 1983).

BORNAT, J., 'Home and Work: A New Context for Trade Union History', *Journal of the Oral History Society*, 5(2) (1977).

BOSTON, S., *Women Workers and the Trade Union Movement* (London: Davis-Poynter, 1980).

BRAVERMAN, H., *Labour and Monopoly Capital: The Degradation of Work in the Twentieth Century* (New York: Monthly Review Press, 1974).

BRECHER, J., *Strike!* (Boston: Southend Press, 1977).

BREMNER, D., *Industries of Scotland* (Edinburgh: David & Charles, 1869).

BROOM, J., *John MacLean* (Loanhead, Midlothian: MacDonald, 1973).

BUCHAN, A., *A History of the Scottish Co-operative Women's Guild, 1891–1913* (Glasgow: Scottish Wholesale Co-operative Society, 1913).

BUCKLEY, K. D., *Trade Unionism in Aberdeen, 1878–1900* (Edinburgh: Oliver and Boyd, 1955).

BURGESS, K., *The Challenge of Labour* (London: Croom Helm, 1980).

—— *The Origins of British Industrial Relations* (London: Croom Helm, 1975).

—— 'Workshop of the World: Client Capitalism at its Zenith, 1830–1870', in T. Dickson (ed.), *Scottish Capitalism* (London: Lawrence & Wishart, 1980).

BUTT, J., 'Employment Patterns of the Scottish City', in Gordon (ed.), *Perspectives of the Scottish City*.

—— and WARD, J. (eds.), *Scottish Themes* (Edinburgh: Scottish Academic Press, 1976).

CALLIN, K. M., *History of the Co-operative Women's Guild: Diamond Jubilee, 1892–1952* (Glasgow: Scottish Co-operative Society, 1952).

CAMPBELL, R. H., *The Rise and Fall of Scottish Industry 1707–1939* (Edinburgh: John Donald, 1980).

CANTOR, M., and LAURIE, B. (eds.), *Class, Sex and the Woman Worker* (Westport, Conn.: Greenwood Press, 1977).

CATLING, H., *The Spinning Mule* (Newton Abbot: David & Charles, 1970).

CHALLINOR, R., *The Origins of British Bolshevism* (London: Croom Helm, 1977).

CHAPMAN, D., 'The Establishment of the Jute Industry', *Review of Economic Studies*, 6 (1938–9).

CLEMENTS, R. V., 'British Trade Unions and Popular Political Economy, 1850–1875', *Economic History Review*, 14(1) (1961).

COOKE, A. J., *Baxters of Dundee* (University of Dundee, 1980).

CRAFTS, N. F. R., *British Economic Growth during the Industrial Revolution* (Oxford University Press, 1985).

CRONIN, J. E., *Industrial Conflict in Modern Britain* (London: Croom Helm, 1979).

DAVIDOFF, L., and WESTOVER, B., 'From Queen Victoria to the Jazz Age: Women's World in England, 1880–1939', in L. Davidoff and B. Westover (eds.), *Our Work, Our Lives, Our Words* (London: Macmillan, 1986).

DAVIN, A., 'Feminism and Labour History', in R. Samuel (ed.), *People's History and Socialist Theory* (London: Routledge & Kegan Paul, 1980).

—— 'Imperialism and Motherhood', *History Workshop Journal*, 5 (Spring 1978).

DEVINE, T. M., 'Women Workers 1850–1911', in T. M. Devine (ed.), *Farm Servants and Labour in Lowland Scotland 1770–1914* (Edinburgh: John Donald, 1984).

DICKSON, T., and CLARKE, T., 'Class and Class Consciousness in Early Industrial Capitalism', in T. Dickson (ed.), *Capital and Class in Scotland* (Edinburgh: John Donald, 1982).

DONNACHIE, I., 'Drink and Society 1750–1850: Some Aspects of the Scottish Experience', *Journal of the Scottish Labour History Society*, 13 (May 1979).

DRAKE, B., *Women in Trade Unions* (London: Labour Research Department, 1921).

DUFFY, A. E., 'New Unionism in Britain 1889–1890: A Reappraisal', *Economic History Review*, 2nd ser., 14(2) (1961–2).

DYEHOUSE, C., 'Working-Class Mothers and Infant Mortality in England 1895–1914', *Journal of Social History*, 12 (1978–9).

EDWARDS, R., *Contested Terrain: The Transformation of the Workplace in the Twentieth Century* (London: Heinemann, 1979).

EISENSTEIN, Z. R. (ed.), *Capitalist Patriarchy and the Case for Socialist Feminism* (New York: Monthly Review Press, 1979).

ELBAUM, B., LAZONICK, W., WILLIAMSON, F., and ZEITLIN, J., 'The Labour Process, Market Structure and Marxist Theory', *Cambridge Journal of Economics*, 3, (1979).

ENGELS, F., *The Origin of the Family, Private Property and the State* (New York: Pathfinder Press, 1972).

ENGLANDER, D., 'Landlord and Tenant in Urban Scotland: The Background to the Clyde Rent Strike 1915', *Journal of the Scottish Labour History Society*, 15 (1981).

FELDBERG, R., and GLENN, E. N., ' "Male and Female" Job versus Gender Models in the Sociology of Work', in J. Siltanen and M. Stanworth (eds.), *Women and the Public Sphere* (London: Hutchinson, 1984).

FIELD, J., 'British Historians and the Concept of the Labour Aristocracy', *Radical History Review*, 19 (Winter 1978–9).

FRASER, W. H., 'The Glasgow Cotton Spinners, 1837', in Butt and Ward (eds.), *Scottish Themes*.

—— 'The Labour Party in Scotland', in K. D. Brown (ed.), *The First Labour Party* (London: Croom Helm, 1985).

—— 'A Newspaper for its Generation: The Glasgow Sentinel', *Scottish Labour History Society Journal*, 4 (July 1971).

—— 'Trades Councils in the Labour Movement in 19th Century Scotland', in I. MacDougall (ed.), *Essays in Scottish Labour History* (Edinburgh: John Donald, 1978).

—— 'Trade Unions, Reform and the Election of 1868 in Scotland', *Scottish Historical Review* 50, (1971).

FRIEFELD, M., 'Technological Change and the "Self-Acting" Mule: A Study of Skill and the Sexual Division of Labour', *Social History*, 2(3) (1986).

GILLESPIE, S., *One Hundred Years of Progress: The Scottish Typographical Association 1853–1952* (Glasgow: Maclehose, 1953).

GORDON, G. (ed.), *Perspectives of the Scottish City* (Aberdeen University Press, 1985).

300   *Select Bibliography*

GRAY, R. Q., *The Labour Aristocracy in Victorian Edinburgh* (Oxford: Clarendon Press, 1976).

GUTMAN, H. G., 'Five Letters of Immigrant Workers from Scotland to the United States 1867–69', *Labour History*, 9(3) (1968).

HALL, C., 'The Early Formation of Victorian Domestic Ideology', in S. Burman (ed.), *Fit Work for Women* (London: Croom Helm, 1979).

HALLEY, J. R. L. (ed.), *A History of Halley's Mill 1822–1980* (Dundee: William Halley, 1980).

HAMILTON, H., *The Industrial Revolution in Scotland* (Oxford University Press, 1932).

HAMILTON, M. A., *Mary MacArthur* (London: Leonard Parsons, 1925).

HIGGS, E., 'Women, Occupations and Work in the Nineteenth Century Censuses', *History Workshop Journal*, 23 (Spring 1987).

HILDEN, P., *Working Women and Socialist Politics in France 1880–1914* (Oxford: Clarendon Press, 1986).

HOBSBAWM, E. J., *Labouring Men* (London: Weidenfeld and Nicolson, 1968).

HONEYMAN, T., *Good Templary in Scotland, 1869–94: Its Work and Workers* (Glasgow: Grand Lodge of Scotland, 1894).

HOPKINS, D., 'The Membership of the ILP 1904–1910: A Spatial and Occupational Analysis', *International Review of Social History*, 20 (1975).

HOWELL, D., *British Workers and the Independent Labour Party, 1888–1906* (Manchester University Press, 1982).

HUMPRHIES, J., '. . . The Most Free from Objections: The Sexual Division of Labour and Women's Work in Nineteenth Century England', *Journal of Economic History*, 47 (1987).

—— 'Protective Legislation, the Capitalist State and Working Class Men: The Case of the 1842 Mines Regulation Act', *Feminist Review*, 7 (Spring 1981).

HUTCHINS, B. L., 'Statistics of Women's Life and Employment', *Royal Statistical Society Journal* (June 1909).

JOHN, A. (ed.), *Unequal Opportunities: Women's Employment in England 1800–1918* (Oxford: Blackwell, 1986).

JOHN, A. V., *By the Sweat of their Brow: Women Workers at Victorian Coal Mines* (London: Croom Helm, 1980).

JOHNSTON, R., 'Thompson, Genovese, and Socialist Humanist History', *Historical Workshop Journal*, 6 (Autumn 1978).

JOHNSTON, T., *The History of the Working Classes in Scotland* (Wakefield: E. P. Publishing, 1974).

JOWITT, J. A., and MCIVOR, A. J. (eds.), *Employers and Labour in the English Textile Industries 1850-1939* (London: Routledge & Kegan Paul, 1988).

JOYCE, P., *Work, Society and Politics* (London: Methuen, 1982).

KESSLER-HARRIS, A., 'Organising the Unorganisable: Three Jewish Women and their Union', *Labour History*, 17 (Winter 1976).

KHUN, A., and WOLPE, Ann Marie (eds.), *Feminism and Materialism* (London: Routledge & Kegan Paul, 1978).

KING, E., *Scotland Sober and Scotland Free: The Temperance Movement 1829-1979* (Glasgow Museum and Art Galleries, 1979).

KNIGHT, D., and WILLMOTT, H. (eds.), *Gender and the Labour Process* (Aldershot: Gower, 1986).

KNOX, W., 'The Political and Workplace Culture of the Scottish Working Class 1832-1914', in R. J. Morris and W. H. Fraser (eds.), *Scottish People and Society 1836-1914*, iii (Edinburgh: John Donald, 1990).

LAZONICK, W., 'The Division of Labour and Machinery: The Development of British and US Cotton Spinning', Discussion Paper Series, Institute of Economic Research, Harvard University (May, 1978).

—— 'Industrial Relations and Technical Change: The Case of the Self-Acting Mule', *Cambridge Journal of Economics*, 3 (1979).

—— 'The Subjection of Labour to Capital: The Rise of the Capitalist System', *Review of Radical Political Economics*, 10 (Spring 1978).

LEE, C. H., *British Regional Employment Statistics 1841-1971* (Cambridge University Press, 1979).

LENMAN, B., and DONALDSON, K., 'Partners, Incomes, Investment and Diversification in the Scottish Linen Area, 1850-1914', *Business History*, 13(1) (1971).

—— LYTHE, C., and GAULDIE, E., *Dundee and its Textile Industry 1850-1914* (Dundee: Abertay Historical Association, 1969).

LEWENHAK, S., *Women and Trade Unions* (London: Benn, 1977).

—— 'Women in the Leadership of the STUC, 1897-1970', *Journal of the Scottish Labour History Society*, 7(4) (July 1973).

LEWIS, J., 'The Social History of Social Policy: Infant Welfare in Edwardian England', *Journal of Social Policy*, 9 (1980).

LEWIS, W. A., *Growth and Fluctuations, 1870-1913* (London: Allen and Unwin, 1978).

LIDDINGTON, J., and NORRIS, J., *One Hand Tied Behind Us* (London: Virago, 1978).

LITTLER, C., *The Development of the Labour Process in Capitalist Societies* (London: Heinemann, 1982).

LOGUE, K. T., *Popular Disturbances in Scotland 1780-1815* (Edinburgh: John Donald, 1979).

LOVELL, J., *British Trade Unions 1875-1933* (London: Macmillan, 1977).

LOWN, J., 'Not so much a Factory, more a Form of Patriarchy', in E. Garmarnikow, D. Morgan, J. Purvis, and D. Taylorsen (eds.), *Class, Gender and Work* (London: Heinemann, British Sociological Association, 1983).

MACDOUGALL, I. (ed.), *The Minutes of Edinburgh Trades Council 1859-1973* (Edinburgh: Constable, 1968).

MACINTYRE, S., *A Proletarian Science* (Cambridge University Press, 1980).

MCLAREN, A. A. (ed.), *Social Class in Scotland: Past and Present* (Edinburgh: John Donald, 1976).

MCLEAN, J., *In the Rapids of Revolution* (London: Allison and Busby, 1978).

MARK-LAWSON, J., and WITZ, A., 'From "Family Labour to "Family Wages"', *Social History*, 13(2), 1988.

MEACHAM, S., 'The Sense of an Impending Clash: English Working Class Unrest before the First World War', *American Historical Review*, 77(5) (1972).

MELLING, J., *Rent Strikes* (Edinburgh: Polygon, 1983).

MILKMAN, R. (ed.), *Women, Work and Protest: A Century of U.S. Women's Labour History* (London: Routledge, 1985).

MILTON, N., *John McLean* (London: Pluto, 1973).

MOORHOUSE, H. F., 'The Marxist Theory of the Labour Aristocracy', *Social History*, 3(1) (1978).

—— WILSON, M., and CHAMBERLAIN, C., 'Rent Strikes—Direct Action and the Working Class', *Socialist Register* (1972).

MORGAN, K. O. (ed.), *Essays in Anti-Labour History* (London: Macmillan, 1974).

PELLING, H., *The Social Geography of British Elections 1885-1910* (London: Macmillan, 1967).

PHILLIPS, A., and TAYLOR, B., 'Sex and Skill: Notes towards a Feminist Economics', *Feminist Review*, 6 (1980).

PHILLIPS, G. A., 'The Triple Industrial Alliance in 1914', *Economic History Review*, 24 (1971).

PINCHBECK, I., *Women Workers and the Industrial Revolution, 1750-1850* (London: Virago, 1969).

PRICE, R., 'The New Unionism and the Labour Process, 1888-1920', in W. Mommsen and G. H. G. Hubung (eds.), *The Development of Trade Unionism in Great Britain and Germany, 1880-1914* (London: Allen and Unwin, 1985).

REDDY, W. M., 'The Batteurs and the Informer's Eye: A Labour Dispute under the French Second Empire', *History Workshop Journal*, 7 (Spring 1979).
—— 'The Textile Trade and the Language of the Crowd at Rouen 1752–1871', *Past and Present*, 74 (Feb. 1977).
REID, A., 'Labour, Capital and the State in Britain 1880–1920', in W. Mommsen and G. H. G. Hubung (eds.), *The Development of Trade Unionism in Great Britain and Germany, 1880–1914* (London: Allen and Unwin, 1985).
—— 'Politics and Economics in the Formation of the British Working Class', *Social History*, 3(3) (1978).
REYNOLDS, J., and LAYBOURN, K., 'The Emergence of the ILP in Bradford', *International Review of Social History*, 20 (1975).
REYNOLDS, S., *Britannica's Typesetters* (Edinburgh University Press, 1989).
ROBERTSON, A. J., 'The Decline of the Scottish Cotton Industry', *Business History*, 12(2) (1970).
ROWAN, C., 'Women in the Labour Party, 1906–1920', *Feminist Review*, 12 (1982).
ROWBOTTOM, S., *Hidden from History* (London: Virago, 1973).
SAVILLE, J., 'The Ideology of Labourism', in R. Benewick, R. N. Berki, and B. Parekh (eds.), *Knowledge and Belief in Politics: The Problem of Ideology* (London: Allen and Unwin, 1973).
SCHREINER, O., *Woman and Labour* (London: Virago, 1978).
SCOTT, J., and TILLY, L., 'Women's Work and the Family in Nineteenth Century Europe', *Comparative Studies in Society and History*, 17 (1975).
SIMON, D., 'Master and Servant', in J. Saville (ed.), *Democracy and the Labour Movement* (London: Lawrence and Wishart, 1954).
SINCLAIR, R., *The Faithful Fibre: A History of the Development of the Linen Thread Company* (Glasgow: Linen Thread Co., 1956).
SLAVEN, A., *The Development of the West of Scotland, 1750–1960* (London: Routledge & Kegan Paul, 1975).
SMITH, J., 'Labour Tradition in Glasgow and Liverpool', *History Workshop Journal*, 17 (Spring 1984).
SMOUT, T. C. (ed.), *Comparative Aspects of Scottish and Irish Economic and Social History* (Edinburgh: John Donald, 1977).
SOLDON, N., *Women in British Trade Unions, 1874–1976* (Dublin: Gill and Macmillan, 1978).
Spare Rib, 1974.
STEDMAN JONES, G., 'Class Struggle in the Industrial Revolution', *New Left Review*, 90 (1975).

STEDMAN JONES, G., 'Working Class Culture and Working Class Politics', *Journal of Social History*, 7(4) (1973–4).

TAX, M., *The Rising of the Women* (New York: Monthly Review Press, 1980).

TAYLOR, B., *Eve and the New Jerusalem* (London: Virago, 1983).

TAYLOR, S., 'The Effect of Marriage on Job Possibilities for Women and the Ideology of the Home: Nottingham 1890–1930', *Oral History*, 5(2) (1977).

THOMAS, K., 'The Double Standard', *Journal of the History of Ideas*, 20 (April 1959).

THOMPSON, D., *The Early Chartists* (London: Macmillan, 1971).

—— 'Women and Nineteenth Century Radical Politics: A Lost Dimension', in J. Mitchell and A. Oakley (eds.), *The Rights and Wrongs of Women* (Harmondsworth: Penguin, 1976).

THOMPSON, E. P., 'Homage to Tom McGuire', in A. Briggs and J. Saville (eds.), *Essays in Labour History* (London: Macmillan, 1967).

—— *The Making of the English Working Class* (Harmondsworth: Penguin, 1968).

THOMPSON, P., *The Nature of Work* (London: Macmillan, 1983).

TREBLE, J. H., 'The Market for Unskilled Male Labour in Glasgow, 1891–1914', in I. MacDougall (ed.), *Essays in Scottish Labour History* (Edinburgh: John Donald, 1978).

VOGEL, L., *Marxism and the Oppression of Women: Towards a Unitary Theory* (London: Pluto, 1983).

WALBY, S., *Patriarchy at Work* (Oxford: Blackwell, 1986).

WALKER, W., *Juteopolis: Dundee and its Textile Workers, 1885–1923* (Edinburgh: Scottish Academic Press, 1979).

WEBB, S. and B., *History of Trade Unionism* (London: Longmans, Green, 1920).

WHITELEGG, E., *et al.* (eds.), *The Changing Experience of Women* (Oxford: Robertson, 1982).

WINTER, J. (ed.), *The British Working Class and Modern British History* (Cambridge University Press, 1983).

Women's Co-operative Guild, *Maternity: Letters from Working Women* (London: Virago, 1978).

WOOD, G. H., 'The Statistics of Wages in the UK during the 19th Century: The Cotton Industry', *Journal of the Royal Statistical Society*, 73 (June 1910).

WOOD, I., 'Irish Immigrants and Scottish Radicalism, 1880–1906', in I. MacDougall (ed.), *Essays in Scottish Labour History* (Edinburgh: John Donald, 1978).

WOOD, S. (ed.), *The Degradation of Work?* (London: Hutchinson, 1982).

WRIGLEY, C. A. (ed.), *A History of British Industrial Relations, 1875–1914* (Brighton: Harvester, 1982).

WRIGLEY, E. A. (ed.), *Nineteenth Century Society: Essays in the Use of Quantitative Methods for the Study of Social Data* (Cambridge University Press, 1972).

YOUNG, J. D., *The Rousing of the Scottish Working Class* (London: Croom Helm, 1979).

ZEITLIN, J., 'Craft Control and the Division of Labour: Engineers and Compositors in Britain, 1890–1930', *Cambridge Journal of Economics*, 3(3) (1979).

—— 'Workplace Militancy: A Rejoinder', *History Workshop Journal*, 16 (Autumn 1983).

Unpublished Material

BRASSEY, Z. G., 'The Cotton Spinners in Glasgow and the West of Scotland, 1790–1840: A Study in Early Industrial Relations', M.Litt. thesis, University of Strathclyde, 1972.

BROWN, C., 'The Churches and the Labour Movement in Glasgow, 1880–1914: The "Secularisation" of Social Reform', University of Glasgow, 1979.

BYRES, T. J., 'The Scottish Economy during the "Great Depression", 1873–1896: With Special Reference to the Heavy Industries of the South West', B.Litt. thesis, University of Glasgow, 1963.

COLLINS, B. E. A., 'Aspects of Irish Immigration into Two Scottish Towns (Dundee and Paisley) during the Mid Nineteenth Century', M.Phil thesis, University of Edinburgh, 1979.

COOPER, S., 'John Wheatley: A Study in Labour History', Ph.D. thesis, University of Glasgow, 1973.

MARSHALL, J. C., 'Half Timers', undergraduate dissertation, University of Dundee.

MORGAN, C. E., 'Working Class Women and Labour and Socialist Movements of Mid Nineteenth Century England', Ph.D. thesis, University of Iowa, 1979.

NUGENT M., 'Wages and Conditions in the Clothing Industry in Glasgow, c.1880–1914', undergraduate dissertation, University of Strathclyde, 1980.

Index

clerks 27, 30
  union of 110
  see also office work
clothing industry 26, 27, 36, 102
  wages in 31–2
  see also shirt finishing
Clydebank 255–9
coal industry 21, 23–4, 64
  women in 82, 89, 235–6
Coats Co. 242–3
Collins, William & Co. 91, 93
compositors 34–5, 83, 96, 236, 282
Confédération Général du Travail
  234
Constonholm Weaving Co.,
  Pollokshaws 131
consumer industries 24, 127
co-operative guild, *see* Scottish
  Co-operative Women's Guild
co-operative movement 68, 272–3
cotton industry 15, 30–1, 34, 38,
  39–54, 84, 110, 115, 117, 285
  decline of 27, 119, 123
  see also spinners, weavers
Cox Brothers, Dundee 196, 201, 206
crèches, *see* nurseries
Cullen, Mr Matthew 87
Cunningham, Mr 87
culture, women's workplace 155–6
  see also promenading and banter;
    sign-language

Daily News 93
dancing, *see* promenading and banter
Dennistoun, John, mill 41–3
deskilling 37, 71–3
Dickinson, Sarah 111–12
Dicks, Esther 243–4
Dilke, Lady 224, 233
Dilke, Sir Charles 115
docility, women's perceived 53, 213,
  236–7, 259–60, 281
domestic ideology 2–3, 10–11, 17,
  35, 54, 73–101, 113, 135,
  164–5, 167–8, 171–2, 175–6,
  189–90, 219, 270–4, 276–8,
  283, 285–6, 288
  see also separate spheres
domestic service 21, 26–8, 36, 102,
  278
  unionization in 102
drawing 150
dress, women workers' 160

dressers 149, 192
drink, alcoholic 76, 162
  see also temperance
Dudhope Works, Dundee 188, 192
Dundee 12, 20–1, 27, 30, 82, 112,
  117–19, 131, 133, 137–211,
  225, 232, 240, 276, 285, 288
Dundee Advertiser 176, 204
Dundee and District Domestic Servants'
  Association 102
Dundee and District Mill and Factory
  Operatives' Union 99, 105, 115,
  128, 167, 182–8, 192–3, 197
Dundee and District Union of Jute and
  Flax Workers 119, 194–7,
  199–202, 204
Dundee Committee on Public Morals
  163
Dundee Mill and Factory Workers'
  Association 63, 105
Dundee Social Union 22, 142–5,
  154, 164, 168, 194
Dundee Standing Joint Industrial
  Committee 201
Dundee Textile Union 181, 187
Dundee Trades Council 63, 170,
  180–1, 186–7, 193–5, 197, 208
Dundee Working Men's Club 81,
  171
Dundee Yearbook 164

east of Scotland 23, 105
East of Scotland Mill and Factory
  Workers' Protective Association
  169
Edinburgh 21, 27–8, 30, 36, 66, 89,
  94–6, 213, 225–6, 238, 282
Edinburgh Female Compositors' Society
  96
Edinburgh Trades Council 62–3
Edinburgh Upholsterers' and Sewers'
  Society 105
employers and workplace gender
  segregation 37, 39, 43–4, 50–3,
  176–8
employment:
  definitions of women's 17–19
  diversifications in women's 27
  see also labour market, sexual
    division in
Engels, Friedrich 6–7, 9, 281, 289
engineering 23–4
  deskilling in 37

England 16, 20-1, 23, 26, 39,
    54, 57, 110, 115, 125, 215,
    274
Factory and Workshop Acts 82, 85,
    225
Factory Inquiry Commission 40, 78
family wage 74-5, 79-81, 108, 279,
    281, 286
feminist history 1, 4-6, 8-9, 36, 82,
    113-14, 272
Ferguson, Lady Helen Munro 218
Ferguson's Mill, T. & J., Kilmarnock
    124-6
Fife 138
Forfar 122, 124, 138, 226
Forfarshire 106
Fraser, Helen 198
Friefeld, M. 53

Galbraith's Mill, St Rollox 121, 128
Galloway, George 214
General Federation of Trade Unions
    195, 202, 229
Gilfillan, Revd George 170
Glasgow 27, 30-4, 39-53, 59, 64,
    68, 75, 82, 91-4, 103, 107, 117,
    119-21, 124-5, 128-9, 132,
    164, 213, 224-5, 232, 238, 244,
    268, 277, 285
Glasgow Council for Women's Trades
    216
    see also Scottish Council for
        Women's Trades
Glasgow Forward 206, 242, 245,
    248, 253, 255, 264, 265, 271,
    274, 278-9
Glasgow Herald 94
Glasgow Sentinel 83-4, 103, 121
Glasgow Spinners' Association
    39-44, 56, 77, 99
Glasgow Spinning Co. 50
Glasgow Tailoresses' Society 105
Glasgow Trades Council 57-8,
    63-4, 68-9, 82-3, 87, 105,
    109-10, 112, 121-2, 124, 129,
    132, 212, 214-15, 221, 224,
    243-4, 248
Glasgow Typographical Society 94-5
Glasgow Union of Women Workers
    216-17
Gilroy's Mill, Dundee 196, 205
Govan 118, 269
Grant and Baxter's Mill, Dundee 199

Grant's Mill, Glasgow 123, 125, 127
Gray, R. Q. 67
Great Depression, the (1873-96) 139
Greenock 122, 133
Greenock Trades Council 88
Grimmond's Mill, Dundee 194

hacklemaker 148
Halley's Mill, Dundee 153
handloom weavers 29, 120-1
    see also weavers
Hardie, Keir 67, 265
Hawick 105, 122, 132, 232
heavy industry 21, 24, 27, 45,
    59-69
    see also engineering, iron and steel
        industry
Hendry and Sons, Ebenezer, Mill,
    Bridgeton 121
Highlands, migrants from 56, 142
holiday pay, dispute over 178
homeworkers 31, 103, 217, 225
hosiery trade 122
housing:
    conditions of 143-5
    employers' provision of 143, 251
    legislation 273
    see also rent strikes
Howden, John 68
Hunter, A. J. 214
Hutchins, Barbara 231

illegitimate births, women's work and
    86
Independent Labour Party 68, 181,
    194, 197, 236, 246, 253-5, 258,
    262-6, 271-5, 277, 279
ingiver 148, 158
    see also apprenticeships, women's
        exclusion from
India 120, 138-9, 203
Industrial Workers of Great Britain
    255-9
Irish immigrants 56, 142
Irish National League 68
iron and steel industry 23-4, 61, 66,
    249
Irwin, Margaret 31-2, 39, 48,
    154-5,
    216, 218, 220

Johnston, Tom 271